# ABE SAPIEN ™

### CREATED BY
### MIKE MIGNOLA

# The DEVIL
# DOES NOT JEST
## AND OTHER STORIES

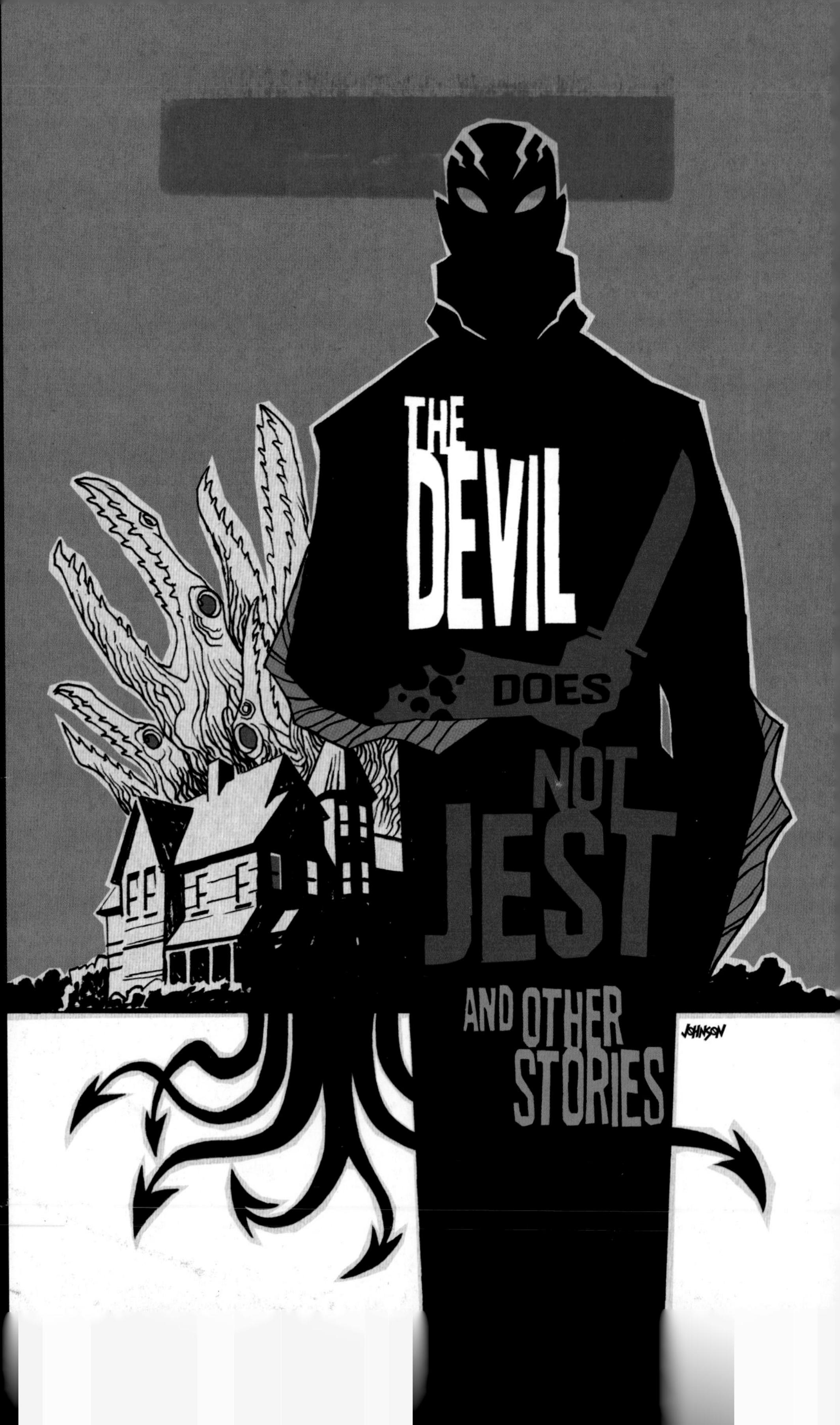
THE DEVIL DOES NOT JEST
AND OTHER STORIES
JOHNSON

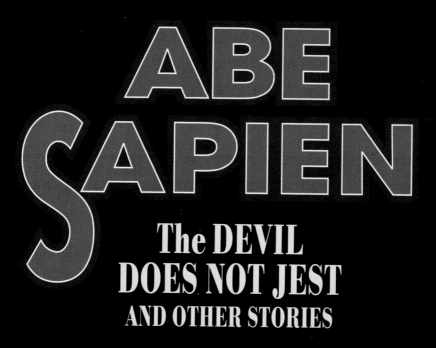

# ABE SAPIEN

## The DEVIL DOES NOT JEST
### AND OTHER STORIES

STORIES BY
**Mike Mignola and John Arcudi**

ART BY
**Patric Reynolds, Peter Snejbjerg, and James Harren**

COLORS BY
**Dave Stewart**

LETTERS BY
**Clem Robins**

COVER ART BY
**Mike Mignola**

SERIES COVERS BY
**Dave Johnson**

EDITOR **Scott Allie**

ASSISTANT EDITOR **Daniel Chabon**

COLLECTION DESIGNER **Amy Arendts**

PUBLISHER **Mike Richardson**

**DARK HORSE BOOKS®**

Neil Hankerson *executive vice president*
Tom Weddle *chief financial officer*
Randy Stradley *vice president of publishing*
Michael Martens *vice president of book trade sales*
Anita Nelson *vice president of business affairs*
Micha Hershman *vice president of marketing*
David Scroggy *vice president of product development*
Dale LaFountain *vice president of information technology*
Darlene Vogel *senior director of print, design, and production*
Ken Lizzi *general counsel*
Davey Estrada *editorial director*
Scott Allie *senior managing editor*
Chris Warner *senior books editor*
Diana Schutz *executive editor*
Cary Grazzini *director of print and development*
Lia Ribacchi *art director*
Cara Niece *director of scheduling*

Special thanks to Jason Hvam.

Published by Dark Horse Books
A division of Dark Horse Comics, Inc.
10956 SE Main Street
Milwaukie, OR 97222

First edition: May 2012
ISBN 978-1-59582-925-2

1 3 5 7 9 10 8 6 4 2
Printed at Midas Printing International, Ltd., Huizhou, China

This book collects *Abe Sapien: The Haunted Boy*,
*Abe Sapien: The Abyssal Plain #1–#2*, and *Abe Sapien: The Devil Does Not Jest #1–#2*.

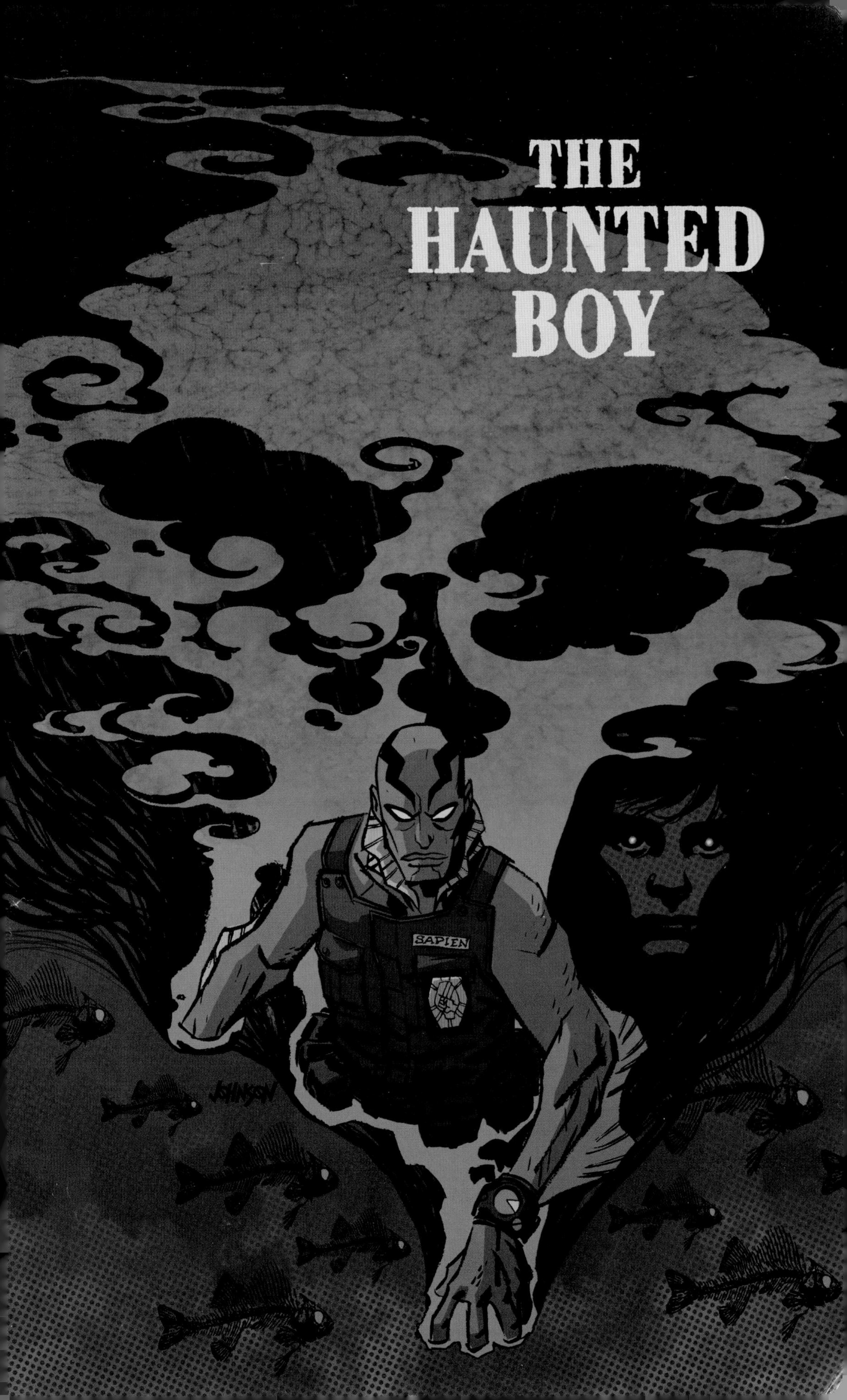
THE
HAUNTED
BOY
SAPIEN
JOHNSON

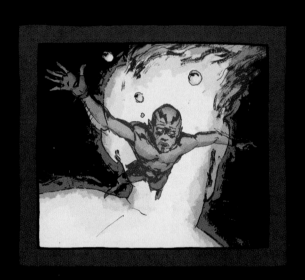

ART BY
**Patric Reynolds**

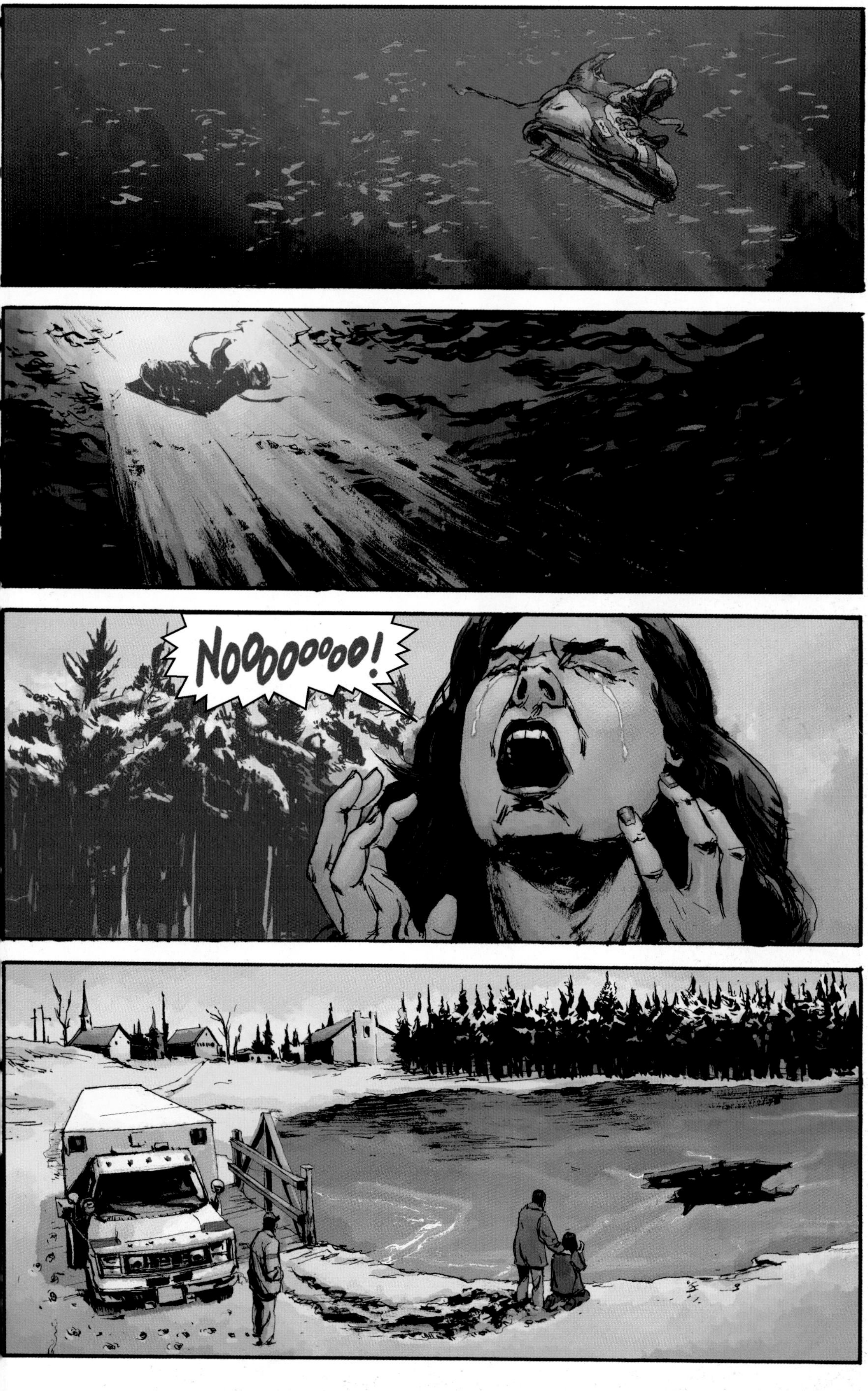
NOOOOOOOO!

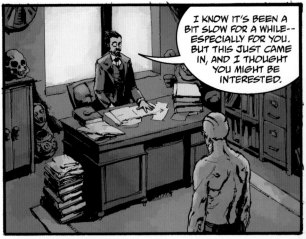

B.P.R.D. HEADQUARTERS, FAIRFIELD, CT. JUNE 1982.

I KNOW IT'S BEEN A BIT SLOW FOR A WHILE-- ESPECIALLY FOR YOU. BUT THIS JUST CAME IN, AND I THOUGHT YOU MIGHT BE INTERESTED.

THANK YOU FOR COMING, ABRAHAM.

UP TO YOU, OF COURSE. LET ME KNOW.

YES SIR.

JANUARY 8 OF THIS YEAR, A STATE TROOPER REPORT WAS FILED FROM HARDIN, VT. TWO TEN-YEAR-OLD BOYS FELL THROUGH THE ICE OVER A LARGE FROZEN POND WHILE SKATING.

ONE BOY WAS SAVED, BUT THE OTHER, ADAM LAZIO, WAS PRONOUNCED DEAD AT THE SCENE.

MRS. LAZIO INITIALLY HAD A GREAT DEAL OF DIFFICULTY COMING TO TERMS WITH HER SON'S DEATH, FILING A LAWSUIT AGAINST THE TOWN OF HARDIN IN MARCH, WHICH SHE LATER DROPPED.

AND THEN, IN LATE MAY--

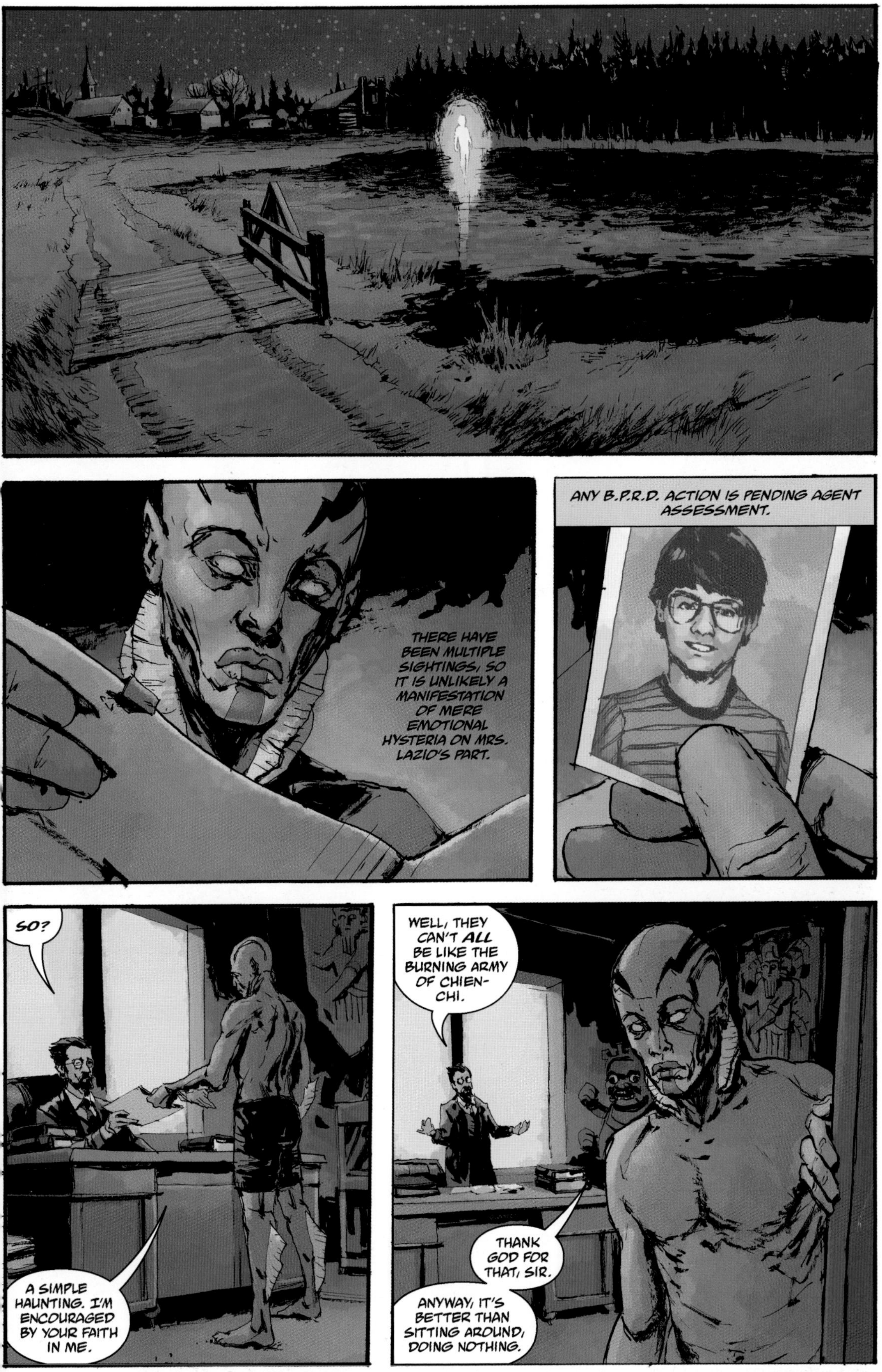
THERE HAVE BEEN MULTIPLE SIGHTINGS, SO IT IS UNLIKELY A MANIFESTATION OF MERE EMOTIONAL HYSTERIA ON MRS. LAZIO'S PART.
ANY B.P.R.D. ACTION IS PENDING AGENT ASSESSMENT.
SO?
A SIMPLE HAUNTING. I'M ENCOURAGED BY YOUR FAITH IN ME.
WELL, THEY CAN'T ALL BE LIKE THE BURNING ARMY OF CHIEN-CHI.
THANK GOD FOR THAT, SIR.
ANYWAY, IT'S BETTER THAN SITTING AROUND, DOING NOTHING.

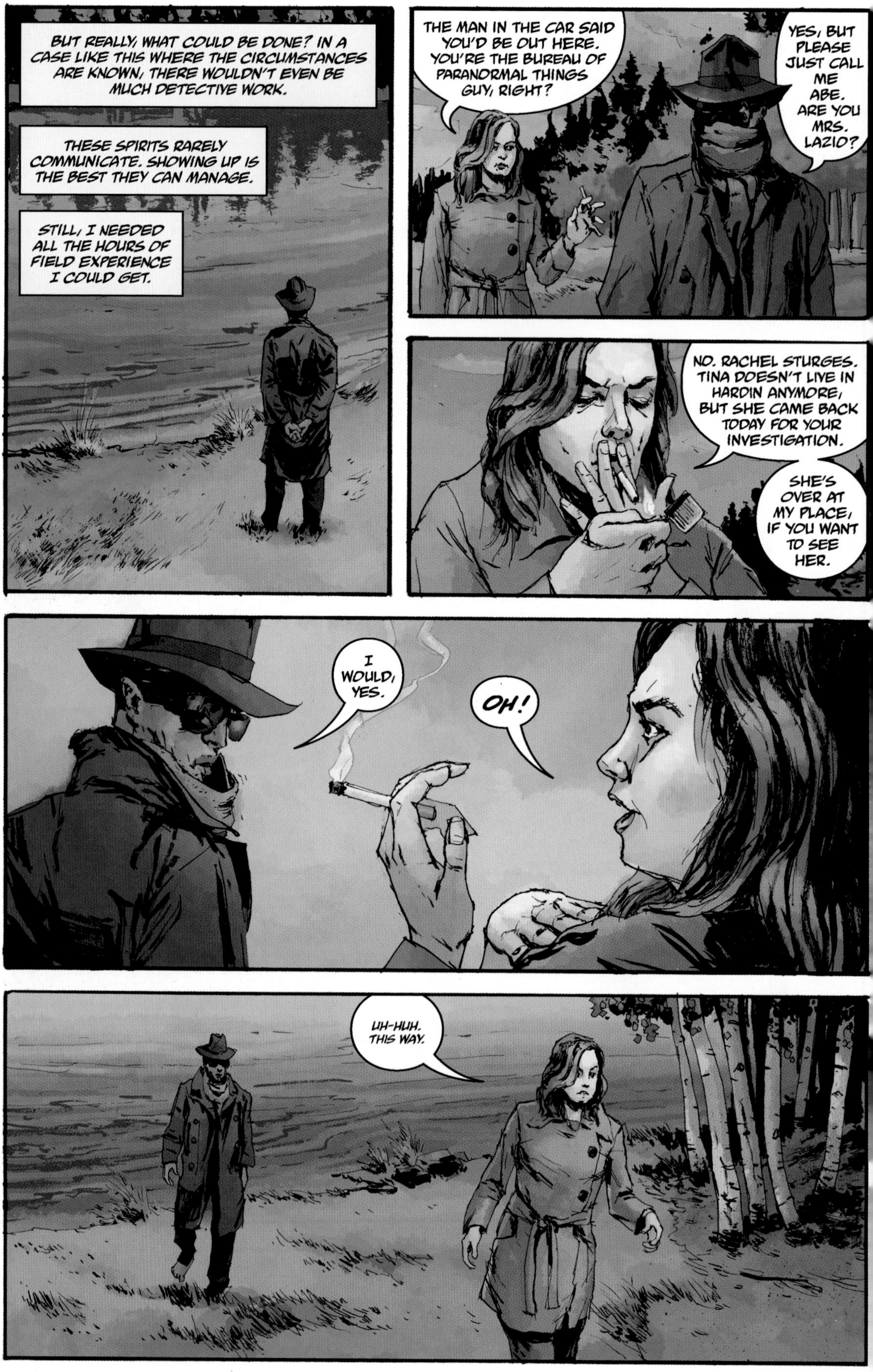
BUT REALLY, WHAT COULD BE DONE? IN A CASE LIKE THIS WHERE THE CIRCUMSTANCES ARE KNOWN, THERE WOULDN'T EVEN BE MUCH DETECTIVE WORK.
THESE SPIRITS RARELY COMMUNICATE. SHOWING UP IS THE BEST THEY CAN MANAGE.
STILL, I NEEDED ALL THE HOURS OF FIELD EXPERIENCE I COULD GET.
THE MAN IN THE CAR SAID YOU'D BE OUT HERE. YOU'RE THE BUREAU OF PARANORMAL THINGS GUY, RIGHT?
YES, BUT PLEASE JUST CALL ME ABE. ARE YOU MRS. LAZIO?
NO. RACHEL STURGES. TINA DOESN'T LIVE IN HARDIN ANYMORE, BUT SHE CAME BACK TODAY FOR YOUR INVESTIGATION.
SHE'S OVER AT MY PLACE, IF YOU WANT TO SEE HER.
I WOULD, YES.
OH!
UH-HUH. THIS WAY.

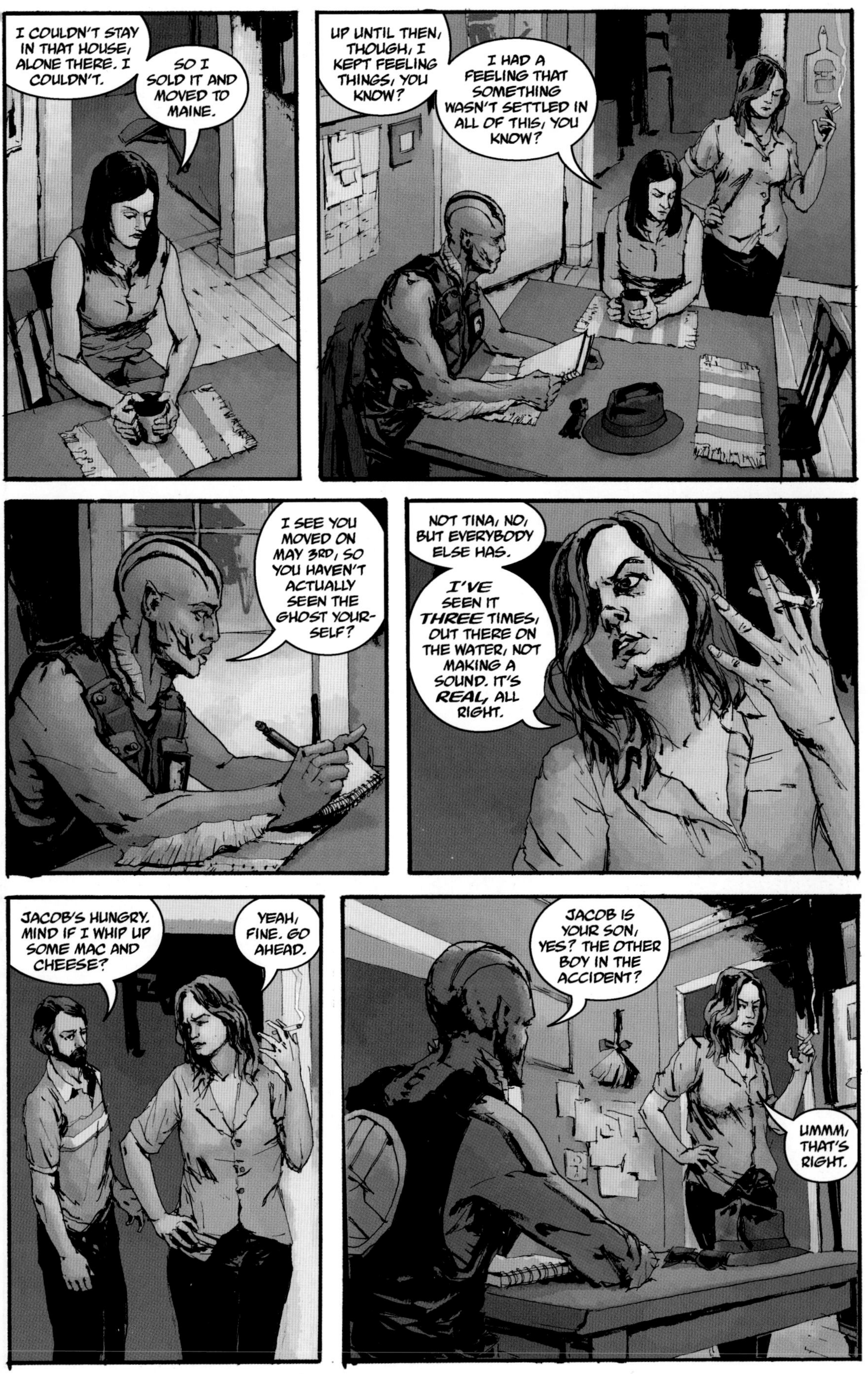
I COULDN'T STAY IN THAT HOUSE, ALONE THERE. I COULDN'T.
SO I SOLD IT AND MOVED TO MAINE.
UP UNTIL THEN, THOUGH, I KEPT FEELING THINGS, YOU KNOW?
I HAD A FEELING THAT SOMETHING WASN'T SETTLED IN ALL OF THIS, YOU KNOW?
I SEE YOU MOVED ON MAY 3RD, SO YOU HAVEN'T ACTUALLY SEEN THE GHOST YOUR-SELF?
NOT TINA, NO, BUT EVERYBODY ELSE HAS.
I'VE SEEN IT THREE TIMES, OUT THERE ON THE WATER, NOT MAKING A SOUND. IT'S REAL, ALL RIGHT.
JACOB'S HUNGRY. MIND IF I WHIP UP SOME MAC AND CHEESE?
YEAH, FINE. GO AHEAD.
JACOB IS YOUR SON, YES? THE OTHER BOY IN THE ACCIDENT?
UMMM, THAT'S RIGHT.

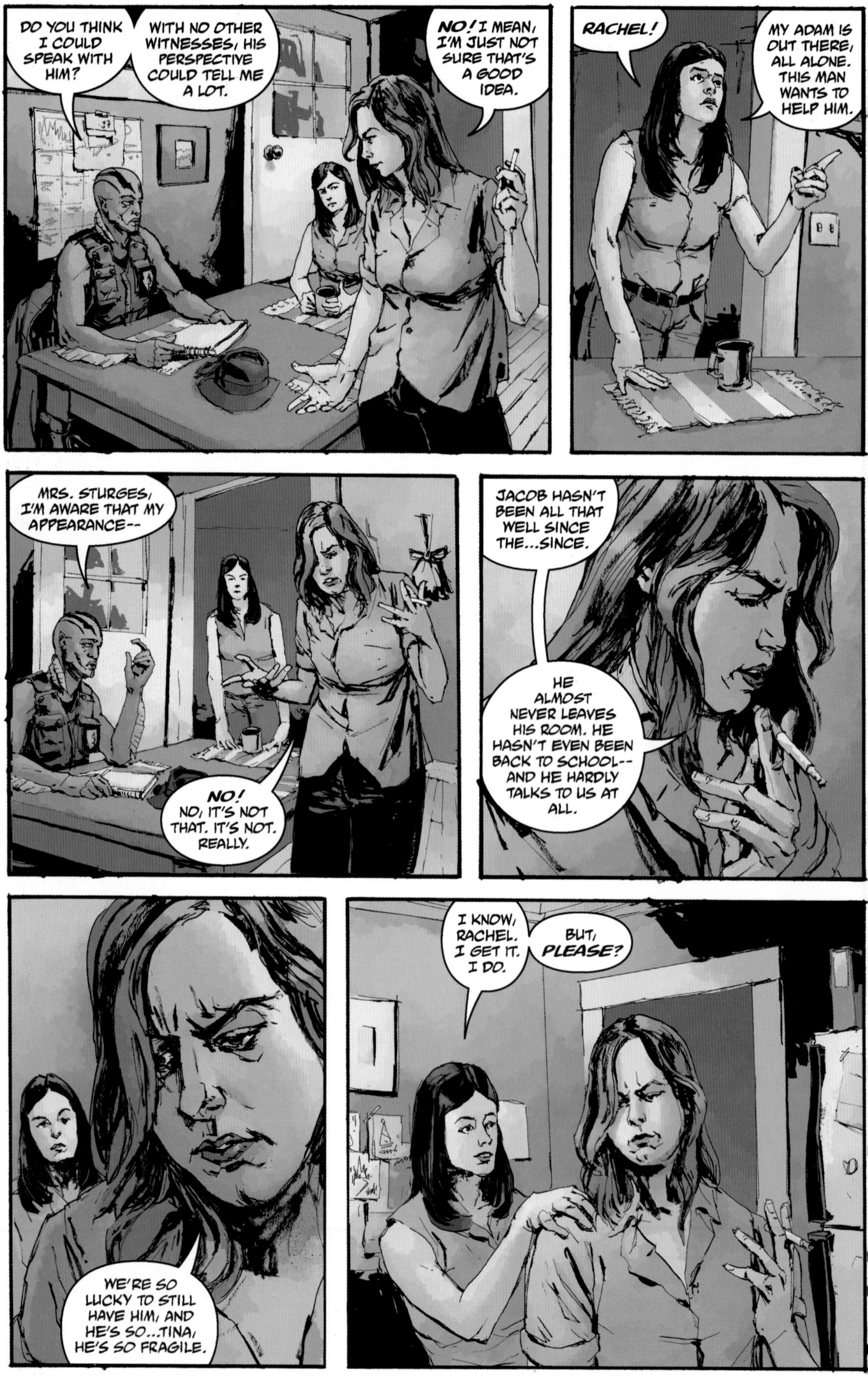
DO YOU THINK I COULD SPEAK WITH HIM?
WITH NO OTHER WITNESSES, HIS PERSPECTIVE COULD TELL ME A LOT.
NO! I MEAN, I'M JUST NOT SURE THAT'S A GOOD IDEA.
RACHEL!
MY ADAM IS OUT THERE, ALL ALONE. THIS MAN WANTS TO HELP HIM.
MRS. STURGES, I'M AWARE THAT MY APPEARANCE--
NO! NO, IT'S NOT THAT. IT'S NOT. REALLY.
JACOB HASN'T BEEN ALL THAT WELL SINCE THE...SINCE.
HE ALMOST NEVER LEAVES HIS ROOM. HE HASN'T EVEN BEEN BACK TO SCHOOL-- AND HE HARDLY TALKS TO US AT ALL.
WE'RE SO LUCKY TO STILL HAVE HIM, AND HE'S SO...TINA, HE'S SO FRAGILE.
I KNOW, RACHEL. I GET IT. I DO.
BUT, PLEASE?

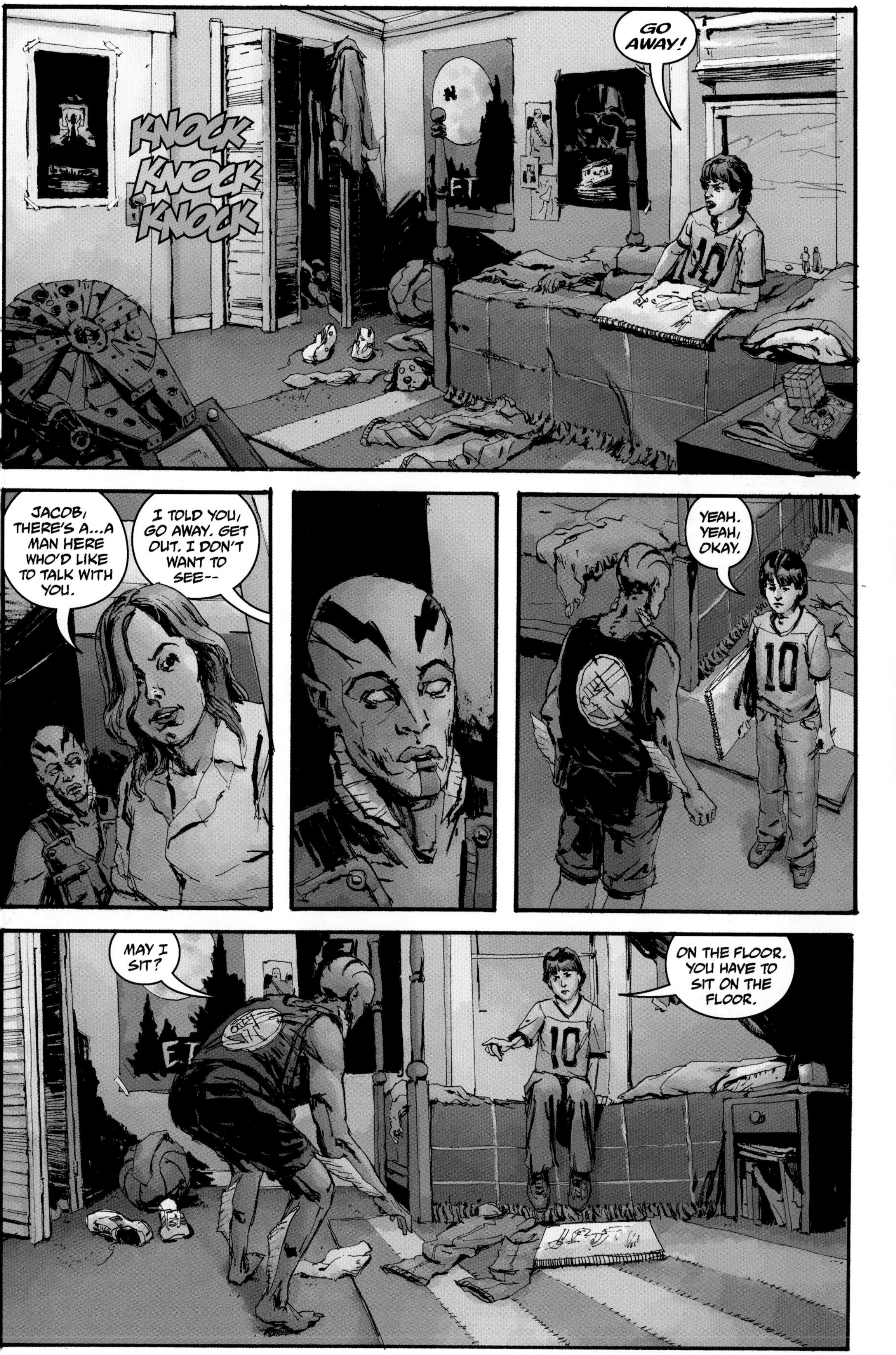

KNOCK
KNOCK
KNOCK
GO AWAY!
JACOB, THERE'S A...A MAN HERE WHO'D LIKE TO TALK WITH YOU.
I TOLD YOU, GO AWAY. GET OUT. I DON'T WANT TO SEE--
YEAH. YEAH, OKAY.
MAY I SIT?
ON THE FLOOR. YOU HAVE TO SIT ON THE FLOOR.

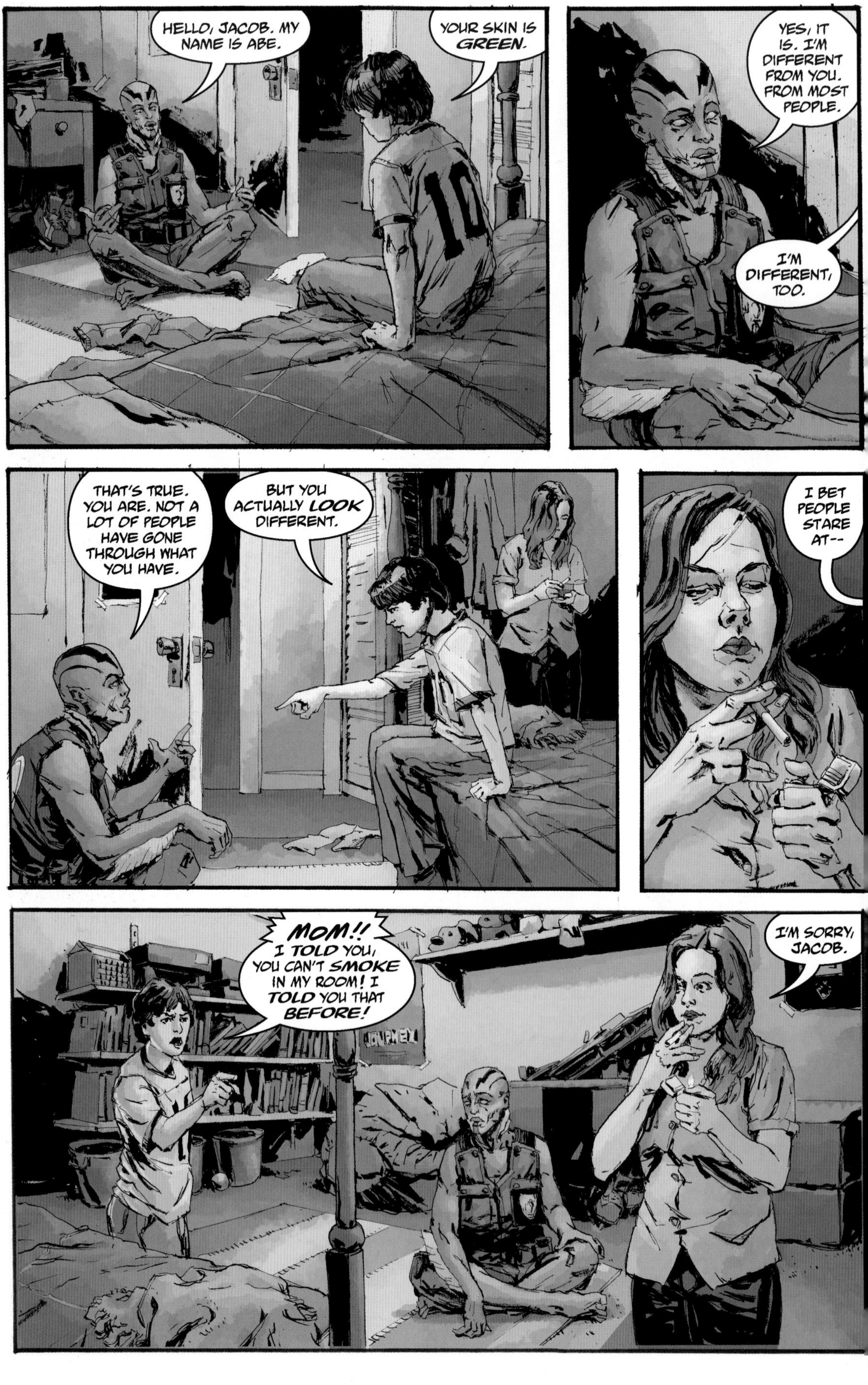
HELLO, JACOB. MY NAME IS ABE.
YOUR SKIN IS GREEN.
YES, IT IS. I'M DIFFERENT FROM YOU. FROM MOST PEOPLE.
I'M DIFFERENT, TOO.
THAT'S TRUE. YOU ARE. NOT A LOT OF PEOPLE HAVE GONE THROUGH WHAT YOU HAVE.
BUT YOU ACTUALLY LOOK DIFFERENT.
I BET PEOPLE STARE AT--
MOM!! I TOLD YOU, YOU CAN'T SMOKE IN MY ROOM! I TOLD YOU THAT BEFORE!
I'M SORRY, JACOB.

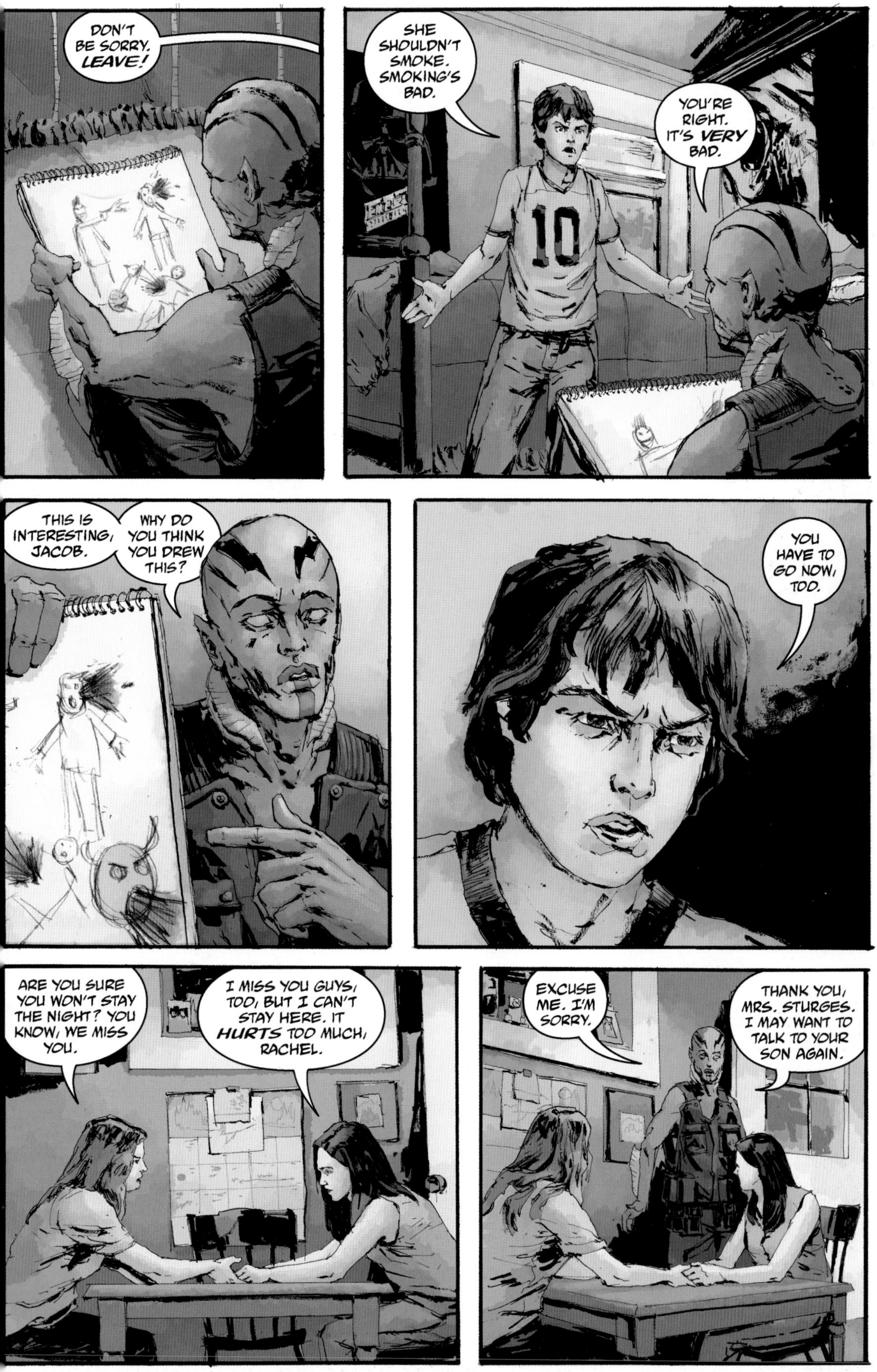
DON'T BE SORRY. LEAVE!
SHE SHOULDN'T SMOKE. SMOKING'S BAD.
YOU'RE RIGHT. IT'S VERY BAD.
THIS IS INTERESTING, JACOB.
WHY DO YOU THINK YOU DREW THIS?
YOU HAVE TO GO NOW, TOO.
ARE YOU SURE YOU WON'T STAY THE NIGHT? YOU KNOW, WE MISS YOU.
I MISS YOU GUYS, TOO, BUT I CAN'T STAY HERE. IT HURTS TOO MUCH, RACHEL.
EXCUSE ME. I'M SORRY.
THANK YOU, MRS. STURGES. I MAY WANT TO TALK TO YOUR SON AGAIN.

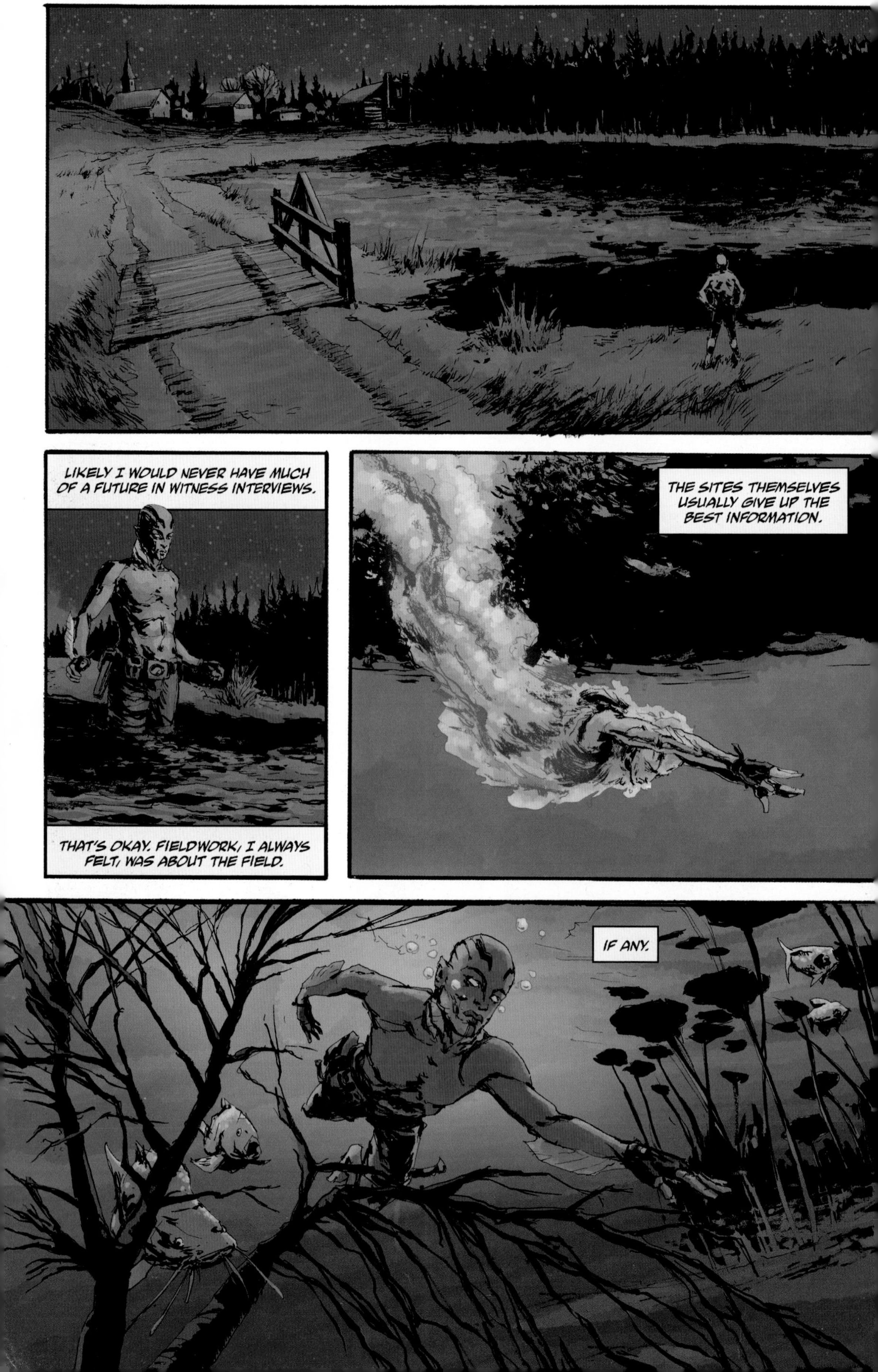
LIKELY I WOULD NEVER HAVE MUCH OF A FUTURE IN WITNESS INTERVIEWS.
THAT'S OKAY. FIELDWORK, I ALWAYS FELT, WAS ABOUT THE FIELD.
THE SITES THEMSELVES USUALLY GIVE UP THE BEST INFORMATION.
IF ANY.

HOW DEEP IS THIS "POND"?

AH! HERE WE ARE.

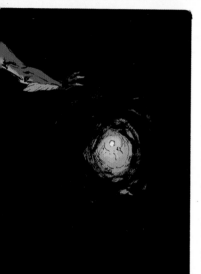

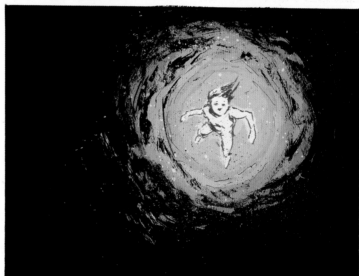

AN UNUSUAL MANIFESTATION, NO DOUBT, BUT ULTIMATELY JUST ANOTHER...

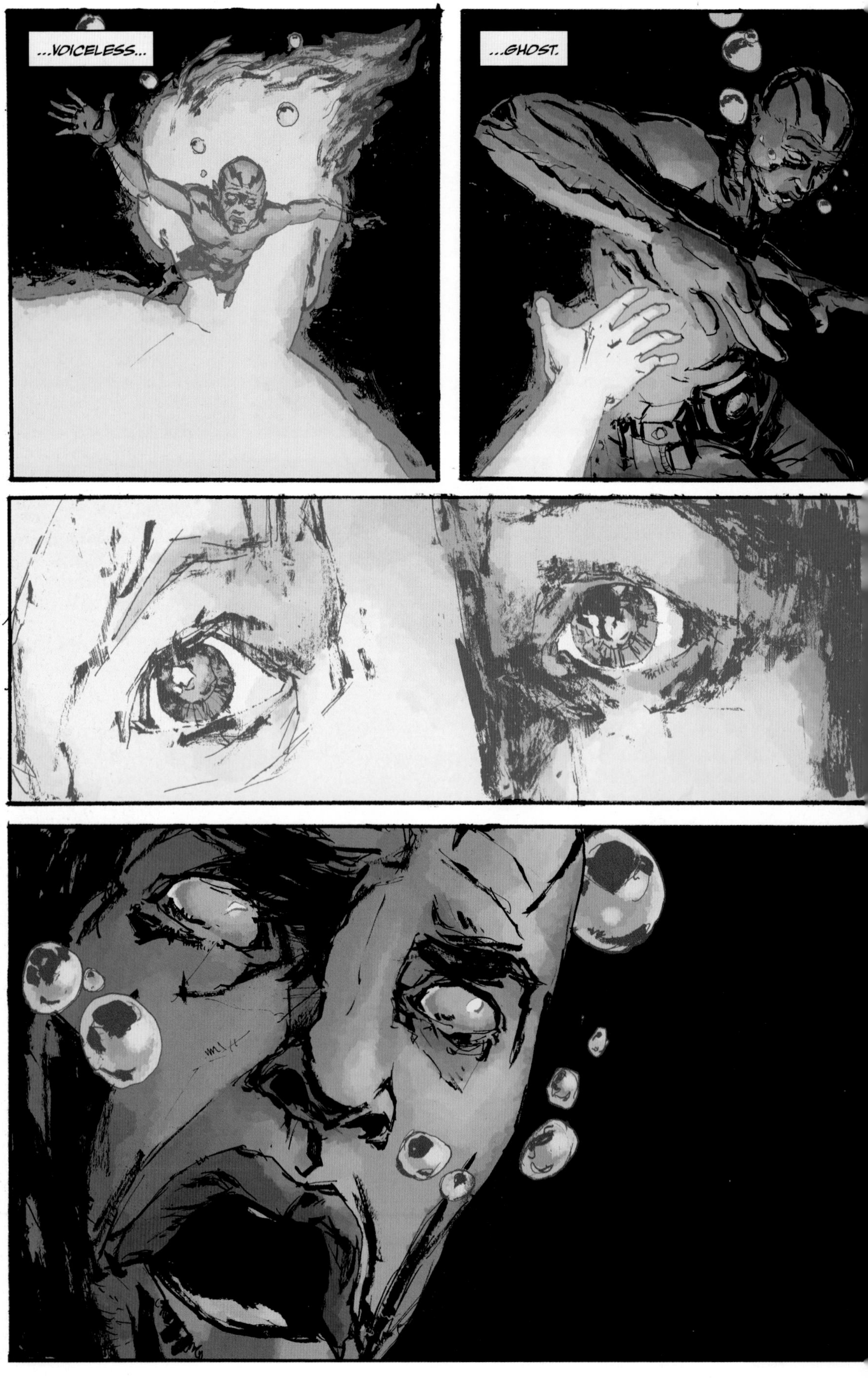
...VOICELESS...
...GHOST.

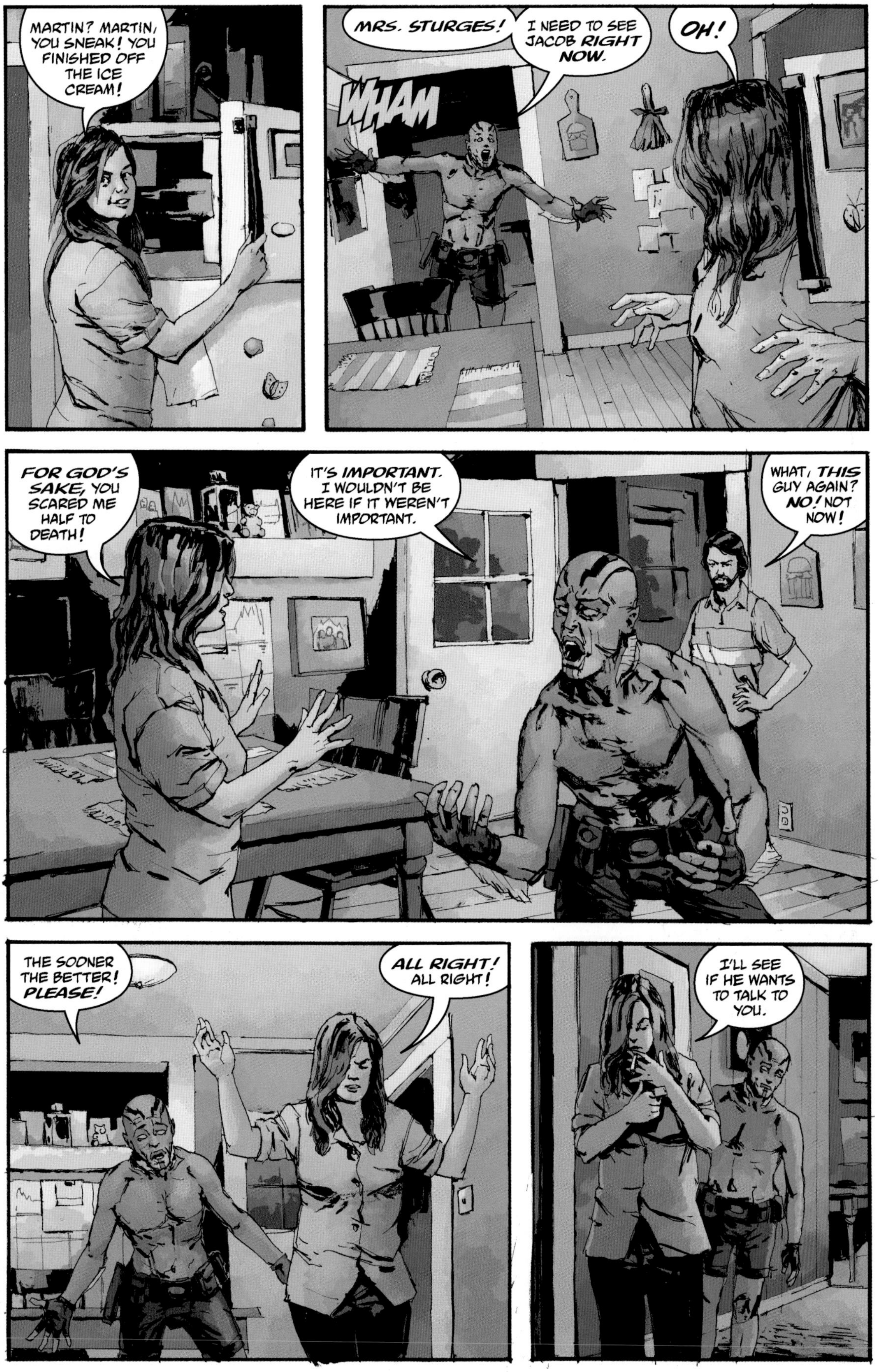
MARTIN? MARTIN, YOU SNEAK! YOU FINISHED OFF THE ICE CREAM!
MRS. STURGES!
I NEED TO SEE JACOB RIGHT NOW.
WHAM
OH!
FOR GOD'S SAKE, YOU SCARED ME HALF TO DEATH!
IT'S IMPORTANT. I WOULDN'T BE HERE IF IT WEREN'T IMPORTANT.
WHAT, THIS GUY AGAIN? NO! NOT NOW!
THE SOONER THE BETTER! PLEASE!
ALL RIGHT! ALL RIGHT!
I'LL SEE IF HE WANTS TO TALK TO YOU.

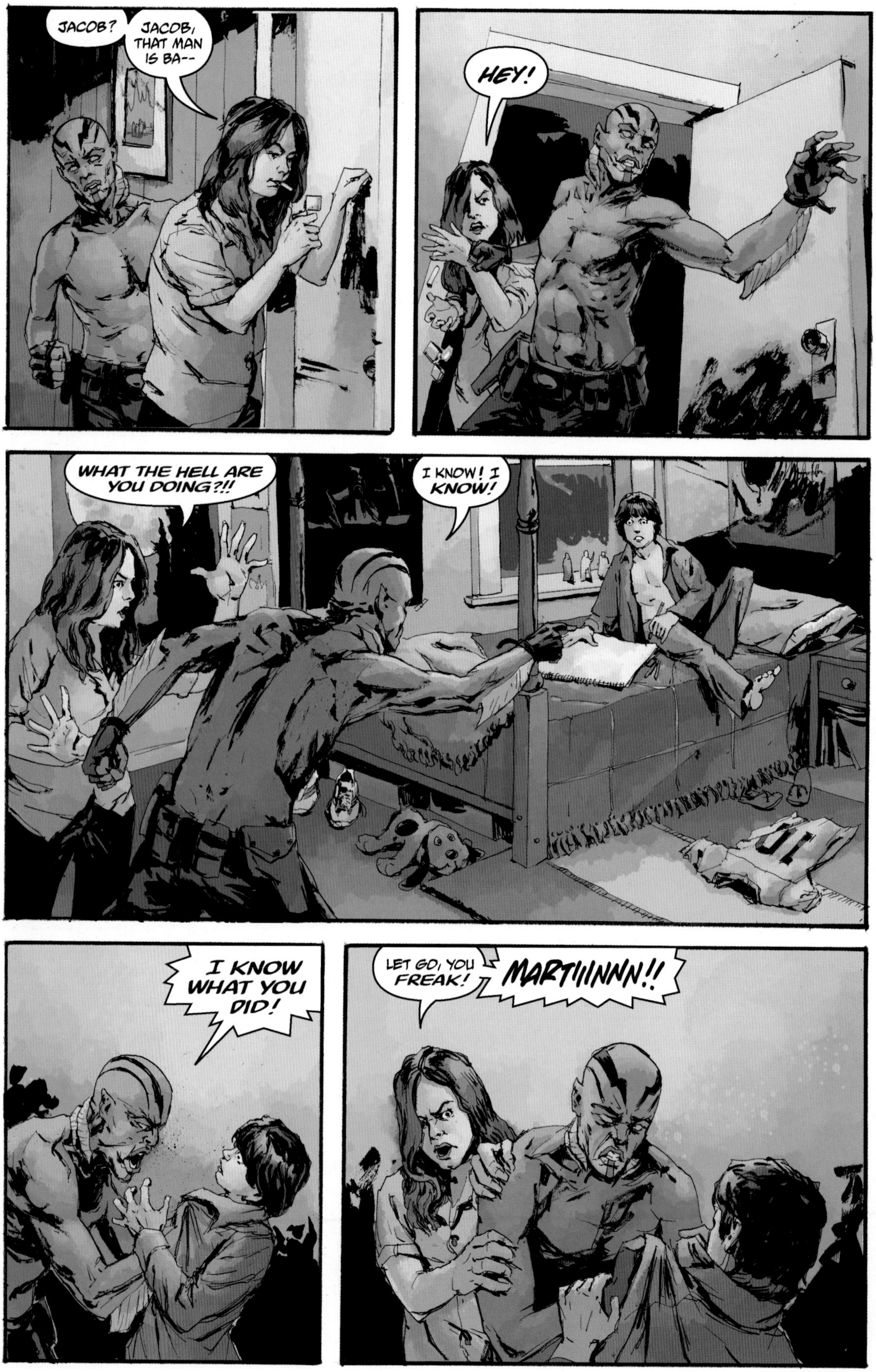
JACOB?
JACOB, THAT MAN IS BA--
HEY!
WHAT THE HELL ARE YOU DOING?!!
I KNOW! I KNOW!
I KNOW WHAT YOU DID!
LET GO, YOU FREAK!
MARTIIINNN!!

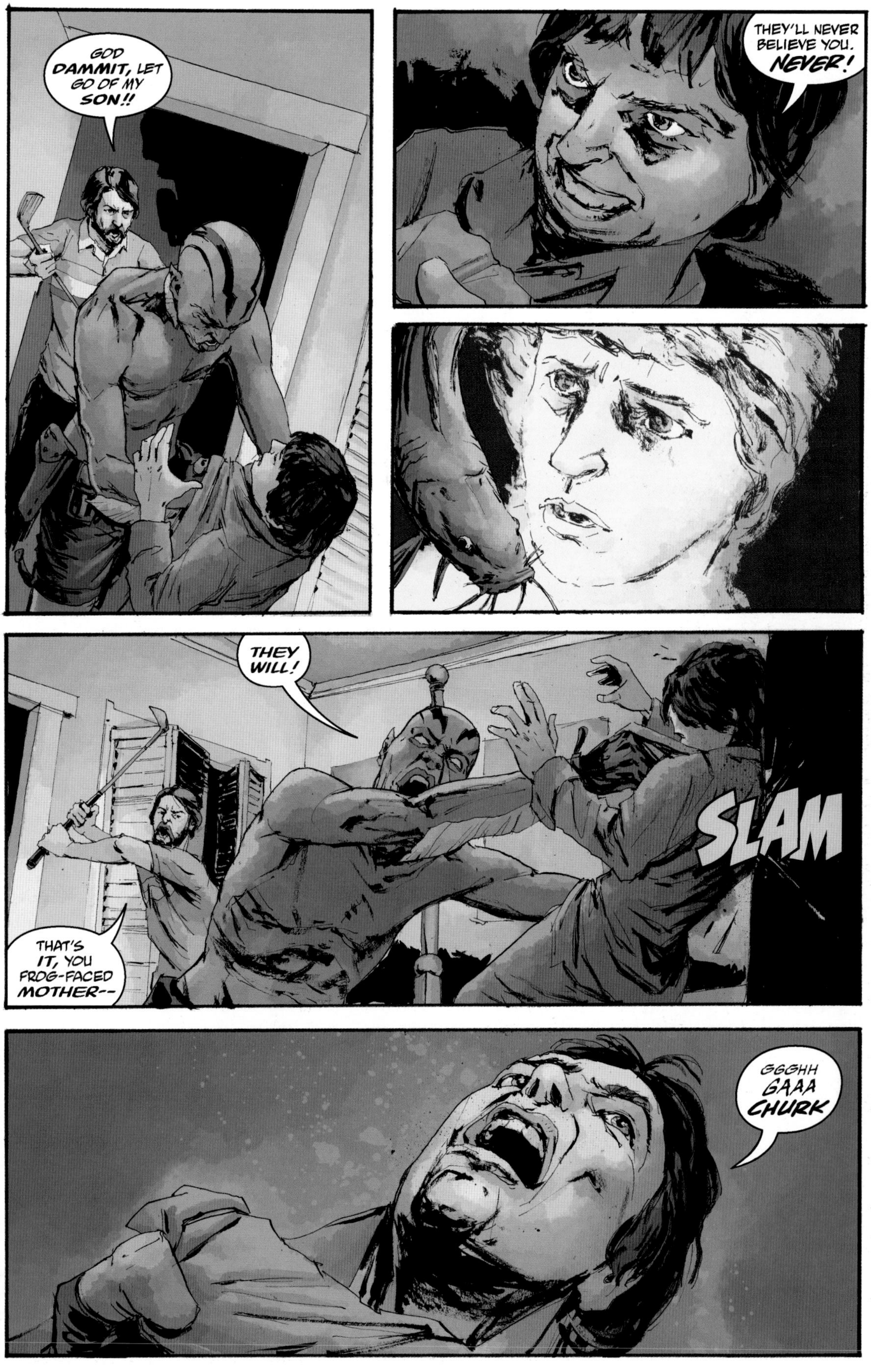
GOD DAMMIT, LET GO OF MY SON!!
THEY'LL NEVER BELIEVE YOU. NEVER!
THEY WILL!
SLAM
THAT'S IT, YOU FROG-FACED MOTHER--
GGGHH GAAA CHURK

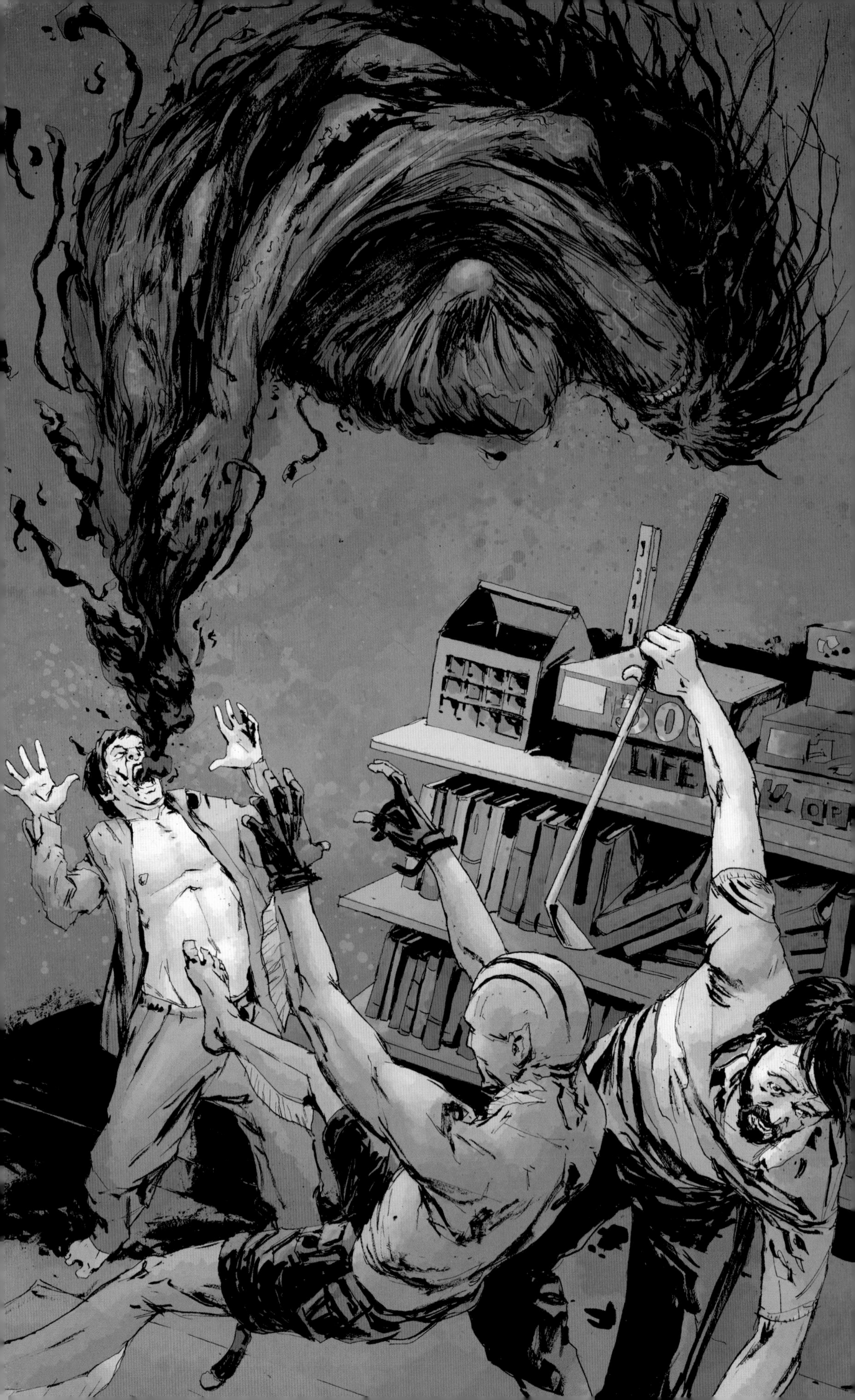
LIFE

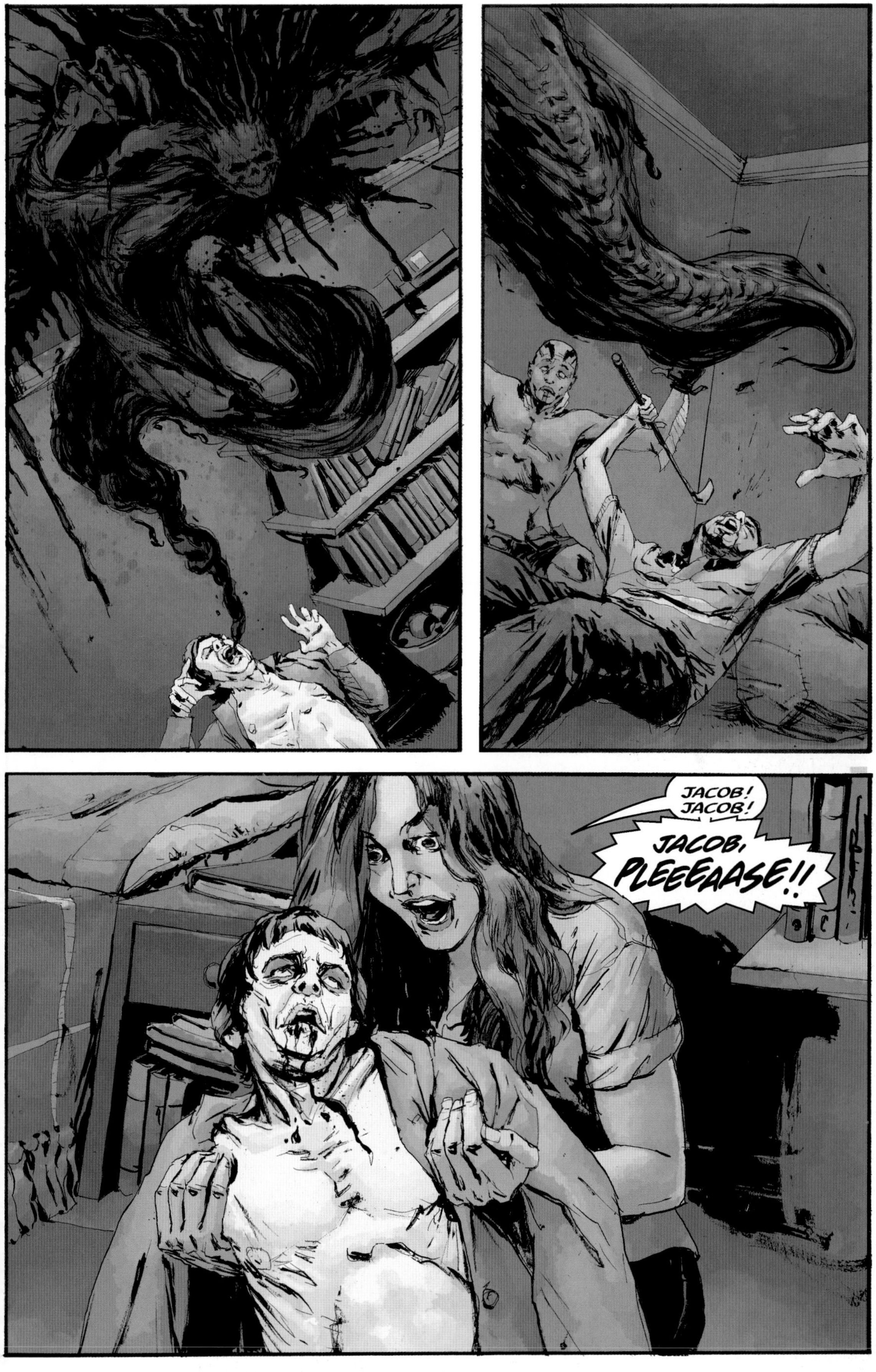
JACOB!
JACOB!
JACOB, PLEEEAASE!!

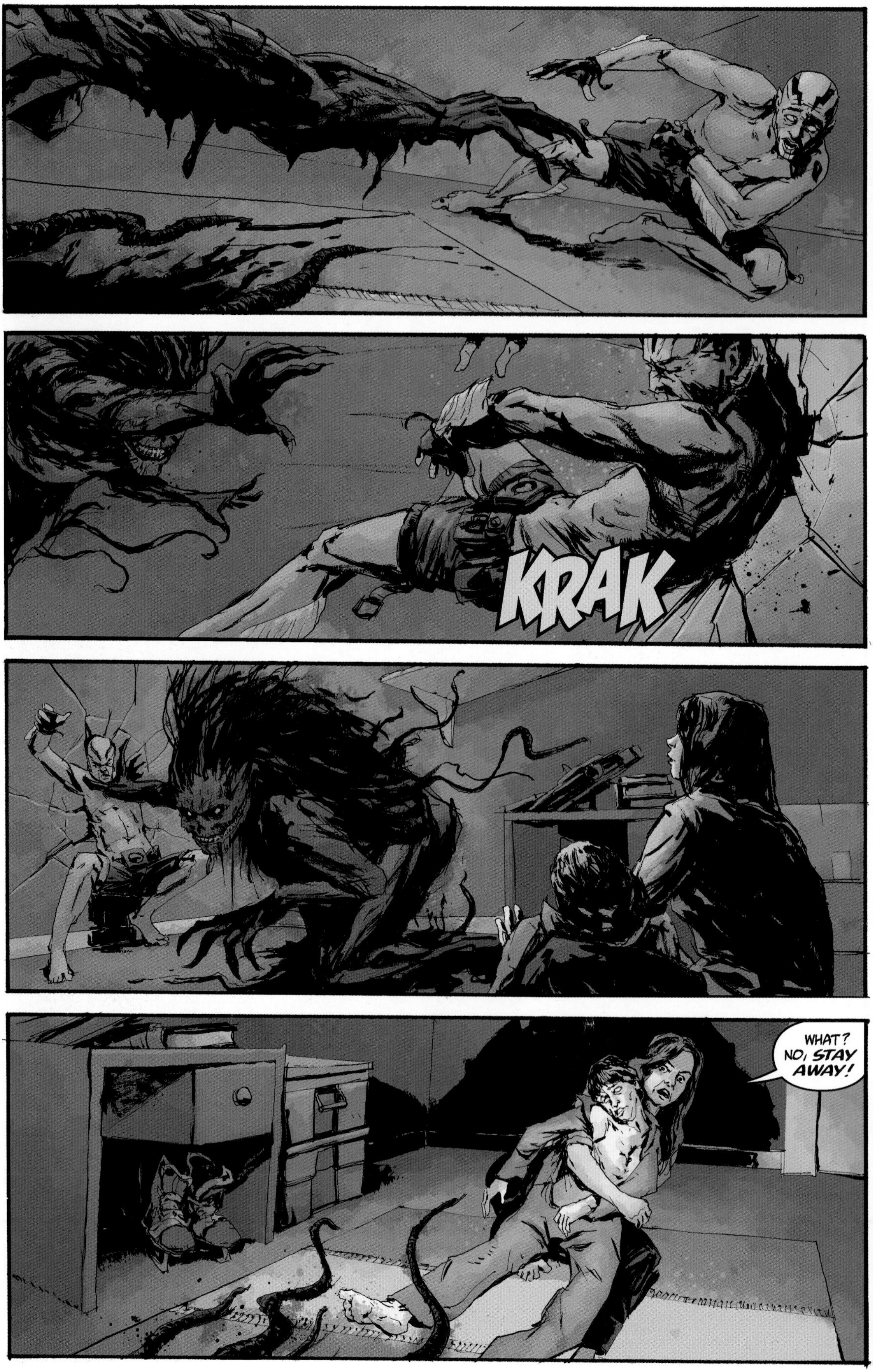
KRAK
WHAT? NO, STAY AWAY!

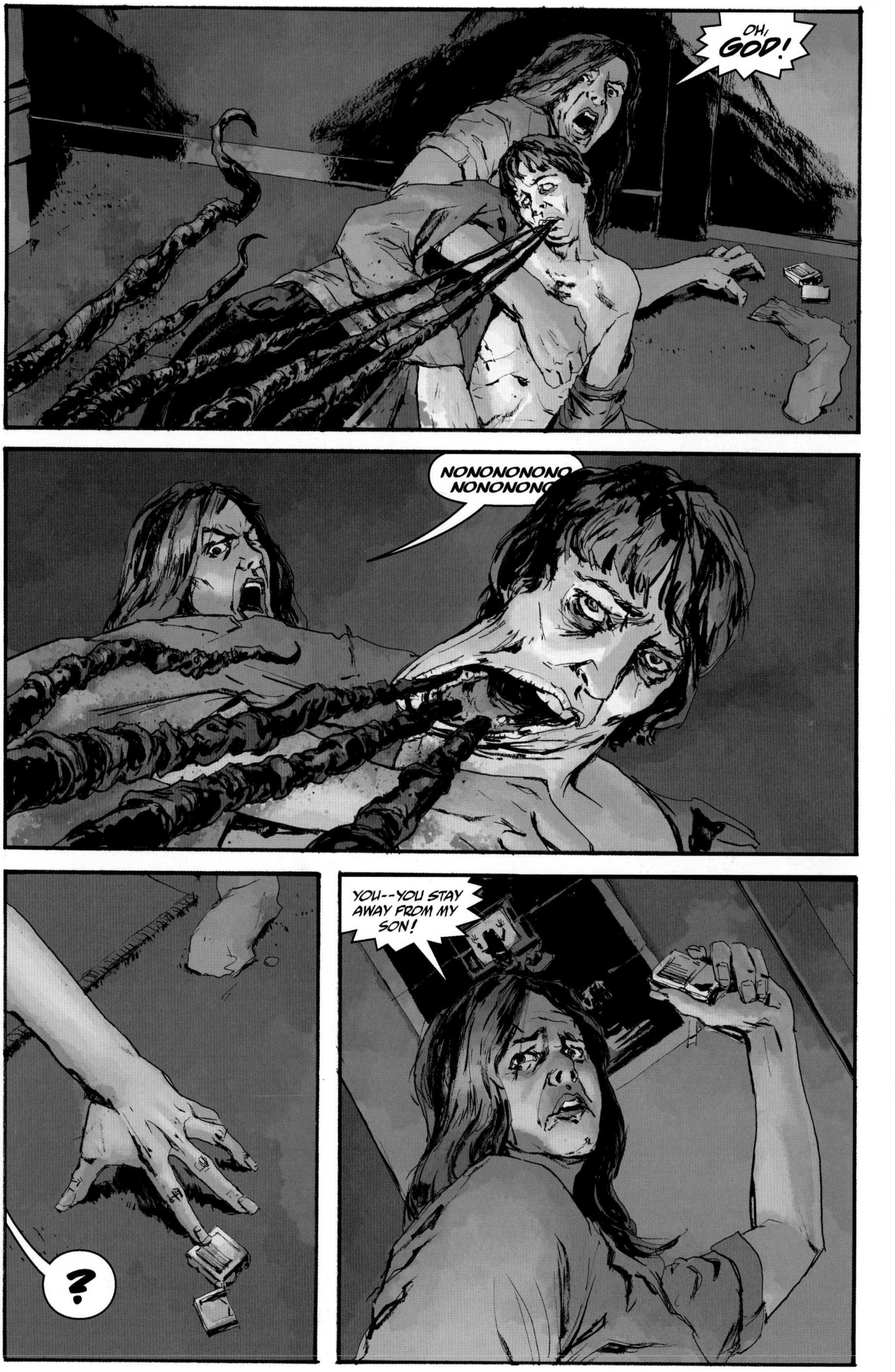
OH, GOD!
NONONONONO NONONONO
?
YOU--YOU STAY AWAY FROM MY SON!

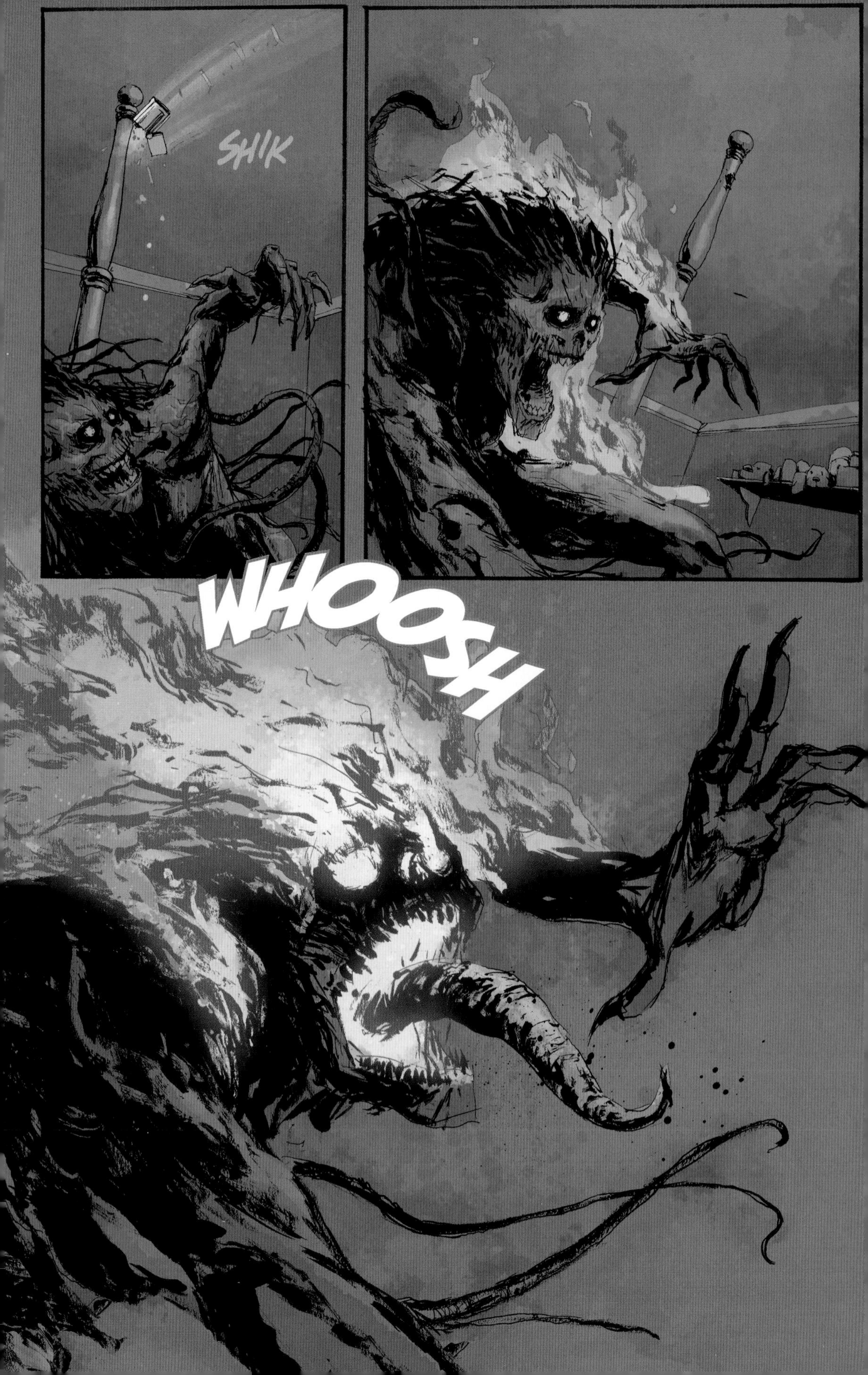
SHIK
WHOOSH

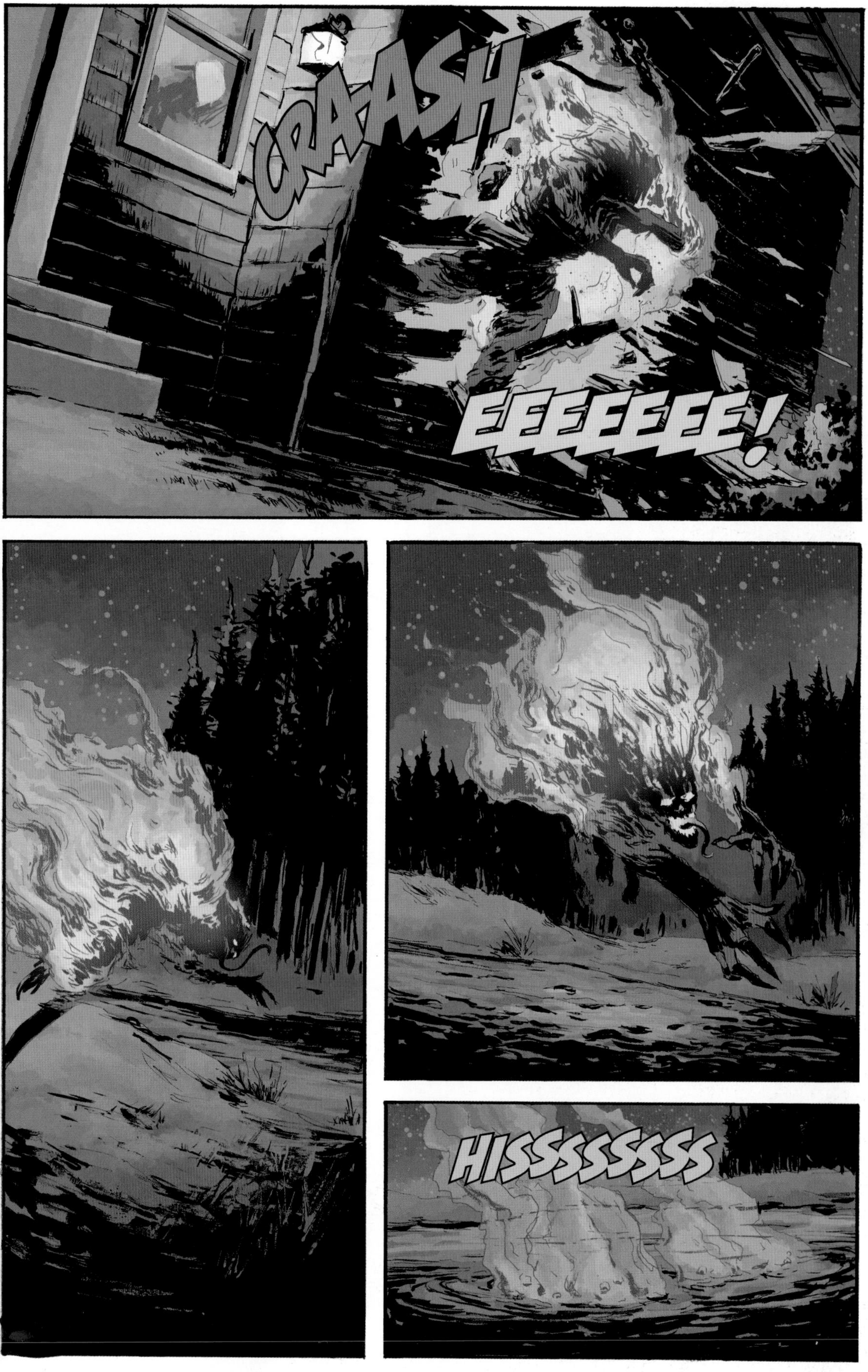
CRAASH
EEEEEEE!
HISSSSSSS

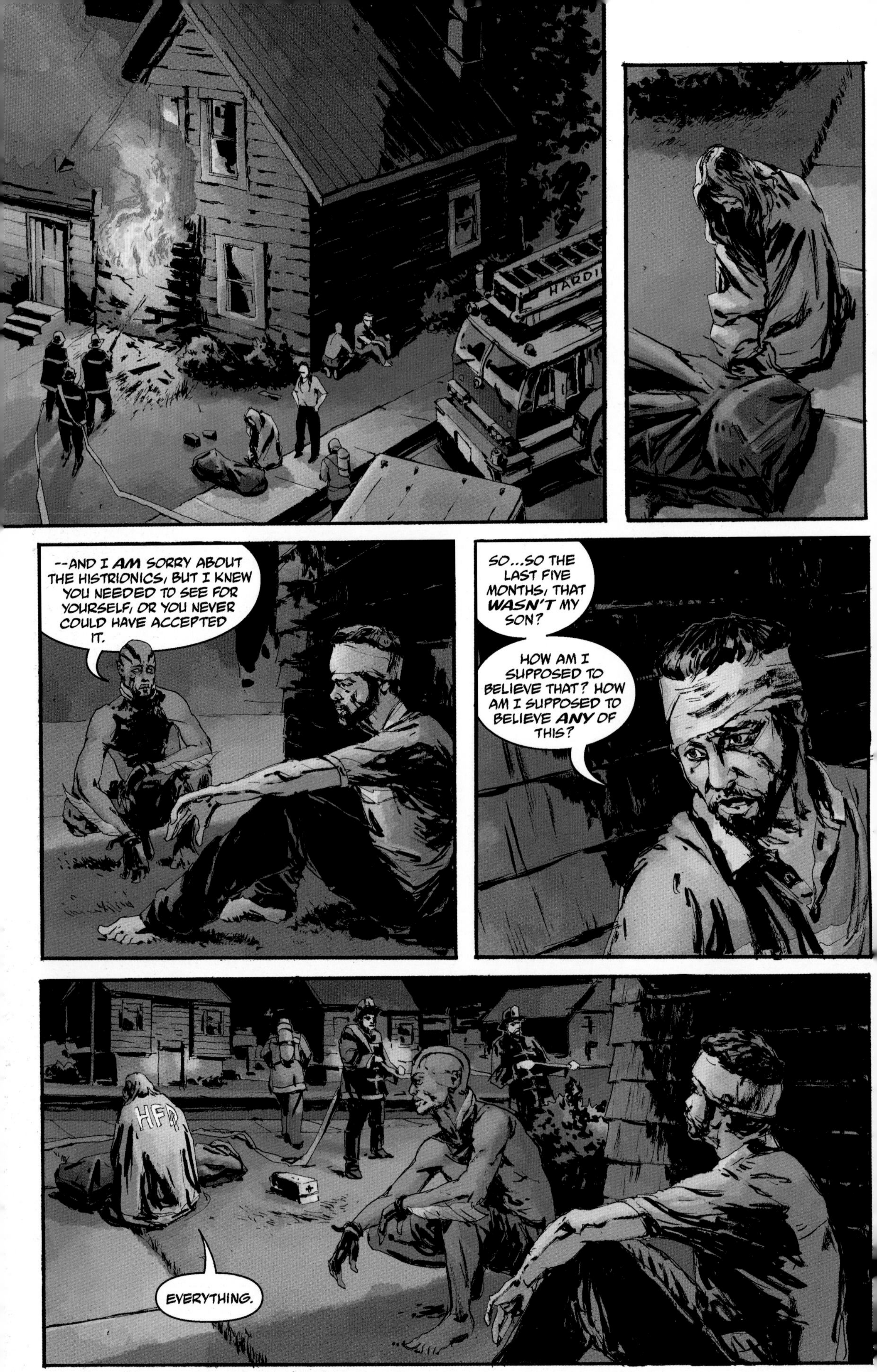
--AND I AM SORRY ABOUT THE HISTRIONICS, BUT I KNEW YOU NEEDED TO SEE FOR YOURSELF, OR YOU NEVER COULD HAVE ACCEPTED IT.
SO...SO THE LAST FIVE MONTHS, THAT WASN'T MY SON?
HOW AM I SUPPOSED TO BELIEVE THAT? HOW AM I SUPPOSED TO BELIEVE ANY OF THIS?
EVERYTHING.

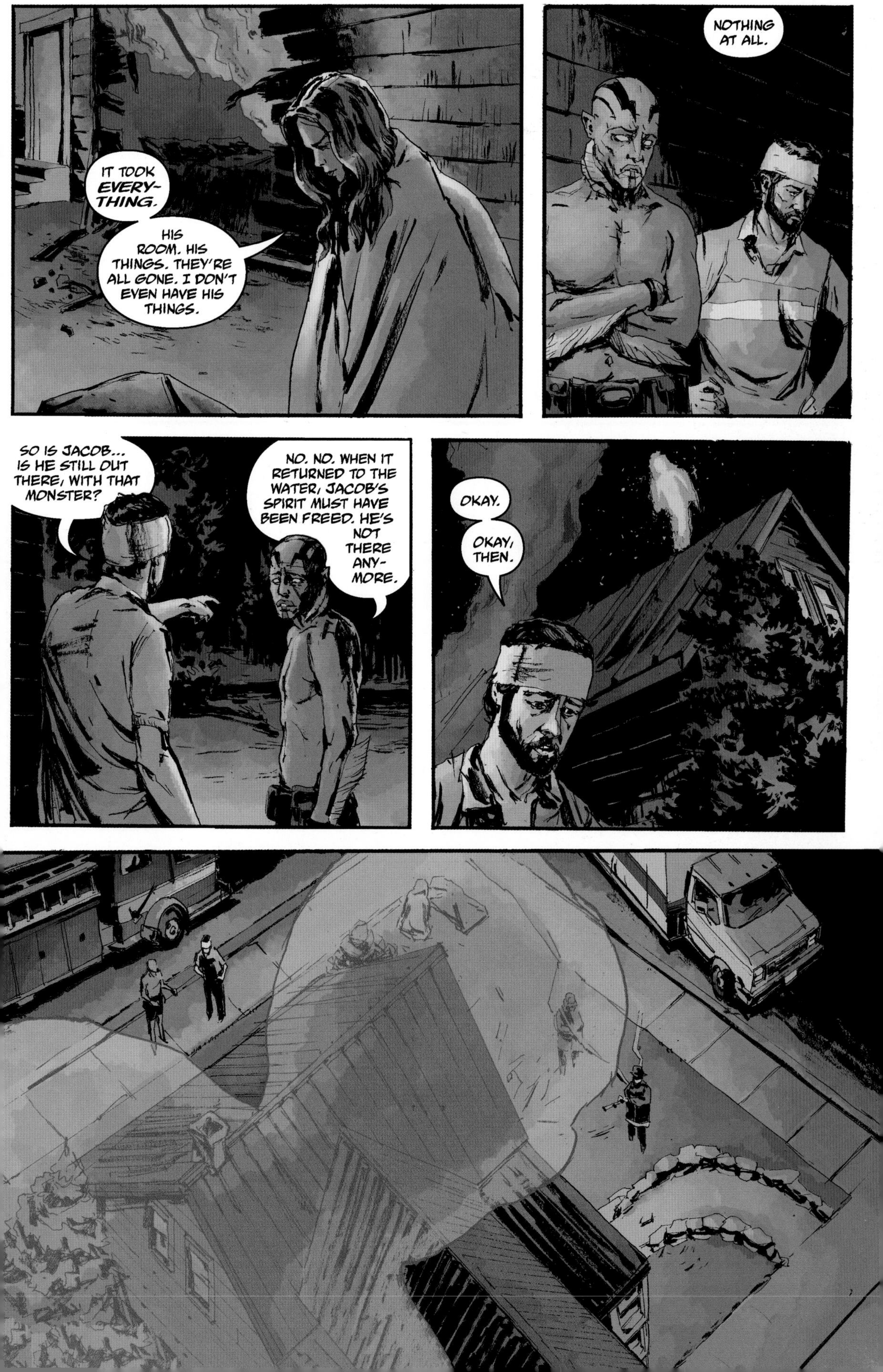
IT TOOK EVERYTHING.
HIS ROOM. HIS THINGS. THEY'RE ALL GONE. I DON'T EVEN HAVE HIS THINGS.
NOTHING AT ALL.
SO IS JACOB... IS HE STILL OUT THERE, WITH THAT MONSTER?
NO. NO. WHEN IT RETURNED TO THE WATER, JACOB'S SPIRIT MUST HAVE BEEN FREED. HE'S NOT THERE ANYMORE.
OKAY.
OKAY, THEN.

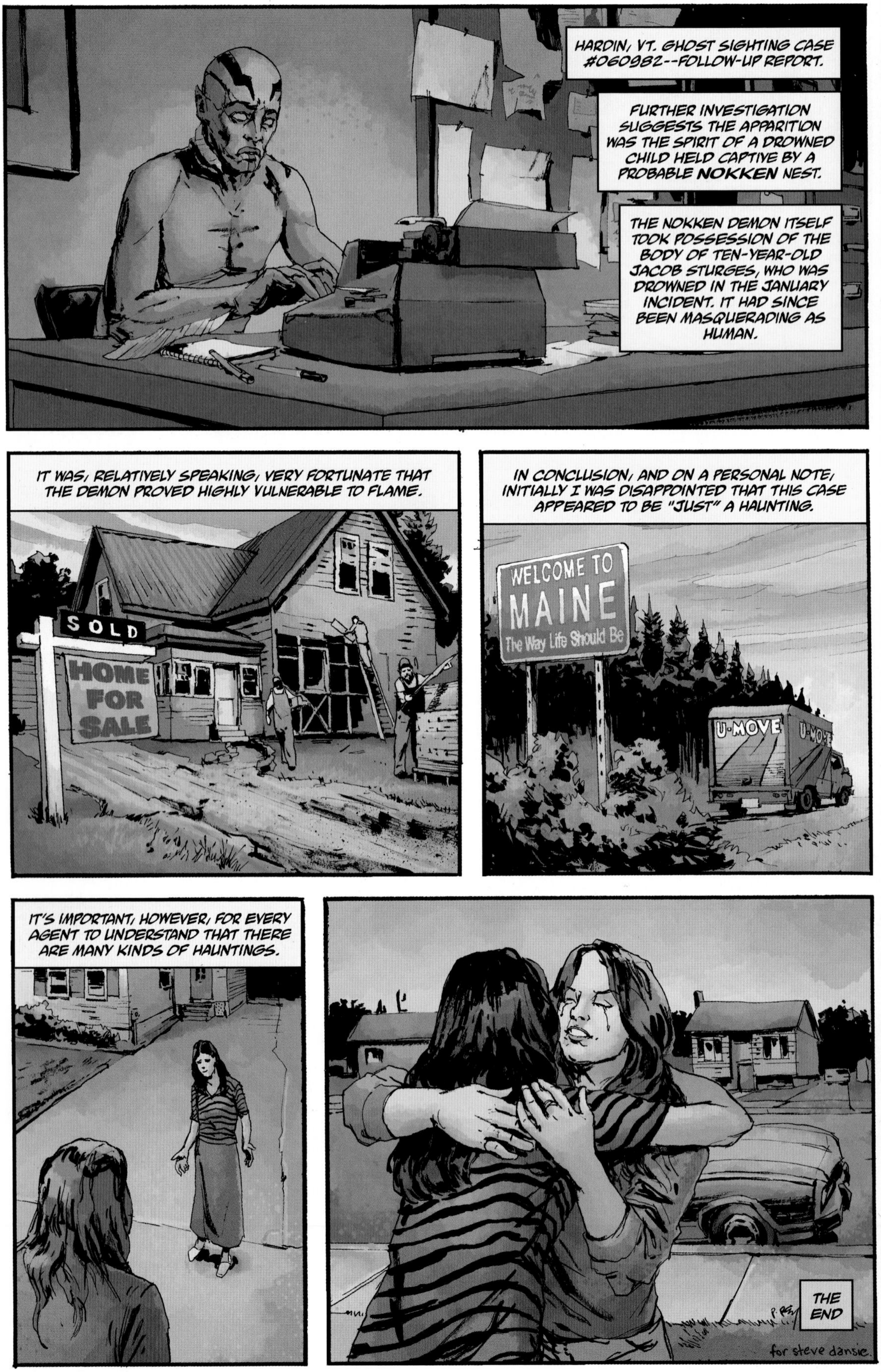
HARDIN, VT. GHOST SIGHTING CASE #060982--FOLLOW-UP REPORT.
FURTHER INVESTIGATION SUGGESTS THE APPARITION WAS THE SPIRIT OF A DROWNED CHILD HELD CAPTIVE BY A PROBABLE NOKKEN NEST.
THE NOKKEN DEMON ITSELF TOOK POSSESSION OF THE BODY OF TEN-YEAR-OLD JACOB STURGES, WHO WAS DROWNED IN THE JANUARY INCIDENT. IT HAD SINCE BEEN MASQUERADING AS HUMAN.
IT WAS, RELATIVELY SPEAKING, VERY FORTUNATE THAT THE DEMON PROVED HIGHLY VULNERABLE TO FLAME.
SOLD
HOME FOR SALE
IN CONCLUSION, AND ON A PERSONAL NOTE, INITIALLY I WAS DISAPPOINTED THAT THIS CASE APPEARED TO BE "JUST" A HAUNTING.
WELCOME TO MAINE
The Way Life Should Be
U-MOVE
IT'S IMPORTANT, HOWEVER, FOR EVERY AGENT TO UNDERSTAND THAT THERE ARE MANY KINDS OF HAUNTINGS.
THE END
for steve dansie.

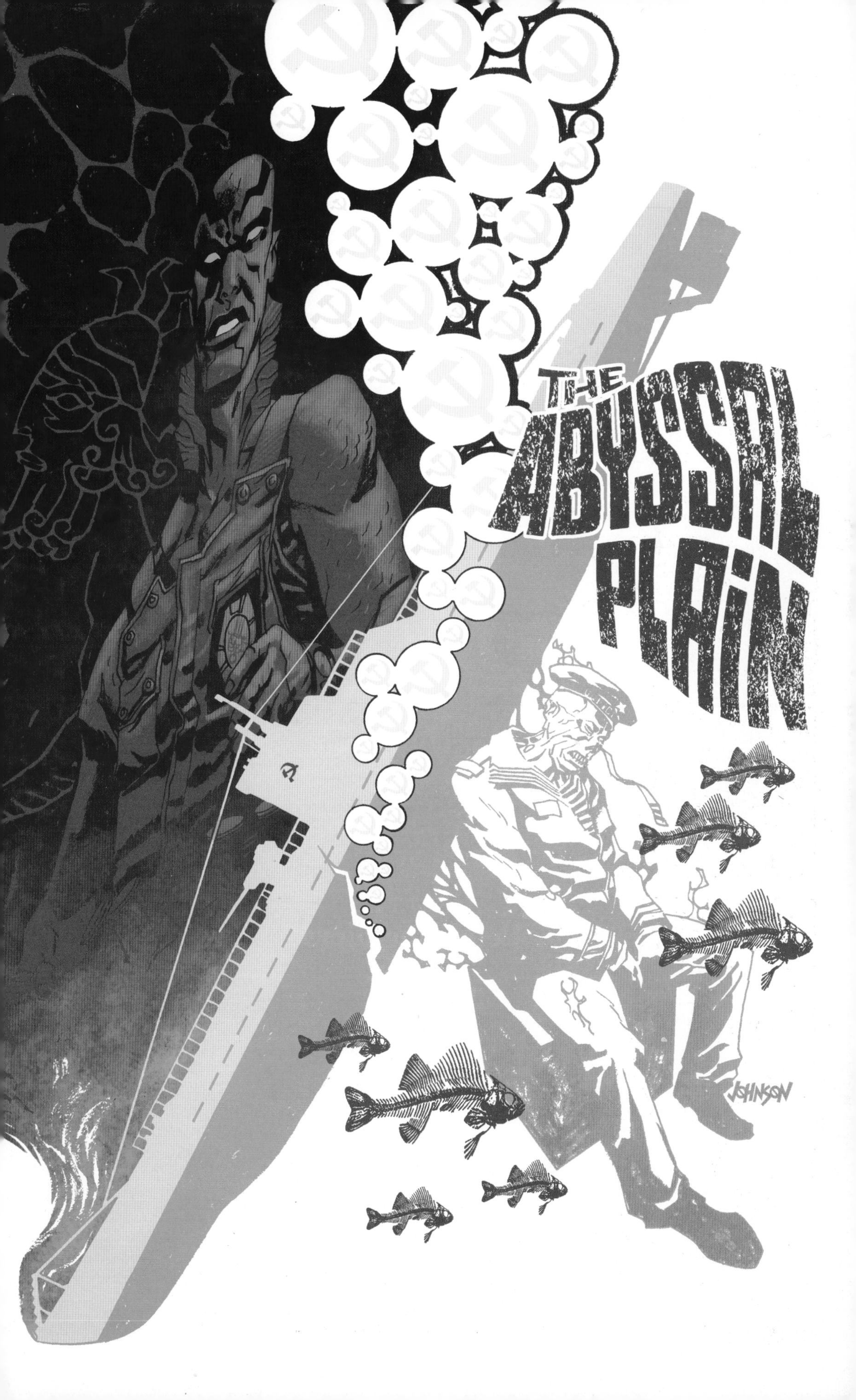
THE ABYSSAL PLAIN
JOHNSON

ART BY
**Peter Snejbjerg**

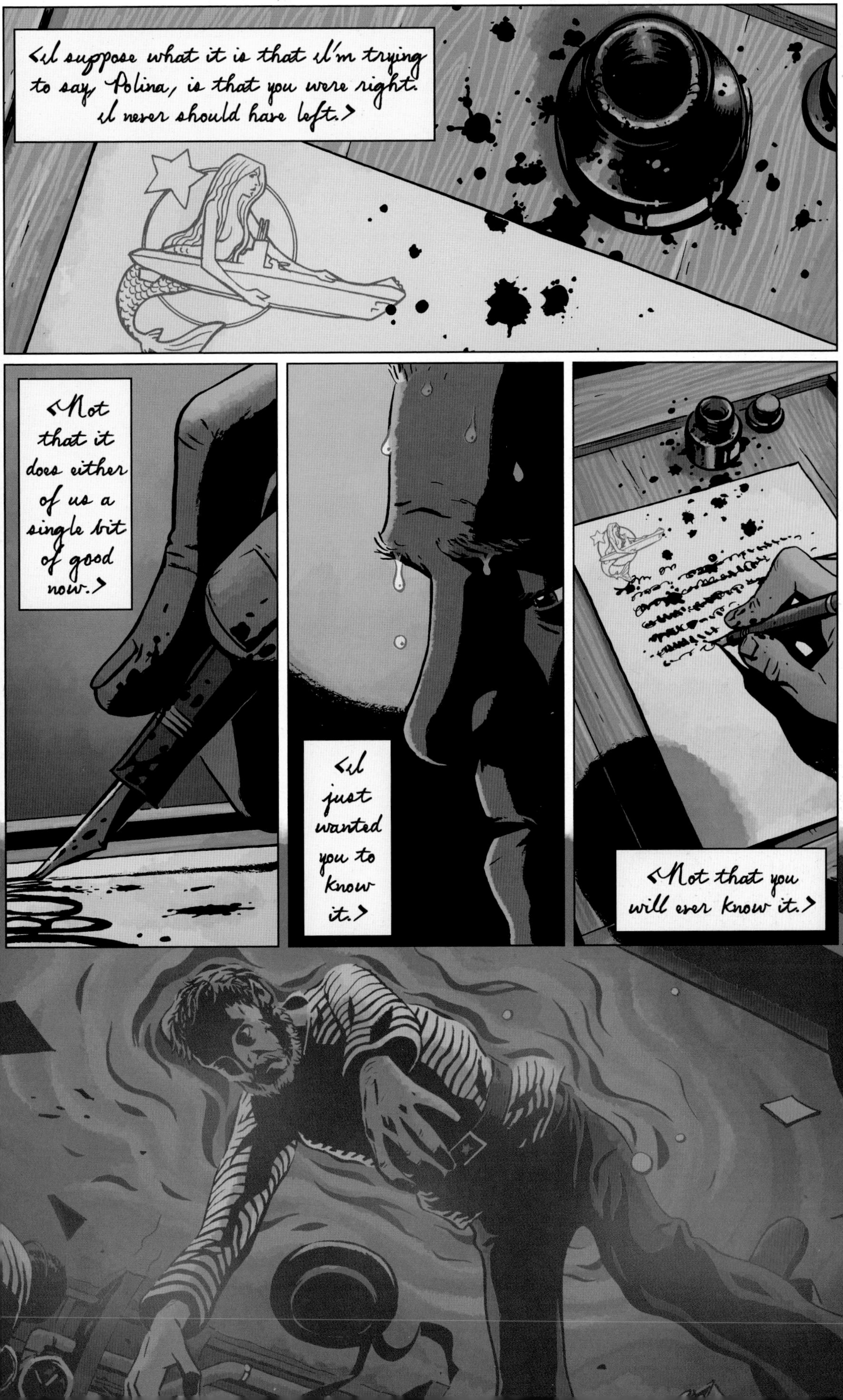
<I suppose what it is that I'm trying to say Polina, is that you were right. I never should have left.>
<Not that it does either of us a single bit of good now.>
<I just wanted you to know it.>
<Not that you will ever know it.>

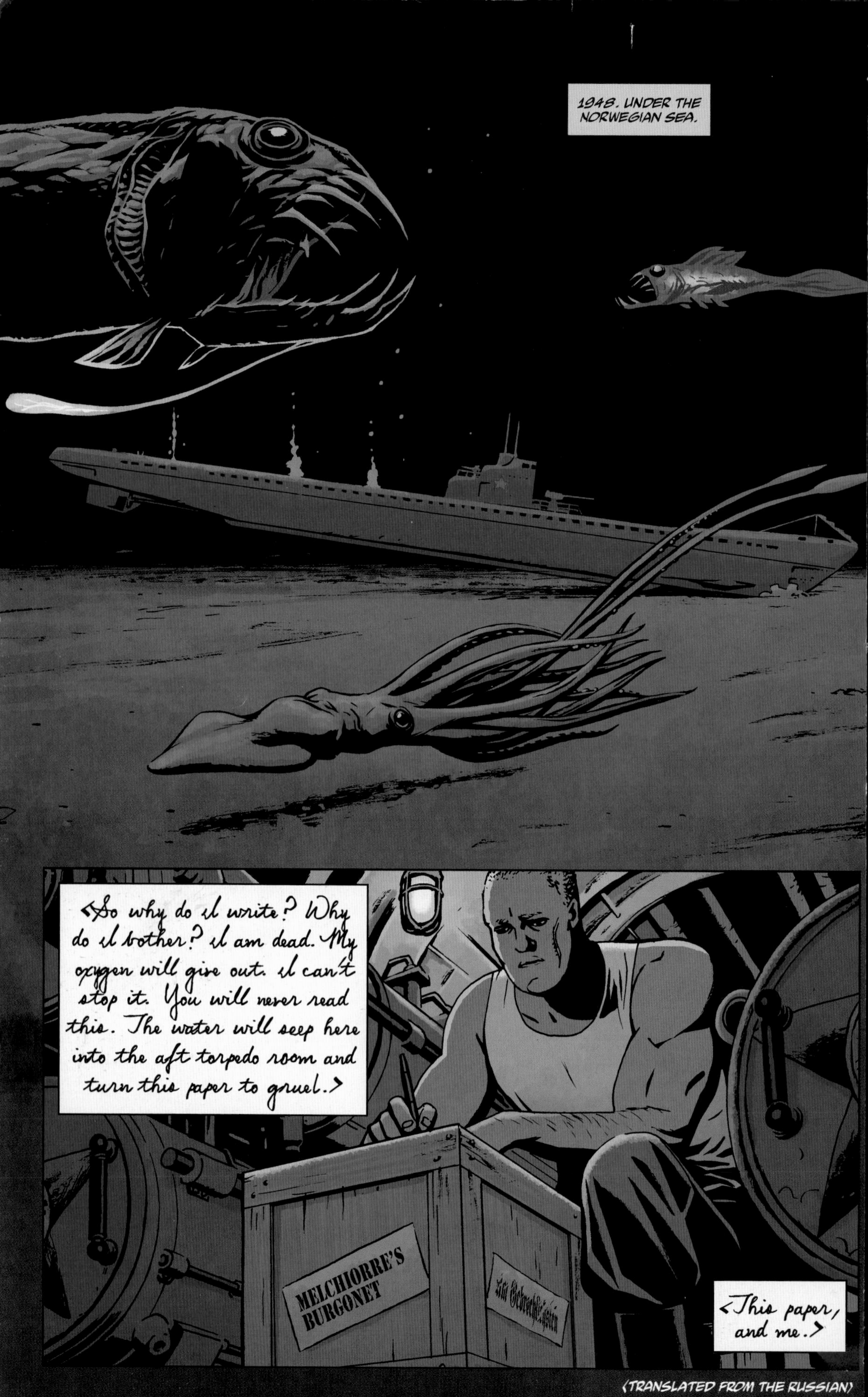
1948. UNDER THE NORWEGIAN SEA.
<So why do I write? Why do I bother? I am dead. My oxygen will give out. I can't stop it. You will never read this. The water will seep here into the aft torpedo room and turn this paper to gruel.>
MELCHIORRE'S BURGONET
<This paper, and me.>

(TRANSLATED FROM THE RUSSIAN)

<𝑒 think, as long as you are alive, you can't really believe that you're going to die. You know it, but you can't believe it.>

<𝑒t's impossible, of course, but 𝑒 have this desperate hope that someone will come and get the submarine out of here. That's in my heart.>

<As long as the generator stays dry...

V:150

P:125

GURGLE

GURGLE

SSSSSSSS

<THE ENGINE ROOM, LORD, THE **GENERATOR!**>

...as long as 𝑒 have light, and oxygen, 𝑒 believe this fantasy.>

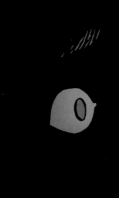

POLINA...

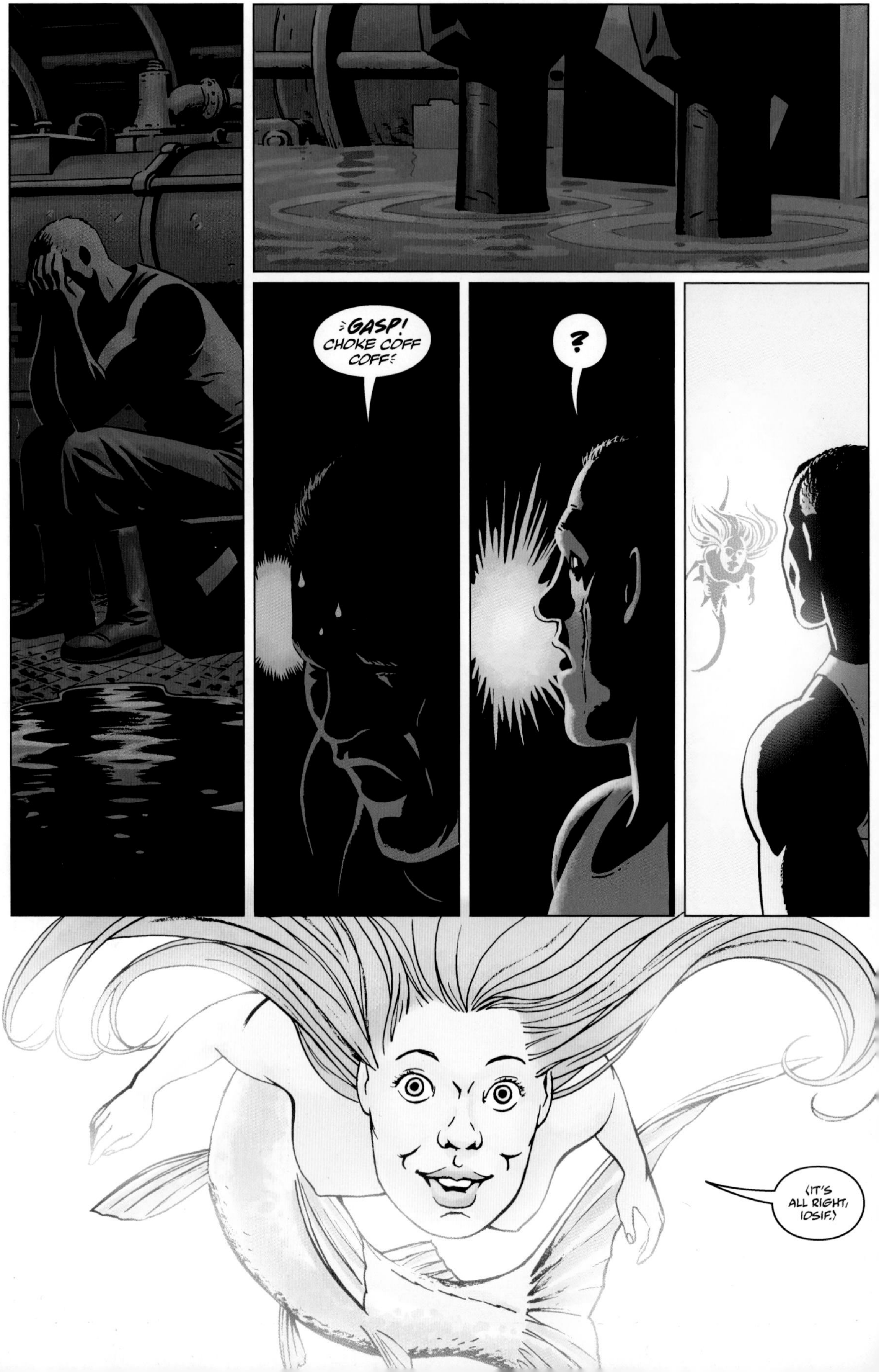
GASP! CHOKE COFF COFF
?
(IT'S ALL RIGHT, IOSIF.)

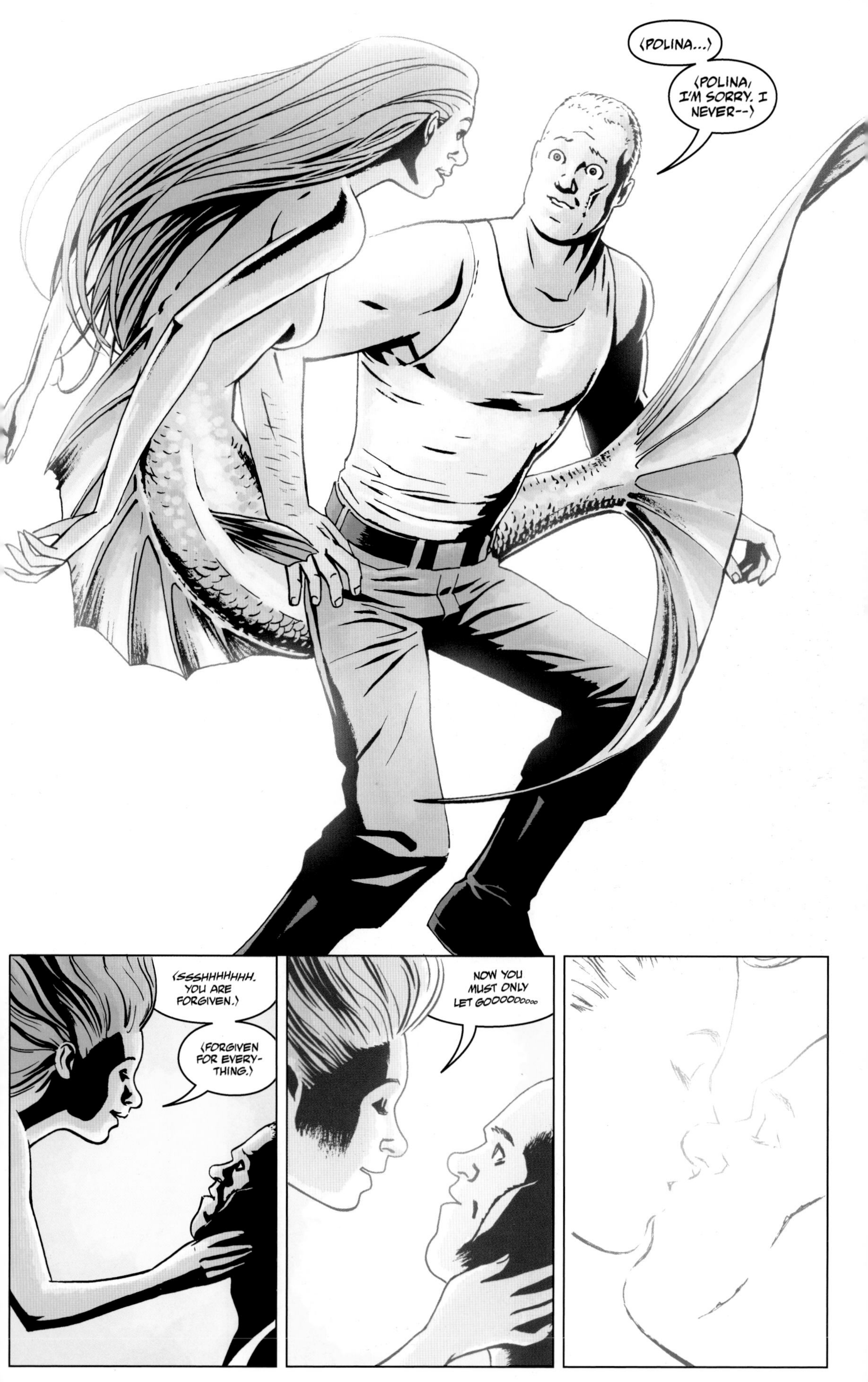
(POLINA...)
(POLINA, I'M SORRY. I NEVER--)
(SSSHHHHHHH. YOU ARE FORGIVEN.)
(FORGIVEN FOR EVERY-THING.)
NOW YOU MUST ONLY LET GOOOOOOooo

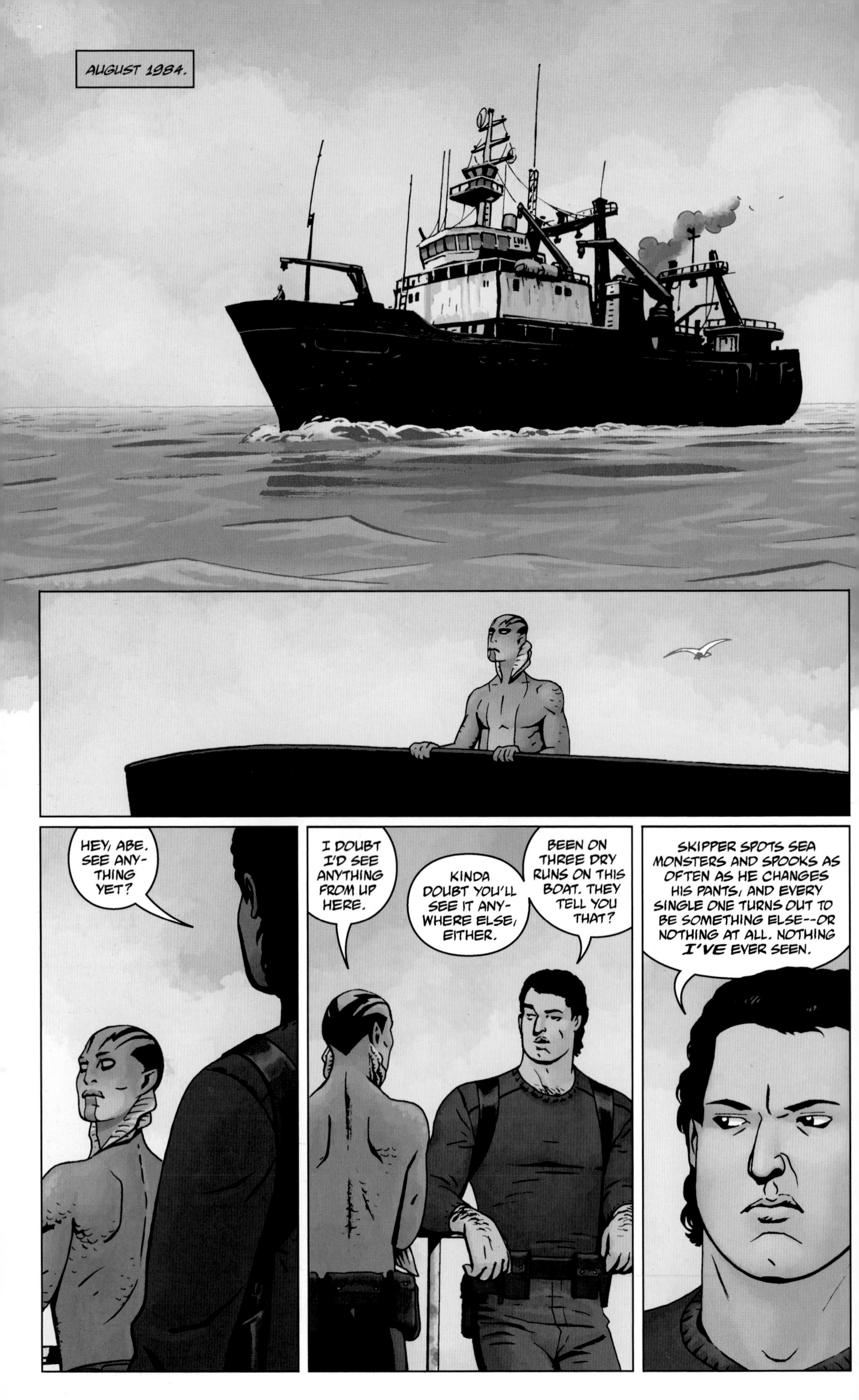
AUGUST 1984.
HEY, ABE. SEE ANY-THING YET?
I DOUBT I'D SEE ANYTHING FROM UP HERE.
KINDA DOUBT YOU'LL SEE IT ANY-WHERE ELSE, EITHER.
BEEN ON THREE DRY RUNS ON THIS BOAT. THEY TELL YOU THAT?
SKIPPER SPOTS SEA MONSTERS AND SPOOKS AS OFTEN AS HE CHANGES HIS PANTS, AND EVERY SINGLE ONE TURNS OUT TO BE SOMETHING ELSE--OR NOTHING AT ALL. NOTHING *I'VE* EVER SEEN.

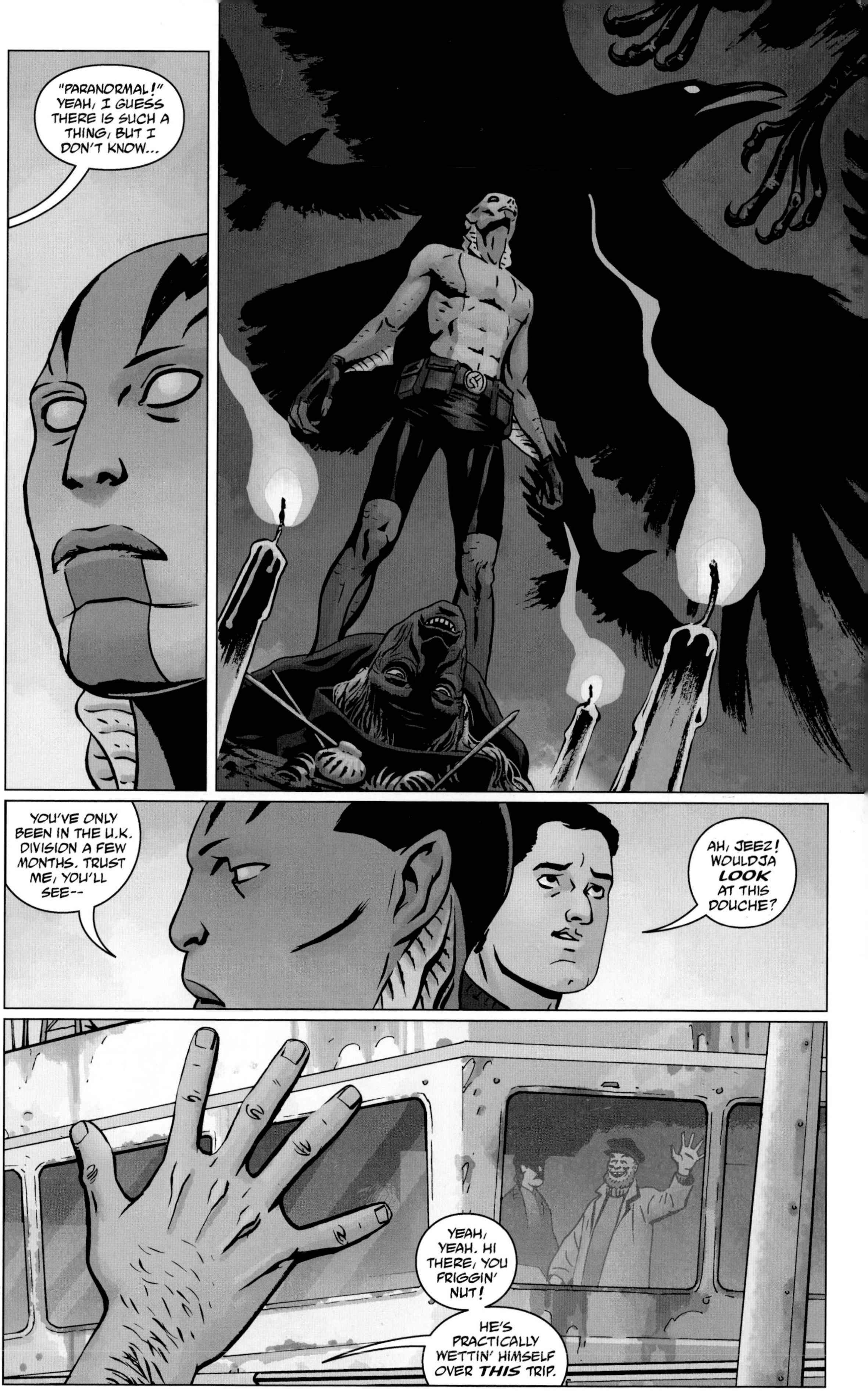
"PARANORMAL!" YEAH, I GUESS THERE IS SUCH A THING, BUT I DON'T KNOW...
YOU'VE ONLY BEEN IN THE U.K. DIVISION A FEW MONTHS. TRUST ME, YOU'LL SEE--
AH, JEEZ! WOULDJA LOOK AT THIS DOUCHE?
YEAH, YEAH. HI THERE, YOU FRIGGIN' NUT!
HE'S PRACTICALLY WETTIN' HIMSELF OVER THIS TRIP.

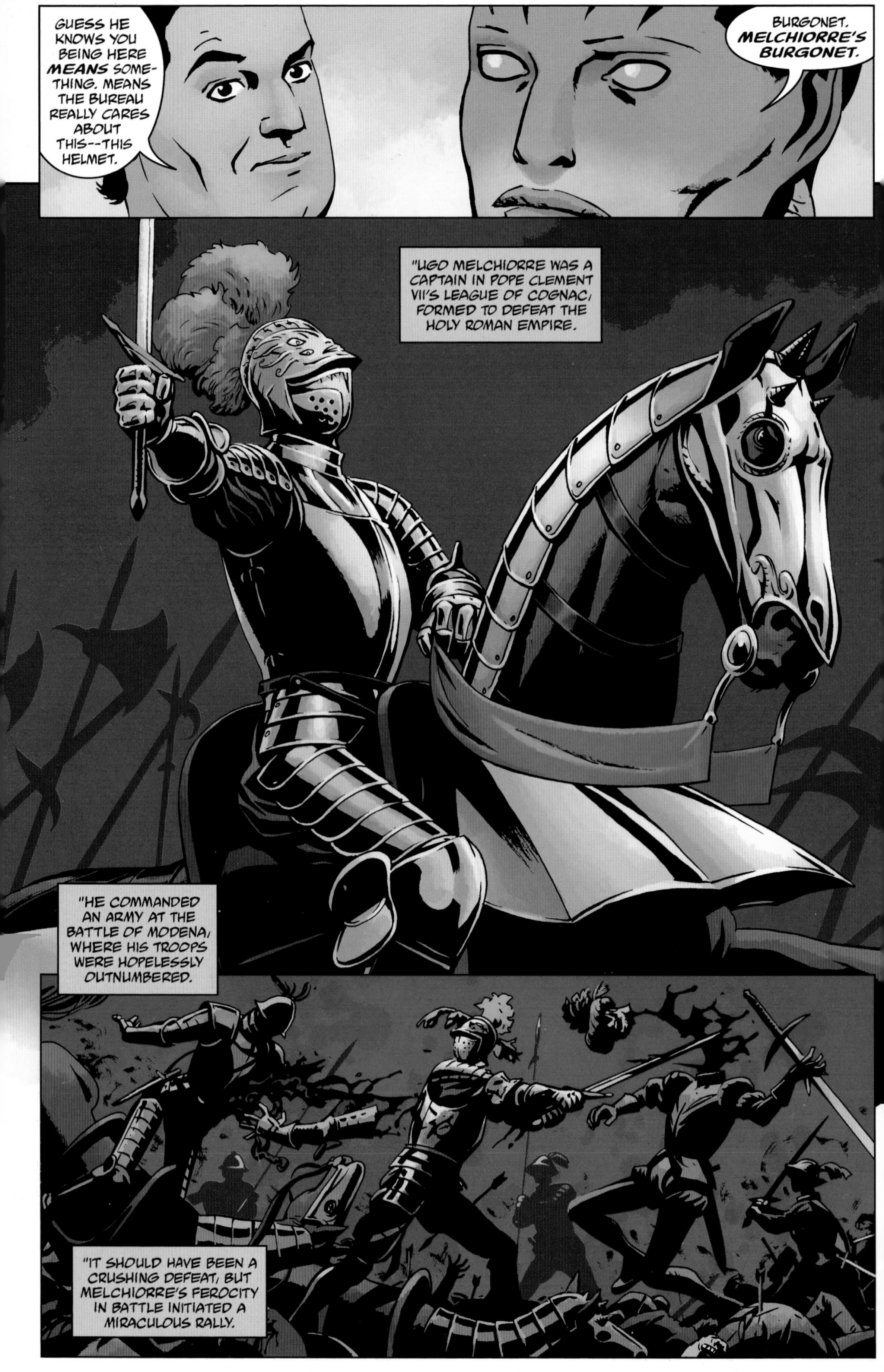
GUESS HE KNOWS YOU BEING HERE **MEANS** SOMETHING. MEANS THE BUREAU REALLY CARES ABOUT THIS--THIS HELMET.
BURGONET. ***MELCHIORRE'S BURGONET.***
"UGO MELCHIORRE WAS A CAPTAIN IN POPE CLEMENT VII'S LEAGUE OF COGNAC, FORMED TO DEFEAT THE HOLY ROMAN EMPIRE.
"HE COMMANDED AN ARMY AT THE BATTLE OF MODENA, WHERE HIS TROOPS WERE HOPELESSLY OUTNUMBERED.
"IT SHOULD HAVE BEEN A CRUSHING DEFEAT, BUT MELCHIORRE'S FEROCITY IN BATTLE INITIATED A MIRACULOUS RALLY.

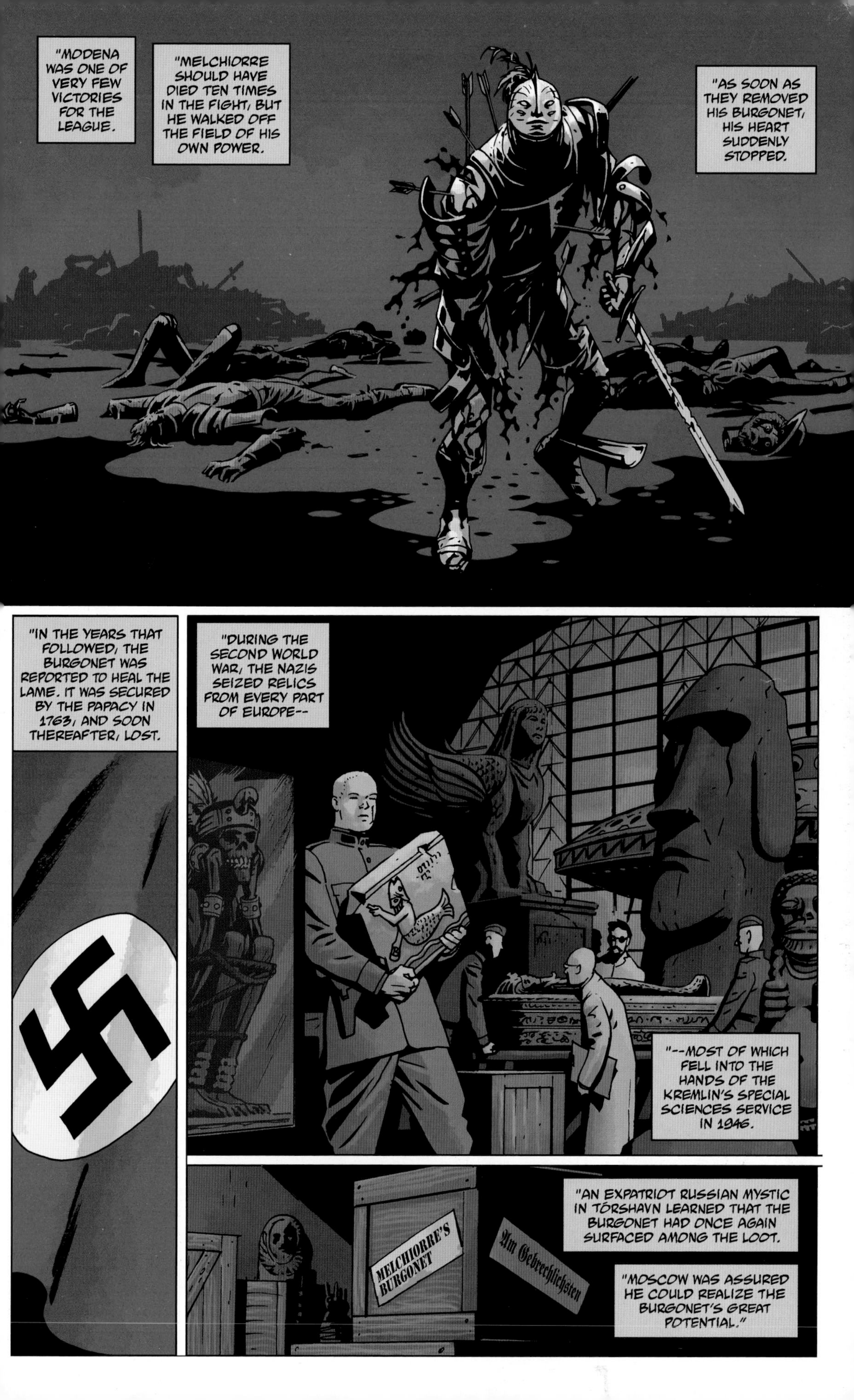
"MODENA WAS ONE OF VERY FEW VICTORIES FOR THE LEAGUE.
"MELCHIORRE SHOULD HAVE DIED TEN TIMES IN THE FIGHT, BUT HE WALKED OFF THE FIELD OF HIS OWN POWER.
"AS SOON AS THEY REMOVED HIS BURGONET, HIS HEART SUDDENLY STOPPED.
"IN THE YEARS THAT FOLLOWED, THE BURGONET WAS REPORTED TO HEAL THE LAME. IT WAS SECURED BY THE PAPACY IN 1763, AND SOON THEREAFTER, LOST.
"DURING THE SECOND WORLD WAR, THE NAZIS SEIZED RELICS FROM EVERY PART OF EUROPE--
"--MOST OF WHICH FELL INTO THE HANDS OF THE KREMLIN'S SPECIAL SCIENCES SERVICE IN 1946.
MELCHIORRE'S BURGONET
Am Gebrechlichsten
"AN EXPATRIOT RUSSIAN MYSTIC IN TÓRSHAVN LEARNED THAT THE BURGONET HAD ONCE AGAIN SURFACED AMONG THE LOOT.
"MOSCOW WAS ASSURED HE COULD REALIZE THE BURGONET'S GREAT POTENTIAL."

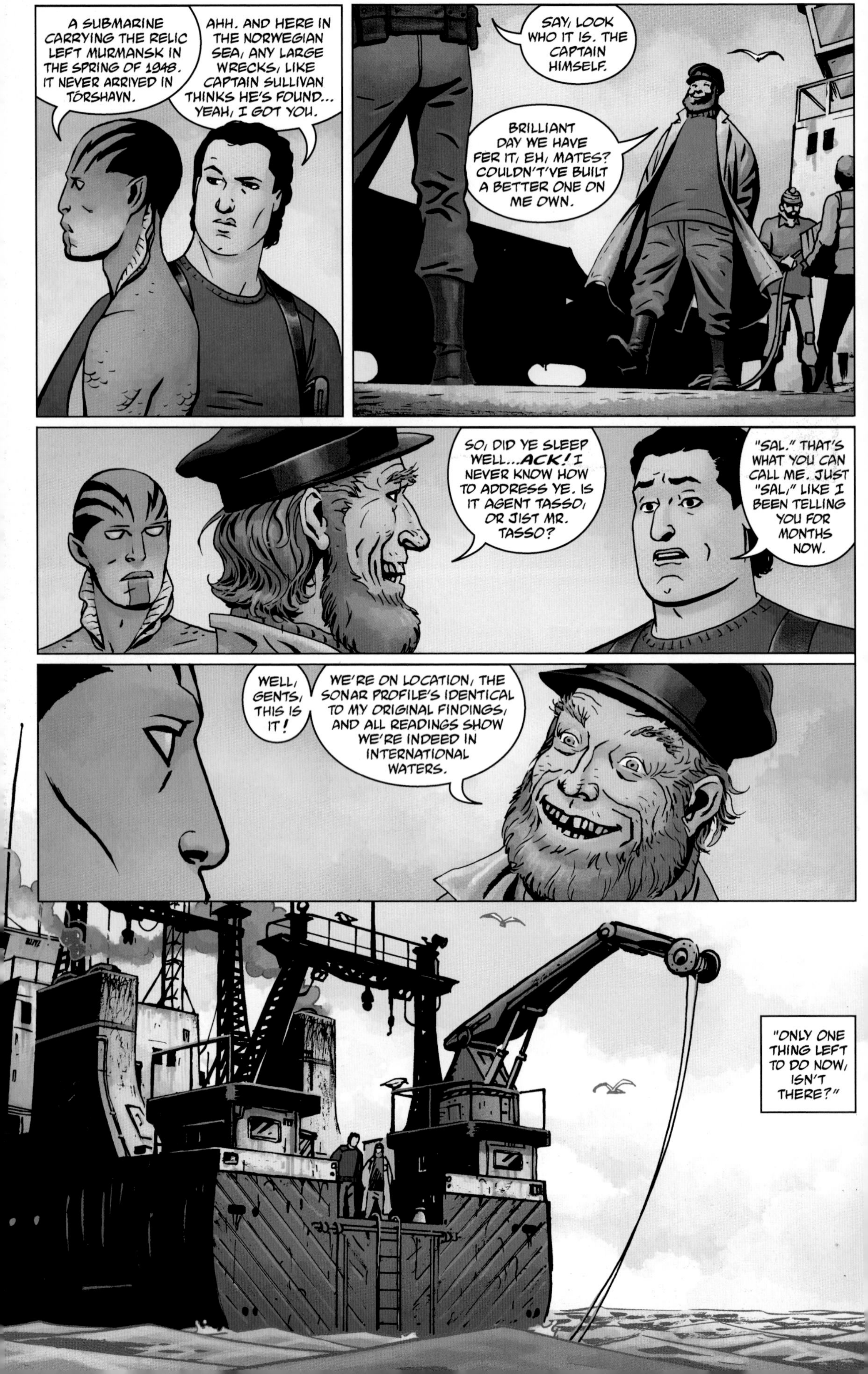
A SUBMARINE CARRYING THE RELIC LEFT MURMANSK IN THE SPRING OF 1948. IT NEVER ARRIVED IN TÓRSHAVN.
AHH. AND HERE IN THE NORWEGIAN SEA, ANY LARGE WRECKS, LIKE CAPTAIN SULLIVAN THINKS HE'S FOUND... YEAH, I GOT YOU.
SAY, LOOK WHO IT IS. THE CAPTAIN HIMSELF.
BRILLIANT DAY WE HAVE FER IT, EH, MATES? COULDN'T'VE BUILT A BETTER ONE ON ME OWN.
SO, DID YE SLEEP WELL...ACK! I NEVER KNOW HOW TO ADDRESS YE. IS IT AGENT TASSO, OR JIST MR. TASSO?
"SAL." THAT'S WHAT YOU CAN CALL ME. JUST "SAL," LIKE I BEEN TELLING YOU FOR MONTHS NOW.
WELL, GENTS, THIS IS IT!
WE'RE ON LOCATION, THE SONAR PROFILE'S IDENTICAL TO MY ORIGINAL FINDINGS, AND ALL READINGS SHOW WE'RE INDEED IN INTERNATIONAL WATERS.
"ONLY ONE THING LEFT TO DO NOW, ISN'T THERE?"

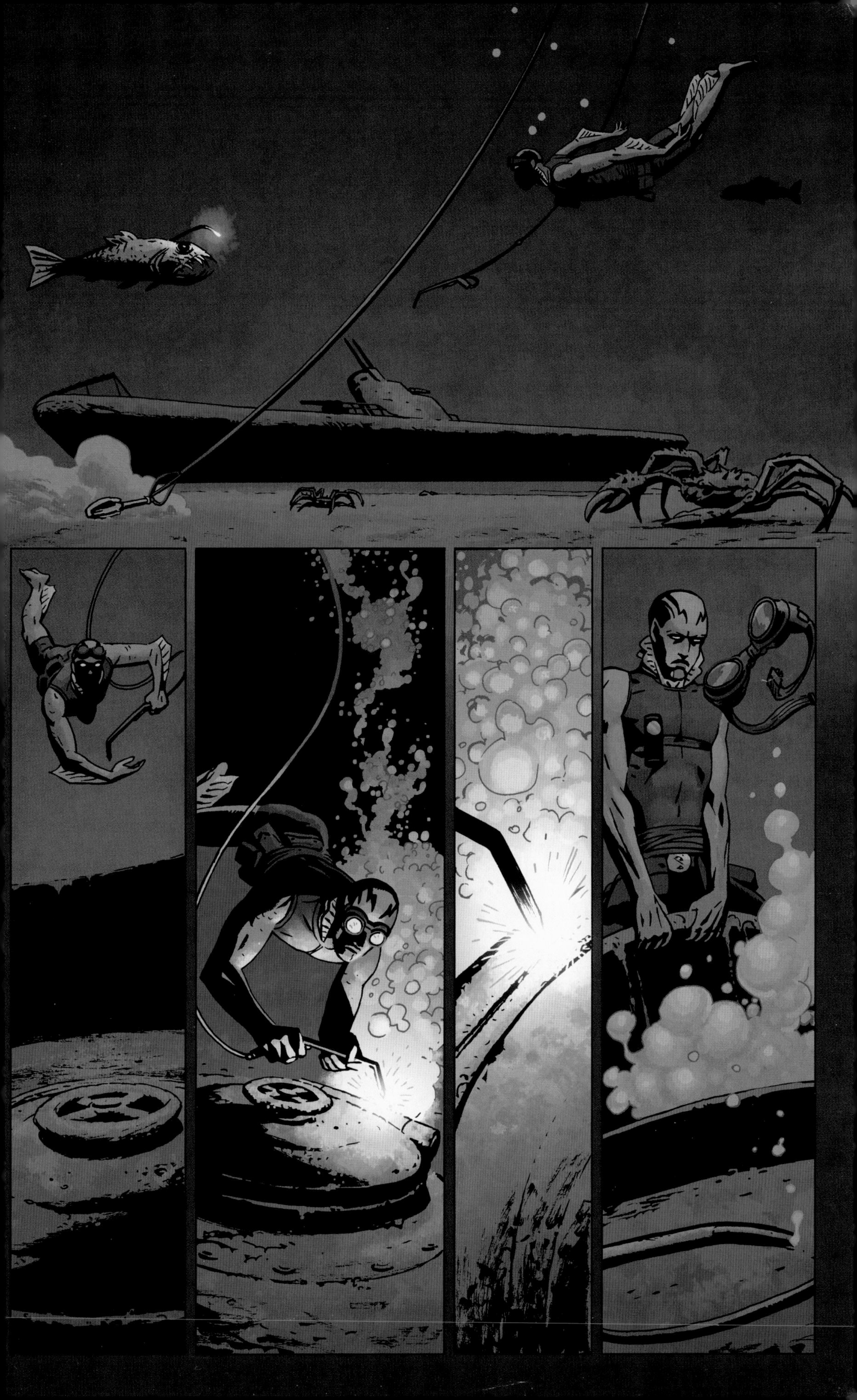

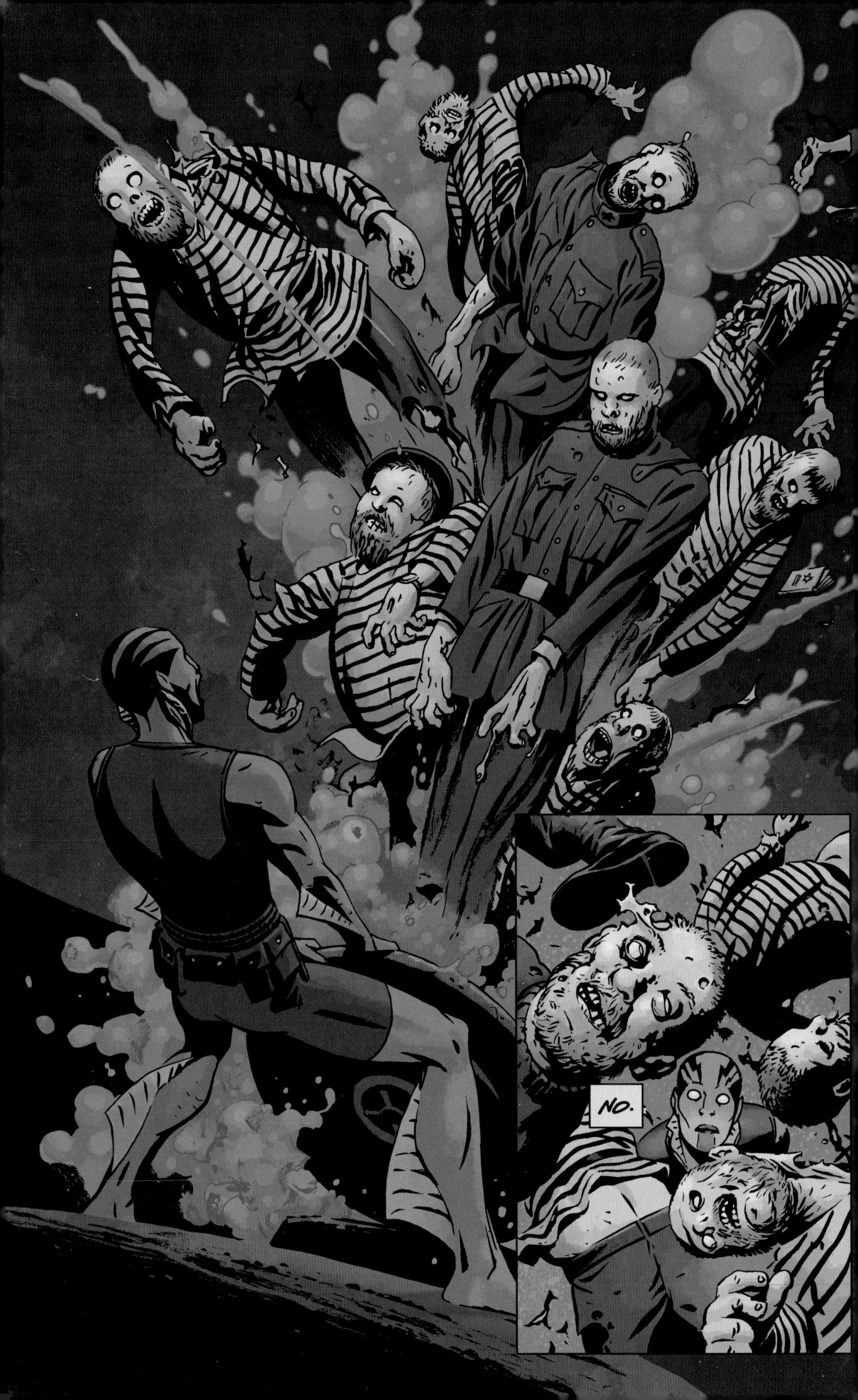
NO.

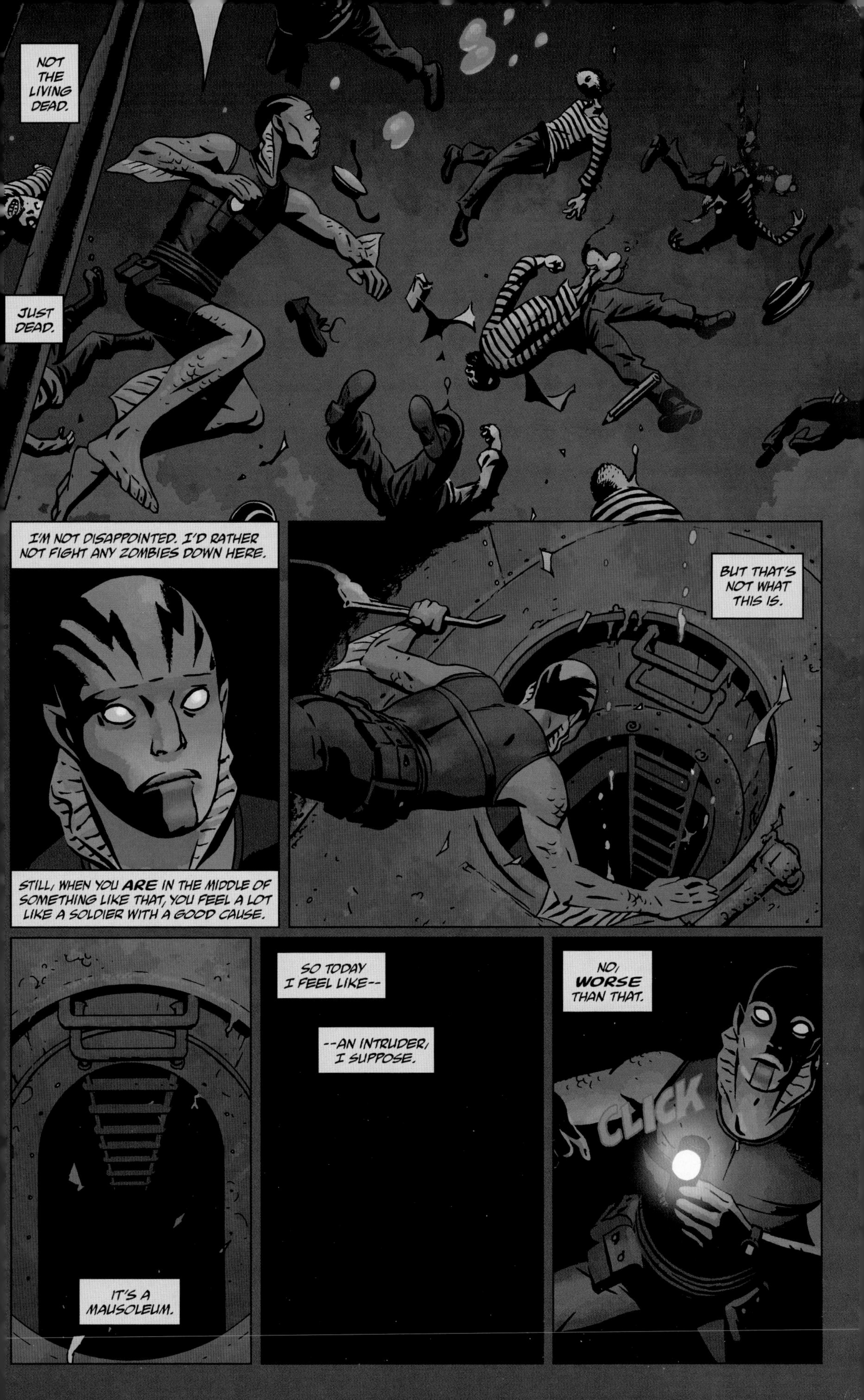
NOT THE LIVING DEAD.
JUST DEAD.
I'M NOT DISAPPOINTED. I'D RATHER NOT FIGHT ANY ZOMBIES DOWN HERE.
STILL, WHEN YOU ARE IN THE MIDDLE OF SOMETHING LIKE THAT, YOU FEEL A LOT LIKE A SOLDIER WITH A GOOD CAUSE.
BUT THAT'S NOT WHAT THIS IS.
IT'S A MAUSOLEUM.
SO TODAY I FEEL LIKE--
--AN INTRUDER, I SUPPOSE.
NO, WORSE THAN THAT.
CLICK

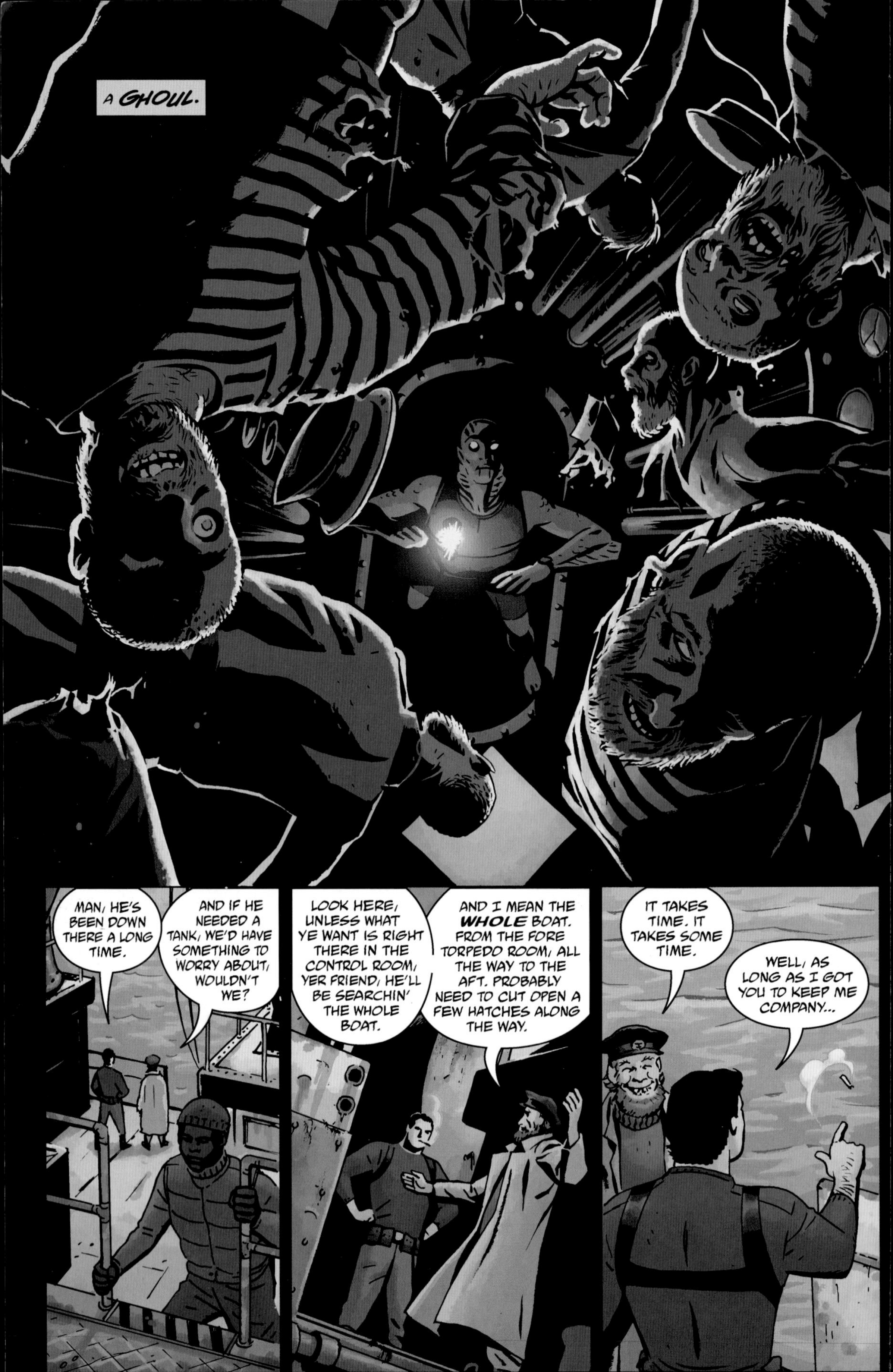

A GHOUL.
MAN, HE'S BEEN DOWN THERE A LONG TIME.
AND IF HE NEEDED A TANK, WE'D HAVE SOMETHING TO WORRY ABOUT, WOULDN'T WE?
LOOK HERE, UNLESS WHAT YE WANT IS RIGHT THERE IN THE CONTROL ROOM, YER FRIEND, HE'LL BE SEARCHIN' THE WHOLE BOAT.
AND I MEAN THE WHOLE BOAT. FROM THE FORE TORPEDO ROOM, ALL THE WAY TO THE AFT. PROBABLY NEED TO CUT OPEN A FEW HATCHES ALONG THE WAY.
IT TAKES TIME. IT TAKES SOME TIME.
WELL, AS LONG AS I GOT YOU TO KEEP ME COMPANY...

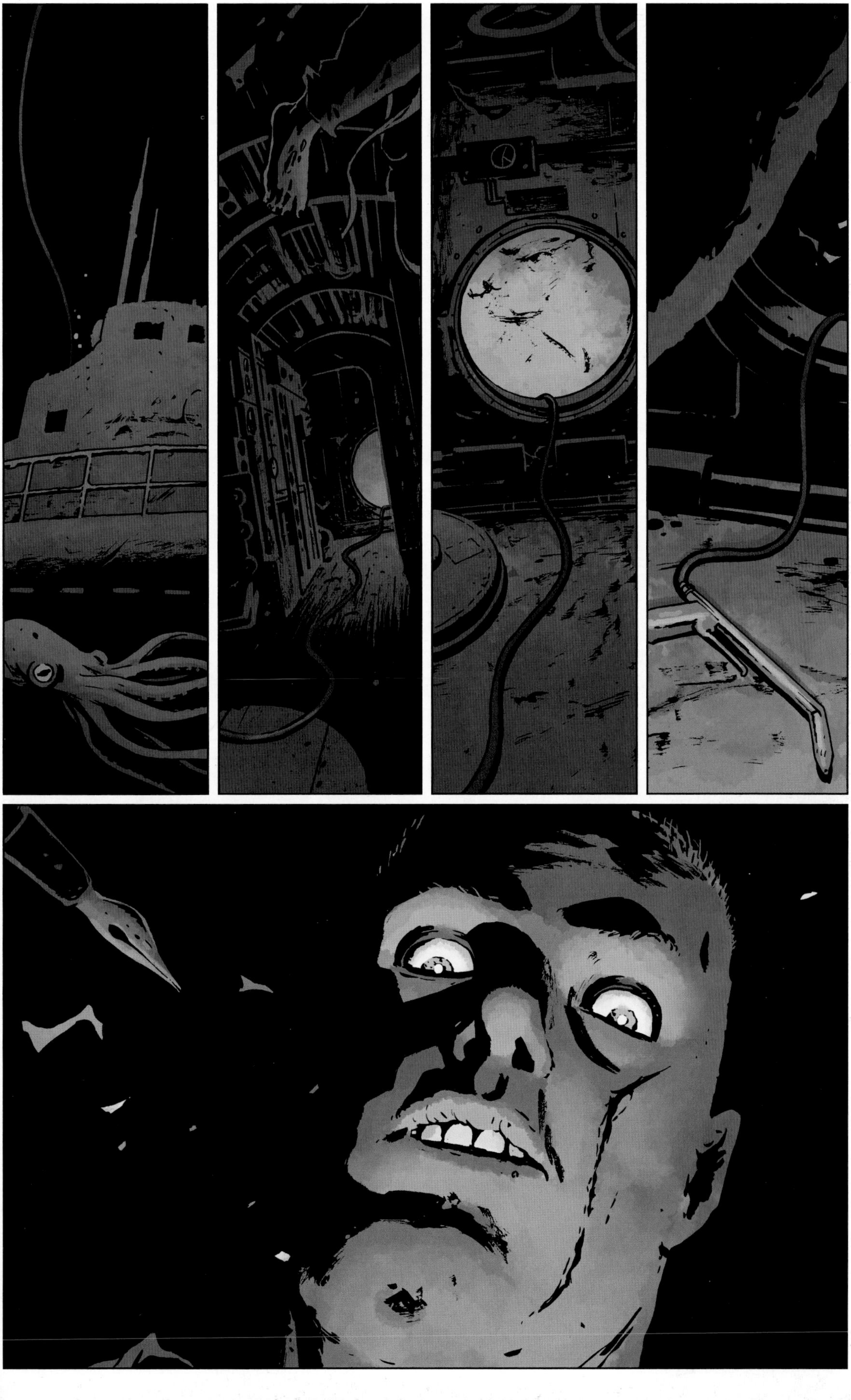

I'M SORRY. YOU HAD A JOB, I KNOW. THAT'S WHY YOU WERE BACK HERE, LOCKED AWAY WITH THIS CRATE.

IT COULDN'T HAVE BEEN COMFORTABLE, AND LOOK WHERE IT GOT YOU.

I DON'T ALWAYS LIKE MY JOB EITHER.

MELCHIORRE'S BURG...ET

Am Gebrex... ichsten

ANYWAY, I HOPE YOU DIDN'T SUFFER TOO MUCH.

I HOPE YOU FOUND PEACE.

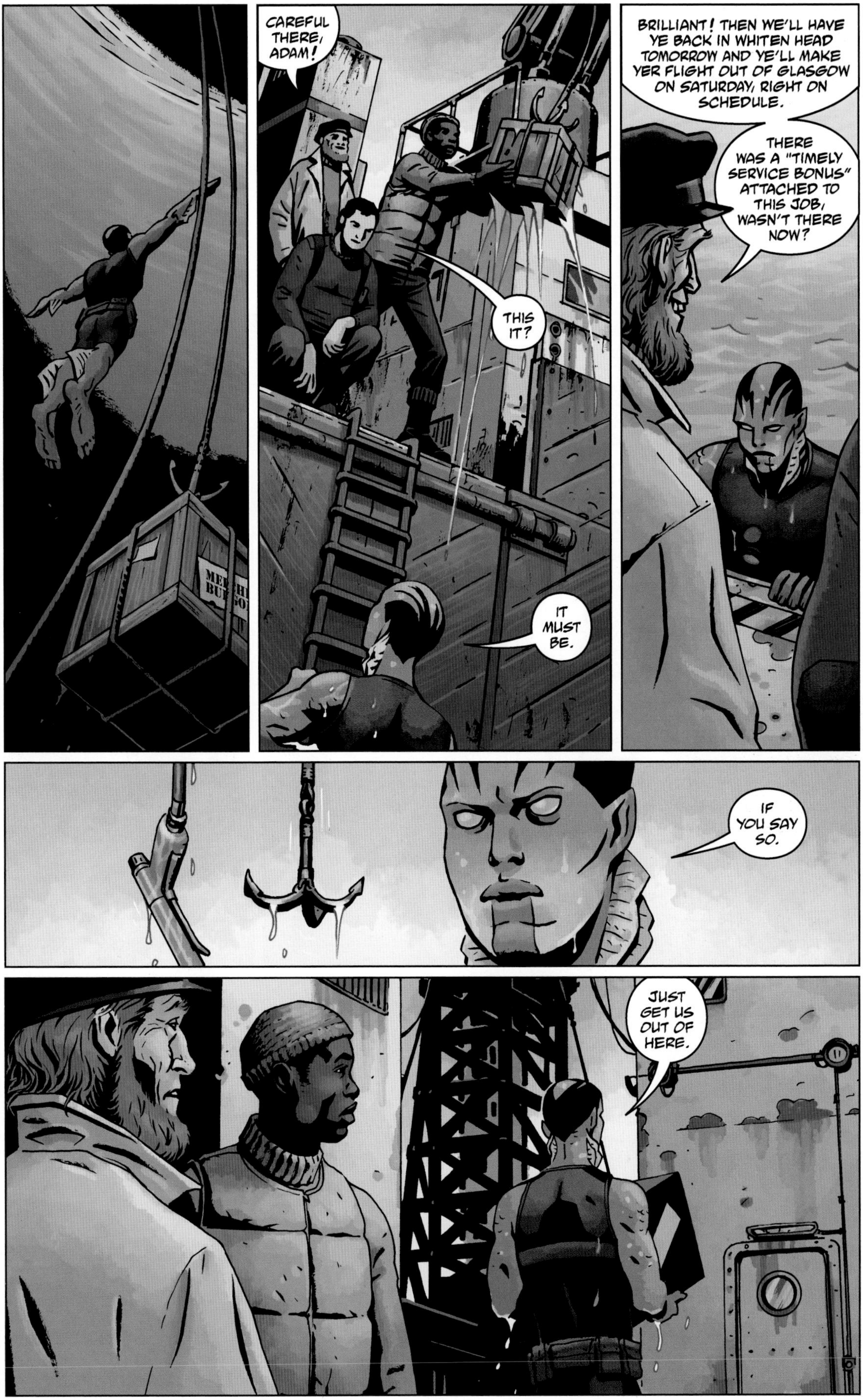
CAREFUL THERE, ADAM!
THIS IT?
IT MUST BE.
BRILLIANT! THEN WE'LL HAVE YE BACK IN WHITEN HEAD TOMORROW AND YE'LL MAKE YER FLIGHT OUT OF GLASGOW ON SATURDAY, RIGHT ON SCHEDULE.
THERE WAS A "TIMELY SERVICE BONUS" ATTACHED TO THIS JOB, WASN'T THERE NOW?
IF YOU SAY SO.
JUST GET US OUT OF HERE.

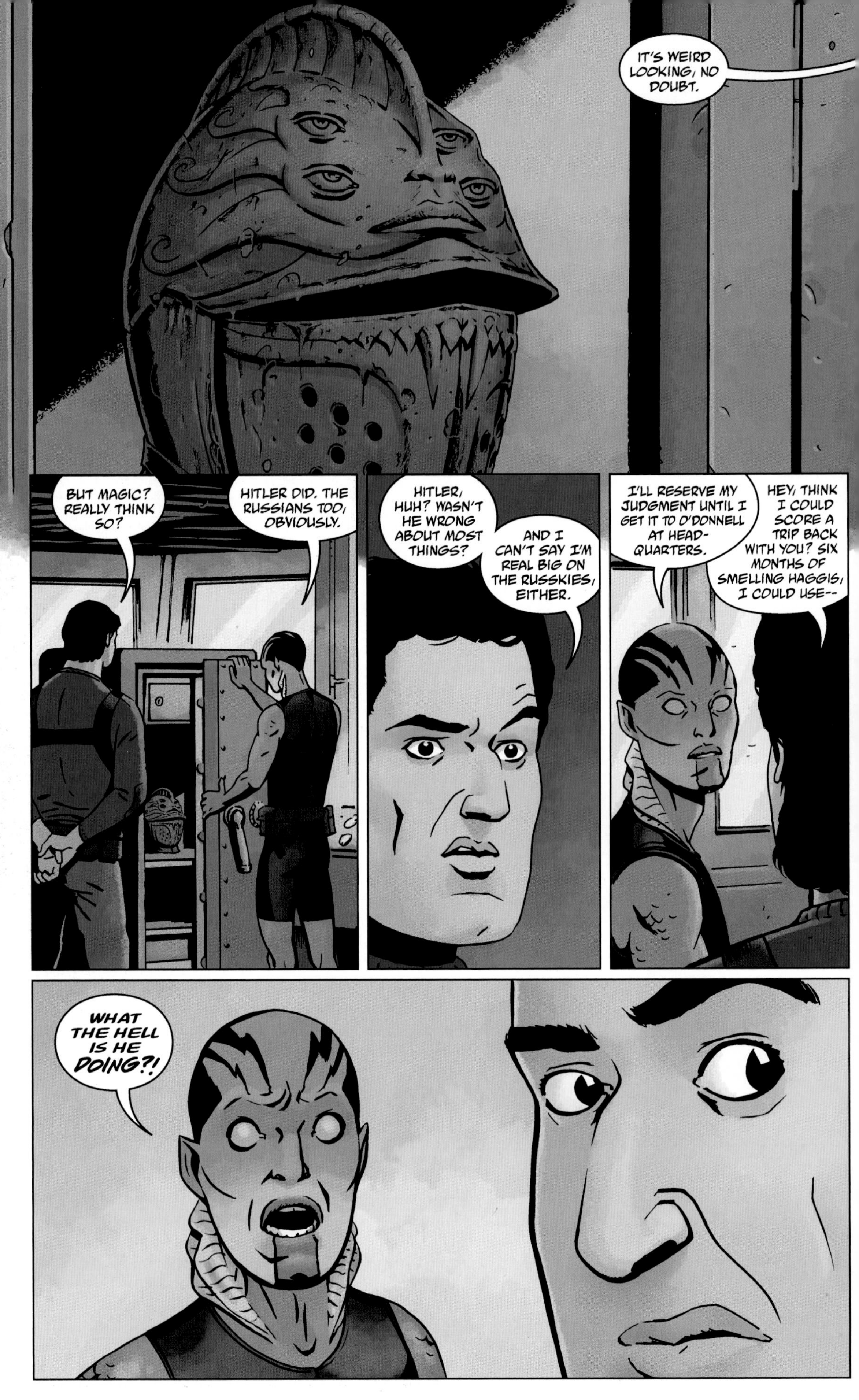
IT'S WEIRD LOOKING, NO DOUBT.
BUT MAGIC? REALLY THINK SO?
HITLER DID. THE RUSSIANS TOO, OBVIOUSLY.
HITLER, HUH? WASN'T HE WRONG ABOUT MOST THINGS?
AND I CAN'T SAY I'M REAL BIG ON THE RUSSKIES, EITHER.
I'LL RESERVE MY JUDGMENT UNTIL I GET IT TO O'DONNELL AT HEAD-QUARTERS.
HEY, THINK I COULD SCORE A TRIP BACK WITH YOU? SIX MONTHS OF SMELLING HAGGIS, I COULD USE--
WHAT THE HELL IS HE DOING?!

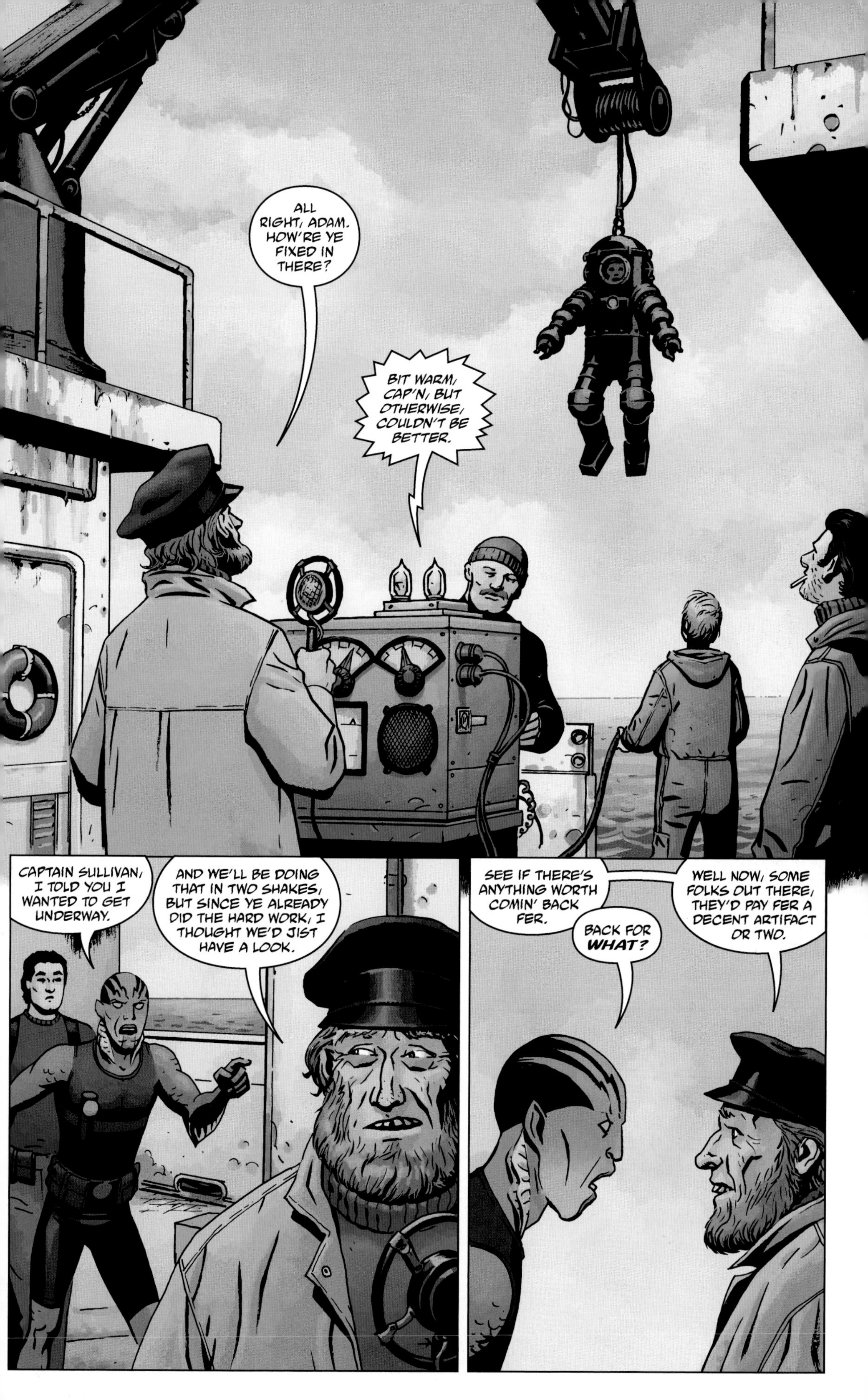
ALL RIGHT, ADAM. HOW'RE YE FIXED IN THERE?
BIT WARM, CAP'N, BUT OTHERWISE, COULDN'T BE BETTER.
CAPTAIN SULLIVAN, I TOLD YOU I WANTED TO GET UNDERWAY.
AND WE'LL BE DOING THAT IN TWO SHAKES, BUT SINCE YE ALREADY DID THE HARD WORK, I THOUGHT WE'D JIST HAVE A LOOK.
SEE IF THERE'S ANYTHING WORTH COMIN' BACK FER.
BACK FOR *WHAT?*
WELL NOW, SOME FOLKS OUT THERE, THEY'D PAY FER A DECENT ARTIFACT OR TWO.

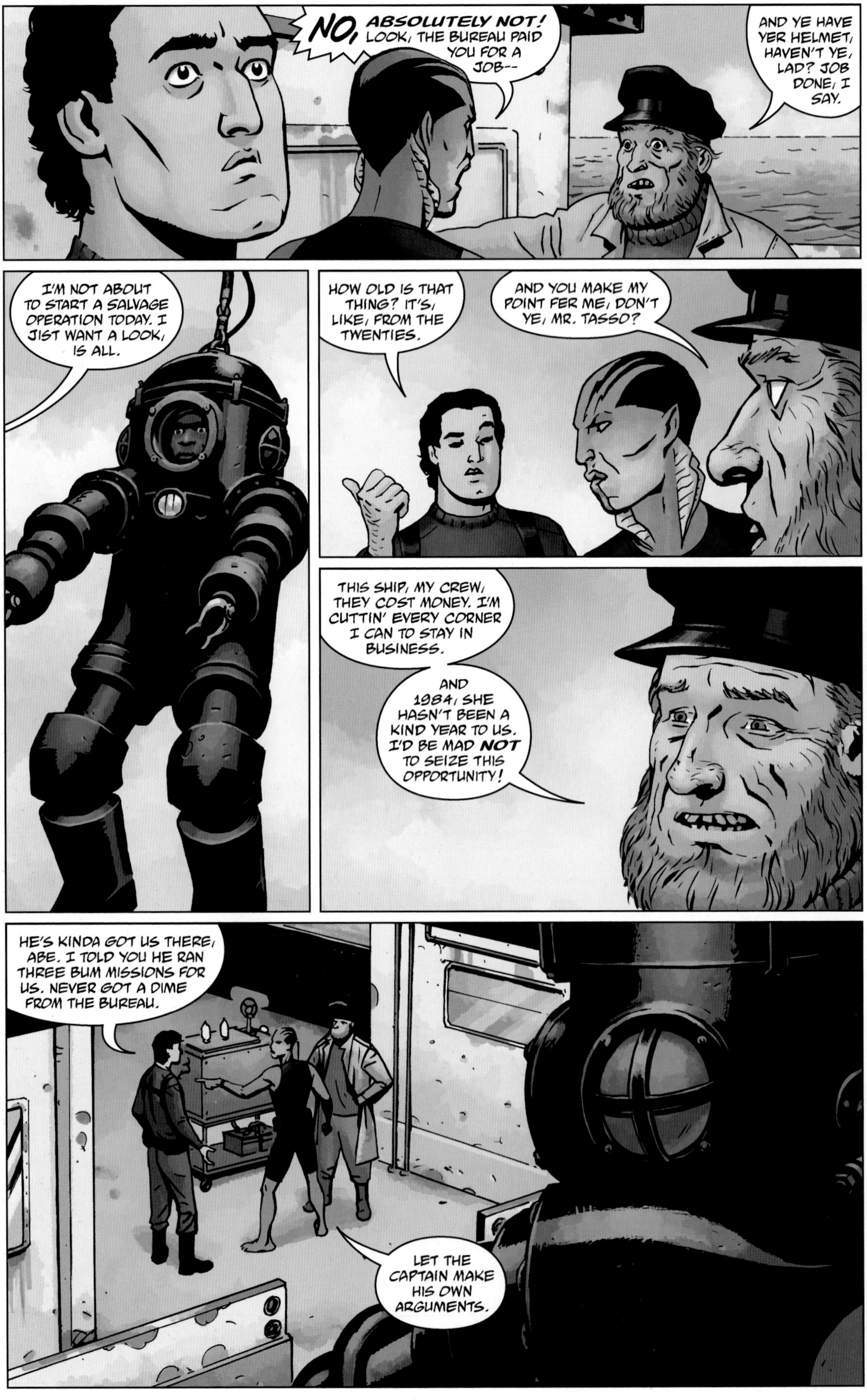
NO, ABSOLUTELY NOT! LOOK, THE BUREAU PAID YOU FOR A JOB--
AND YE HAVE YER HELMET, HAVEN'T YE, LAD? JOB DONE, I SAY.
I'M NOT ABOUT TO START A SALVAGE OPERATION TODAY. I JIST WANT A LOOK, IS ALL.
HOW OLD IS THAT THING? IT'S, LIKE, FROM THE TWENTIES.
AND YOU MAKE MY POINT FER ME, DON'T YE, MR. TASSO?
THIS SHIP, MY CREW, THEY COST MONEY. I'M CUTTIN' EVERY CORNER I CAN TO STAY IN BUSINESS.
AND 1984, SHE HASN'T BEEN A KIND YEAR TO US. I'D BE MAD NOT TO SEIZE THIS OPPORTUNITY!
HE'S KINDA GOT US THERE, ABE. I TOLD YOU HE RAN THREE BUM MISSIONS FOR US. NEVER GOT A DIME FROM THE BUREAU.
LET THE CAPTAIN MAKE HIS OWN ARGUMENTS.

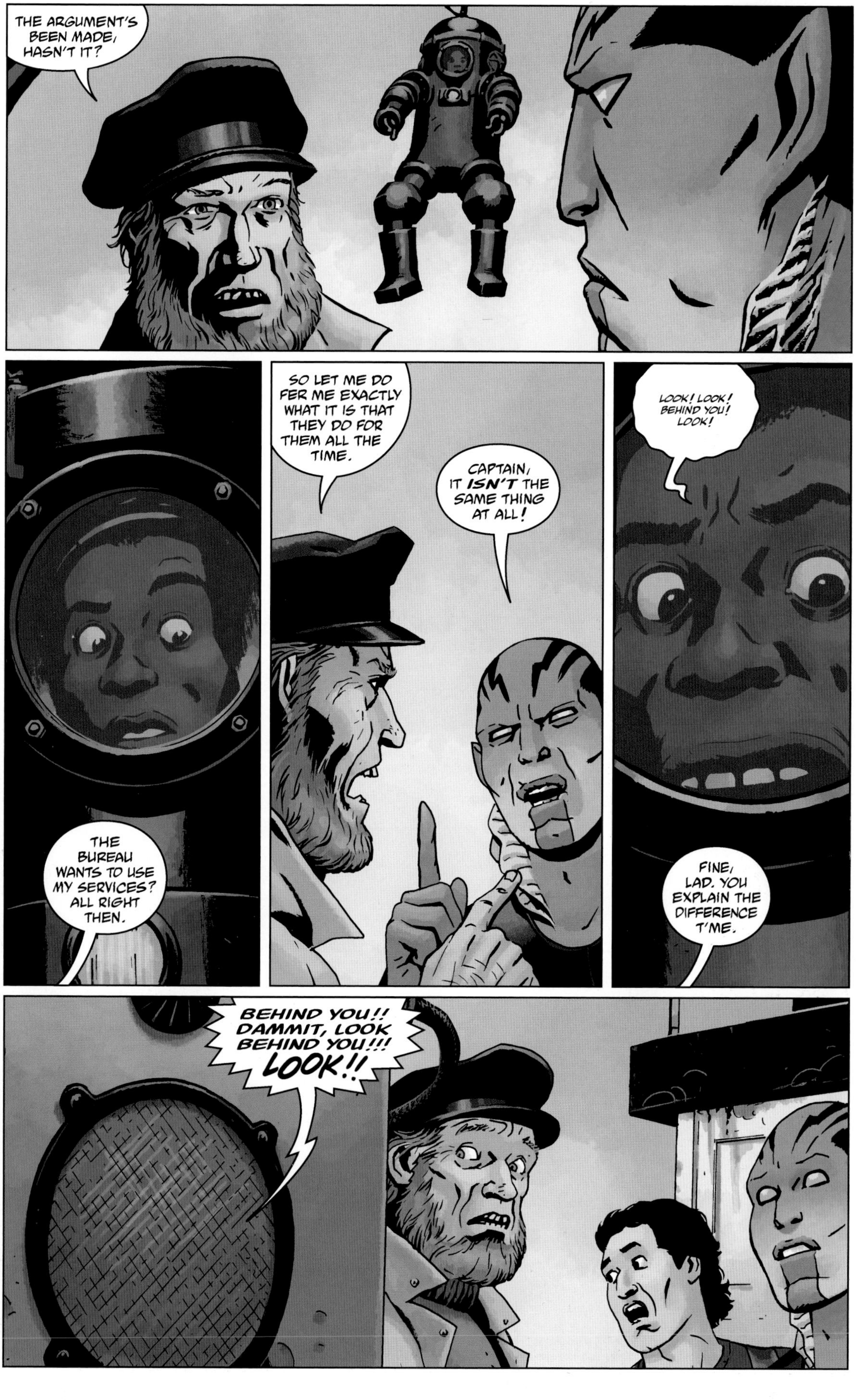
THE ARGUMENT'S BEEN MADE, HASN'T IT?
THE BUREAU WANTS TO USE MY SERVICES? ALL RIGHT THEN.
SO LET ME DO FER ME EXACTLY WHAT IT IS THAT THEY DO FOR THEM ALL THE TIME.
CAPTAIN, IT ISN'T THE SAME THING AT ALL!
LOOK! LOOK! BEHIND YOU! LOOK!
FINE, LAD. YOU EXPLAIN THE DIFFERENCE T'ME.
BEHIND YOU!! DAMMIT, LOOK BEHIND YOU!!! LOOK!!

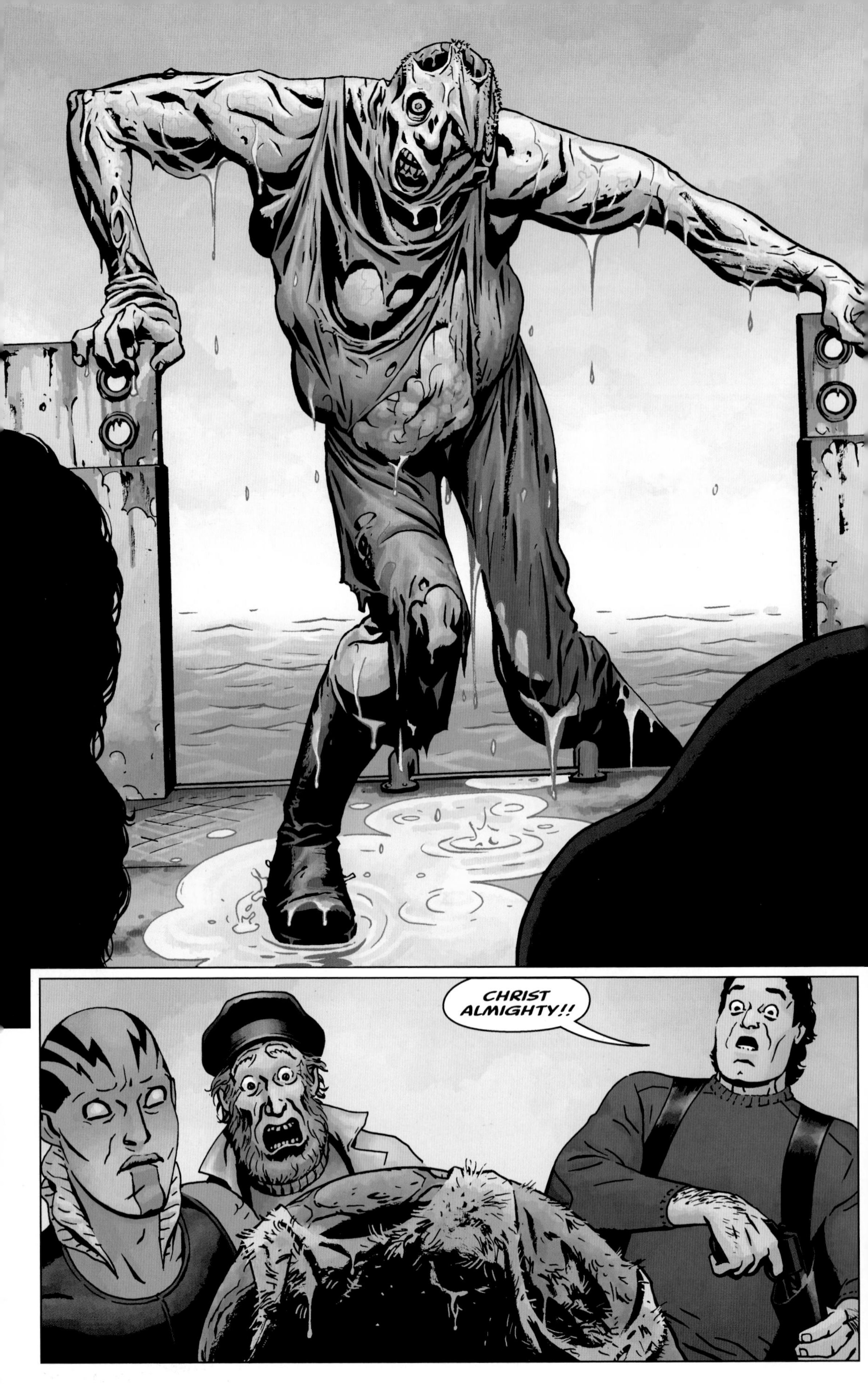
CHRIST ALMIGHTY!!

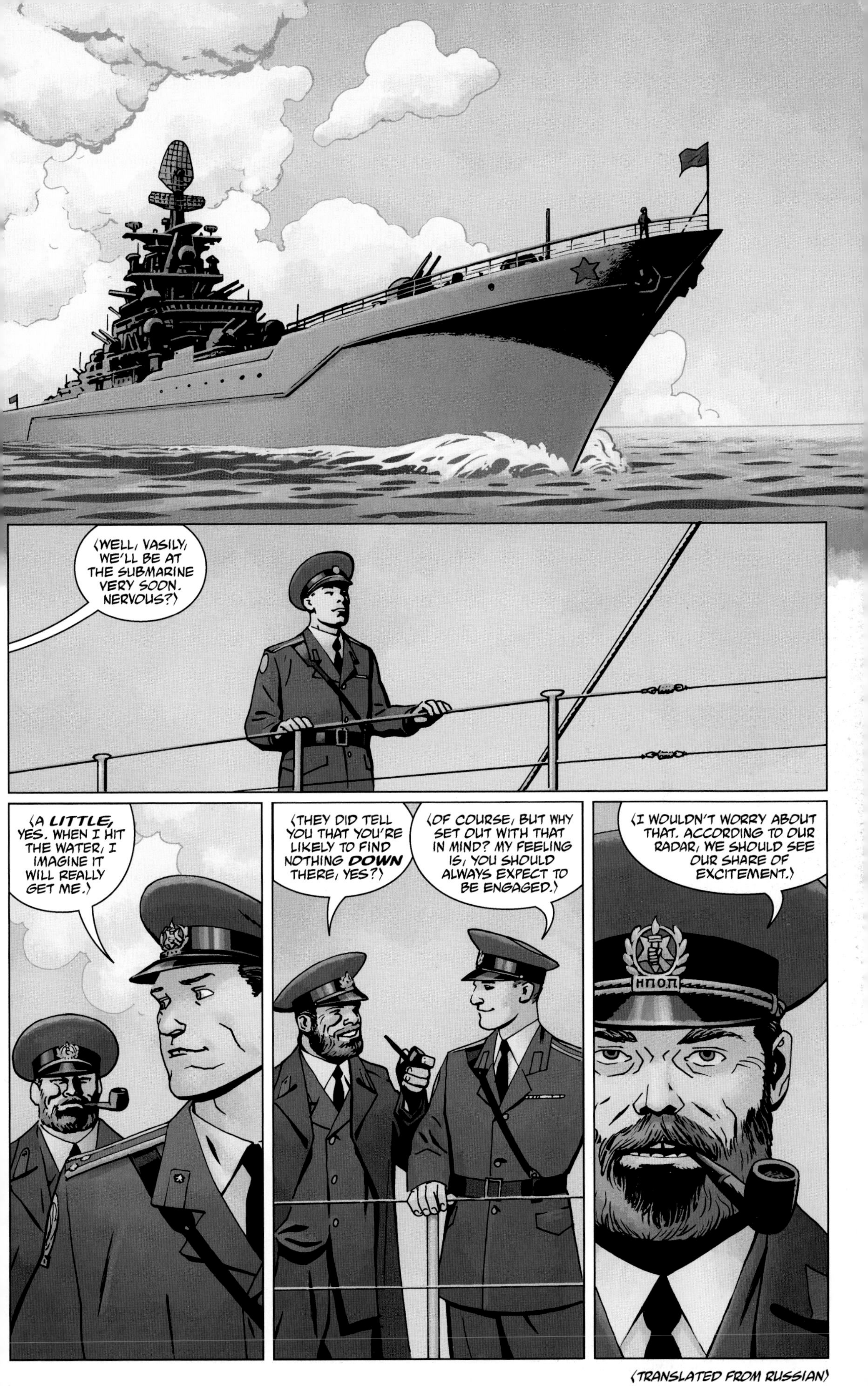

⟨WELL, VASILY, WE'LL BE AT THE SUBMARINE VERY SOON. NERVOUS?⟩
⟨A *LITTLE*, YES. WHEN I HIT THE WATER, I IMAGINE IT WILL REALLY GET ME.⟩
⟨THEY DID TELL YOU THAT YOU'RE LIKELY TO FIND NOTHING *DOWN* THERE, YES?⟩
⟨OF COURSE, BUT WHY SET OUT WITH THAT IN MIND? MY FEELING IS, YOU SHOULD ALWAYS EXPECT TO BE ENGAGED.⟩
НПОП
⟨I WOULDN'T WORRY ABOUT THAT. ACCORDING TO OUR RADAR, WE SHOULD SEE OUR SHARE OF EXCITEMENT.⟩


⟨TRANSLATED FROM RUSSIAN⟩

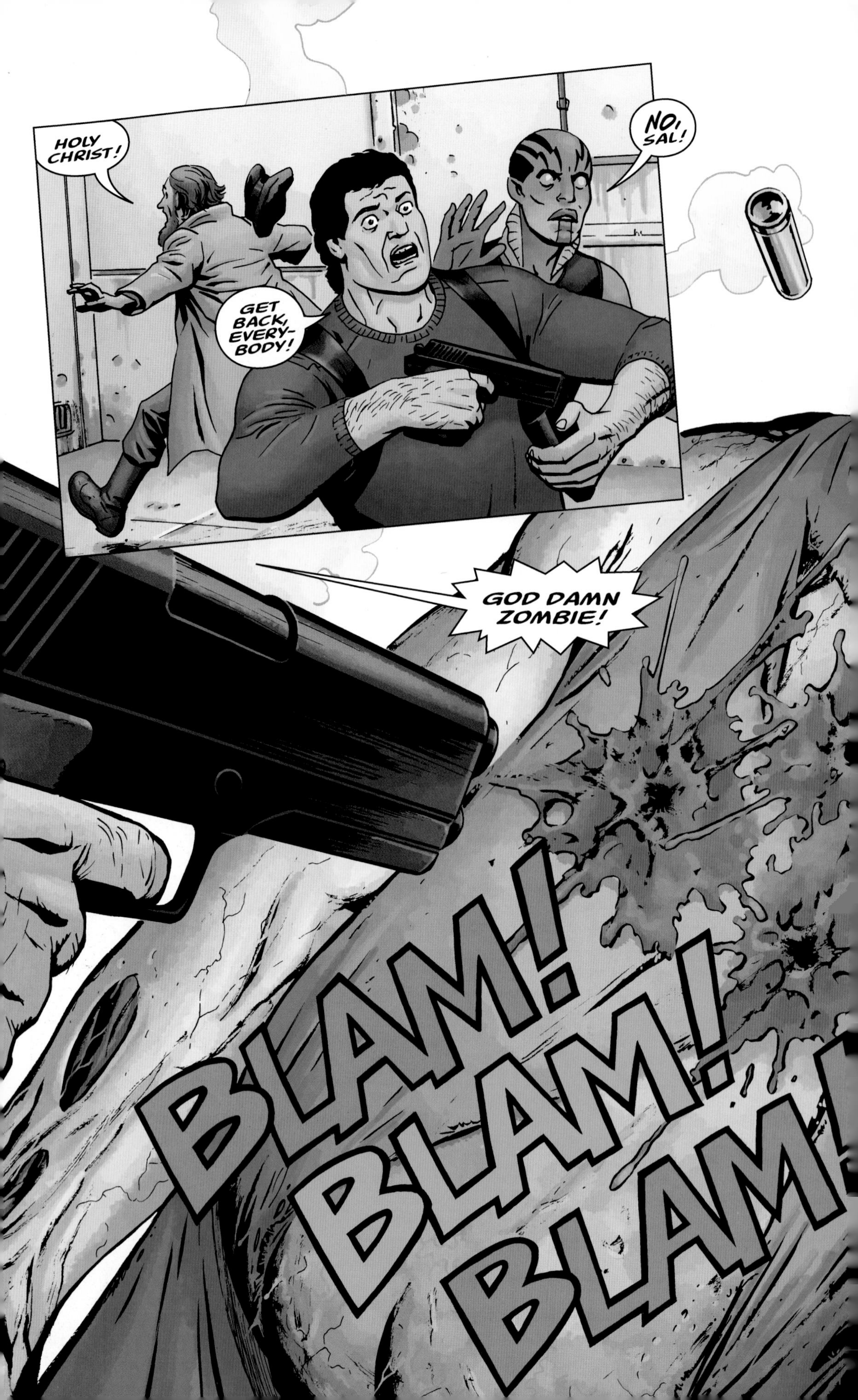
HOLY CHRIST!
NO, SAL!
GET BACK, EVERY-BODY!
GOD DAMN ZOMBIE!
BLAM! BLAM! BLAM!

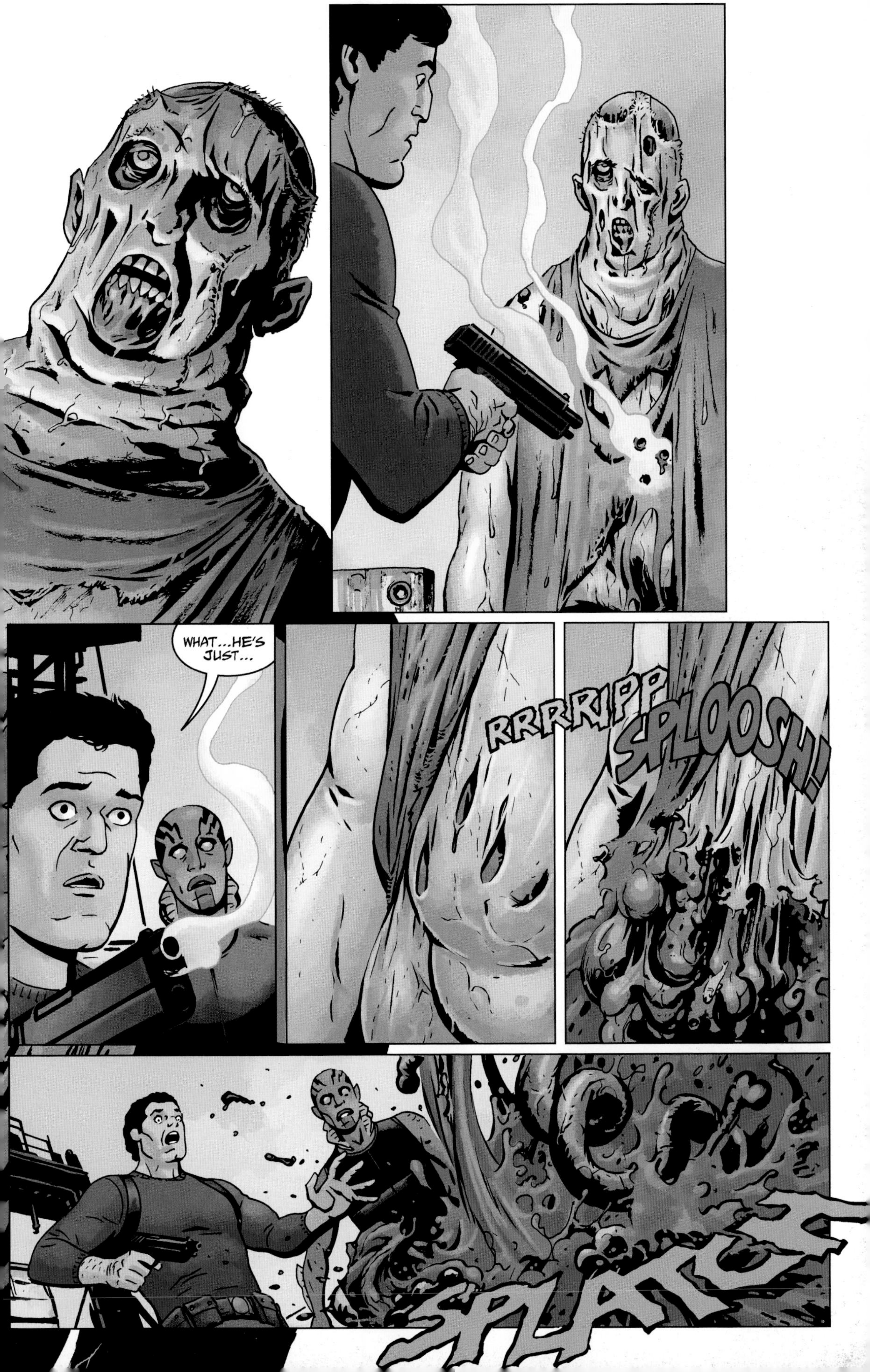
WHAT...HE'S JUST...
RRRRIPP
SPLOOSH!
SPLATCH

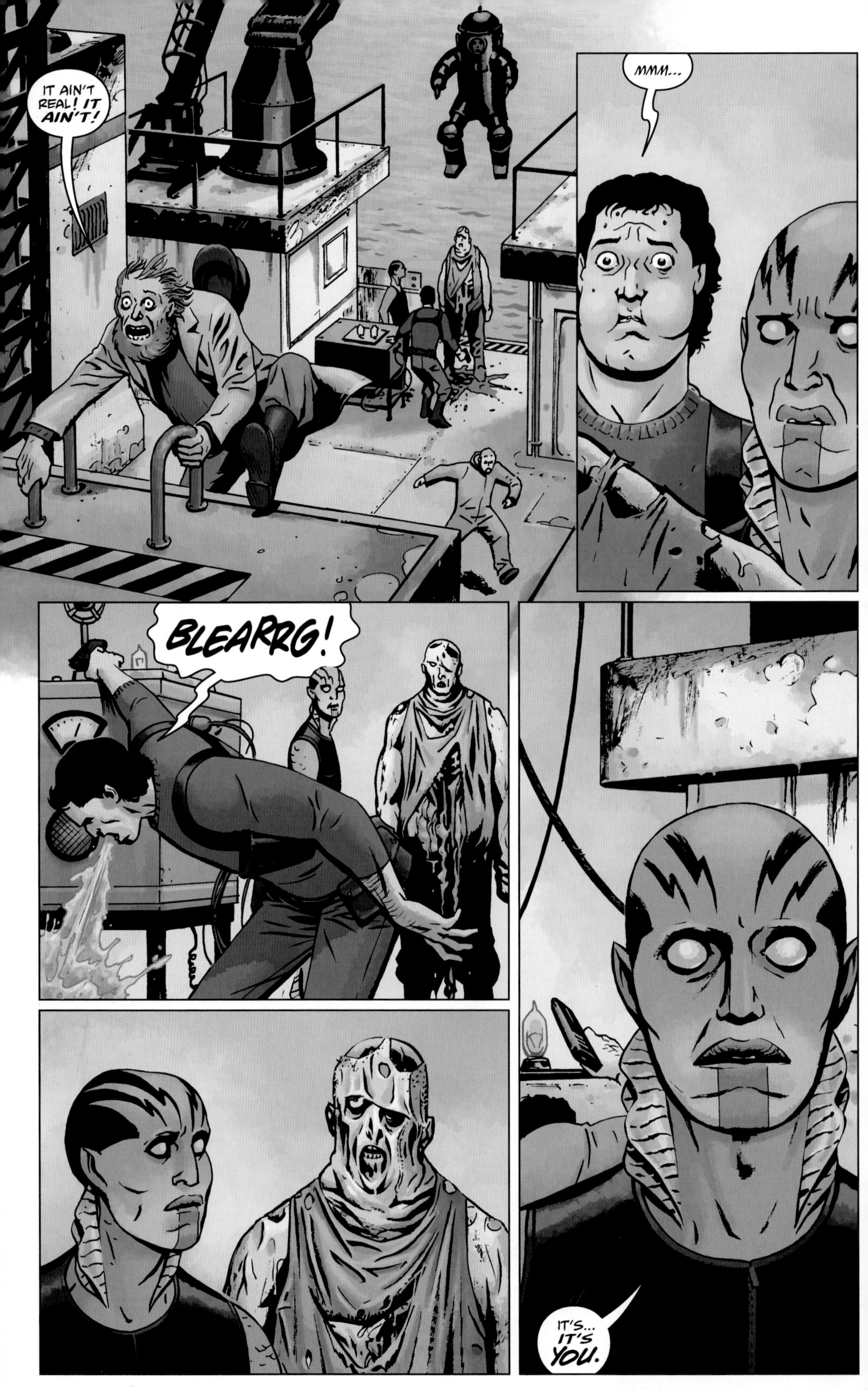
IT AIN'T REAL! IT AIN'T!
MMM...
BLEARRG!
IT'S... IT'S YOU.

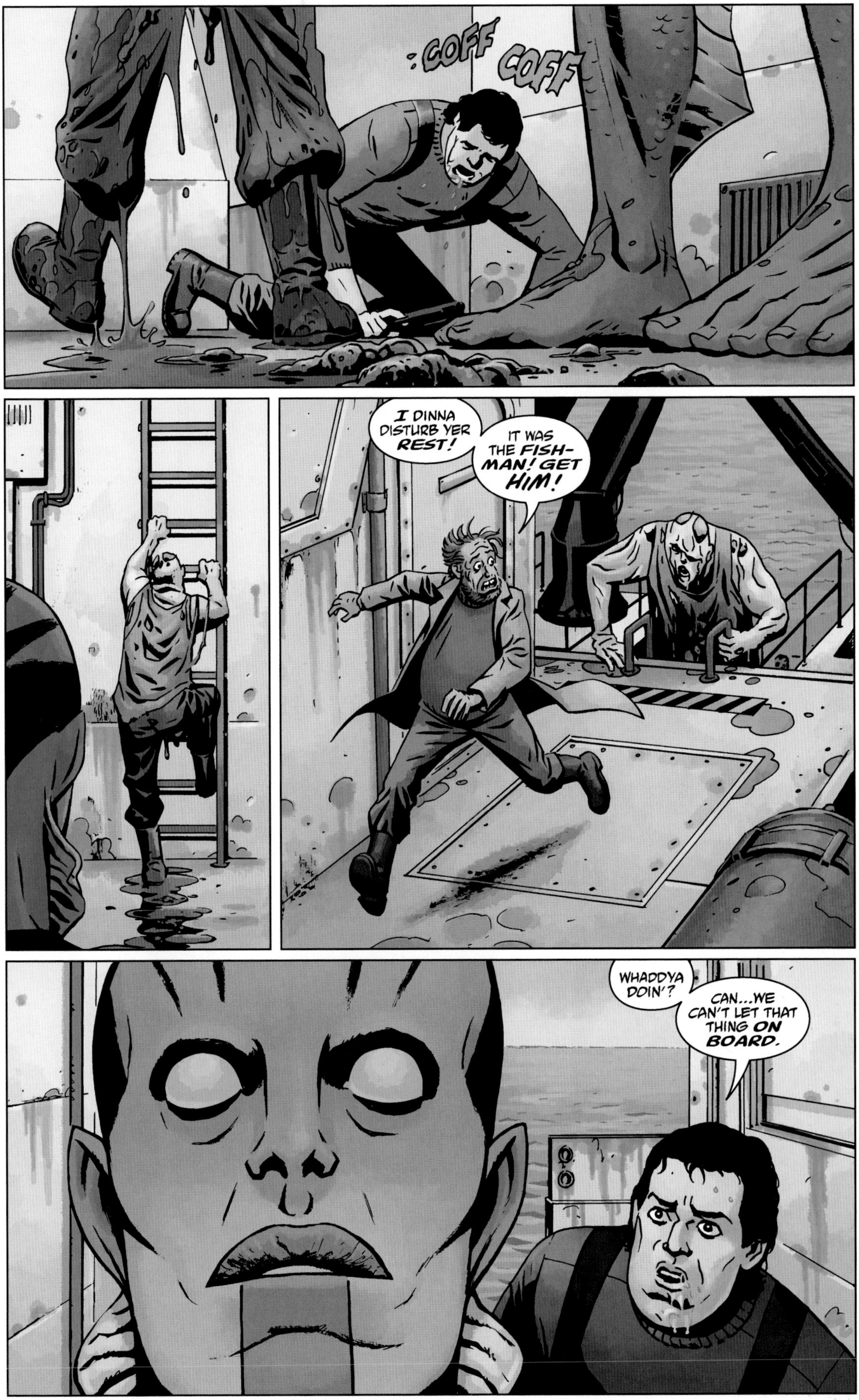
COFF
COFF
I DINNA DISTURB YER REST!
IT WAS THE FISH-MAN! GET HIM!
WHADDYA DOIN'?
CAN...WE CAN'T LET THAT THING ON BOARD.

I WANT TO OBSERVE HIM FOR A MOMENT, AND HE'S OBVIOUSLY NOT HOSTILE.

"HE"? THAT'S NOT A "HE." THAT'S A #*&%IN' ZOMBIE!

YOU'RE OVERREACTING, SAL.

WHY WOULDN'T YOU? IT'S YOUR FIRST TIME, BUT NOT MINE.

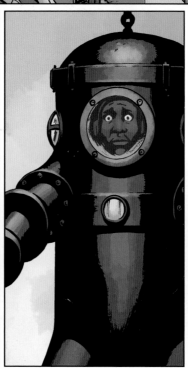

GET ADAM DOWN OUT OF THAT THING.

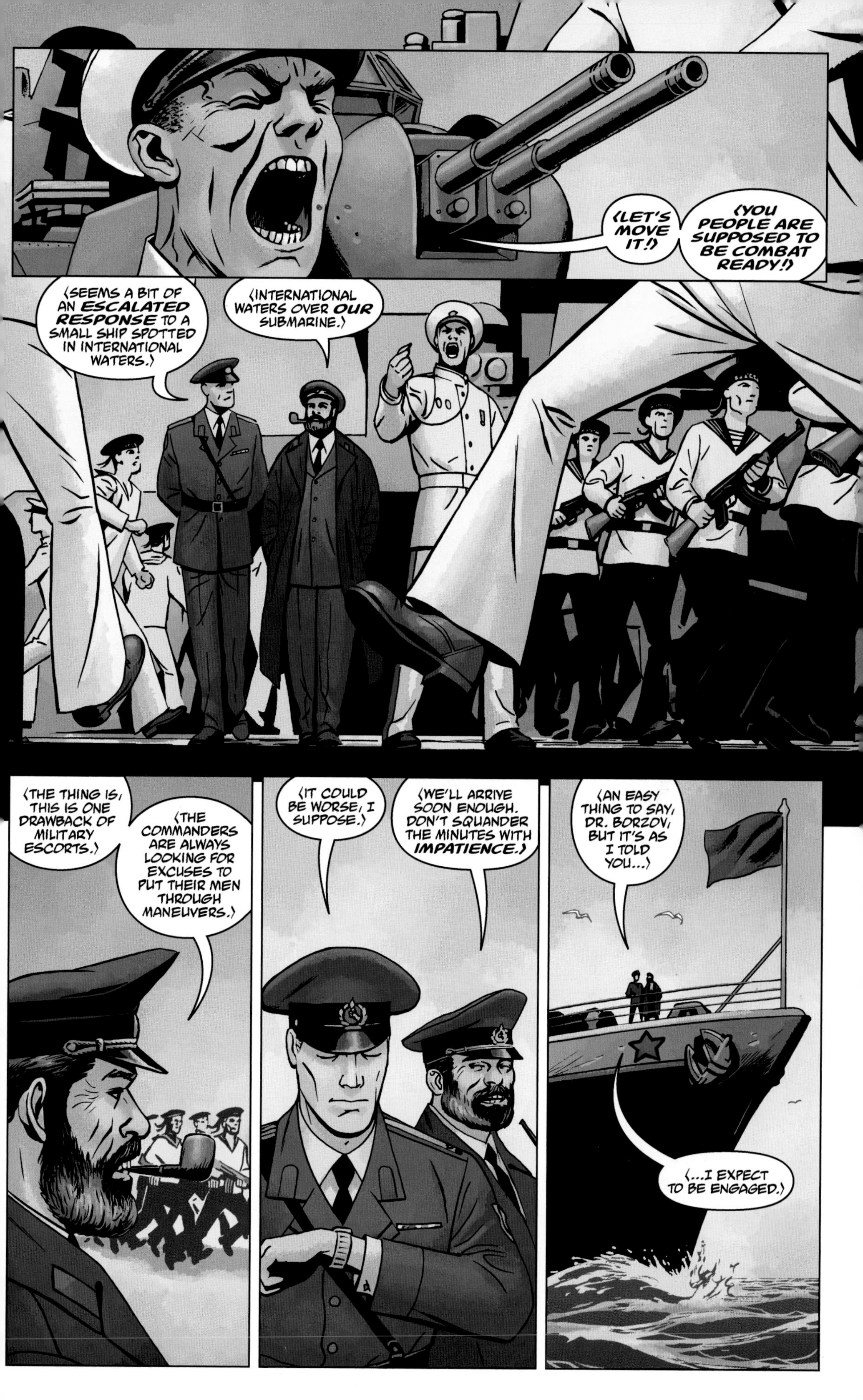
⟨LET'S MOVE IT!⟩
⟨YOU PEOPLE ARE SUPPOSED TO BE COMBAT READY!⟩
⟨SEEMS A BIT OF AN ESCALATED RESPONSE TO A SMALL SHIP SPOTTED IN INTERNATIONAL WATERS.⟩
⟨INTERNATIONAL WATERS OVER OUR SUBMARINE.⟩
⟨THE THING IS, THIS IS ONE DRAWBACK OF MILITARY ESCORTS.⟩
⟨THE COMMANDERS ARE ALWAYS LOOKING FOR EXCUSES TO PUT THEIR MEN THROUGH MANEUVERS.⟩
⟨IT COULD BE WORSE, I SUPPOSE.⟩
⟨WE'LL ARRIVE SOON ENOUGH. DON'T SQUANDER THE MINUTES WITH IMPATIENCE.⟩
⟨AN EASY THING TO SAY, DR. BORZOV, BUT IT'S AS I TOLD YOU...⟩
⟨...I EXPECT TO BE ENGAGED.⟩

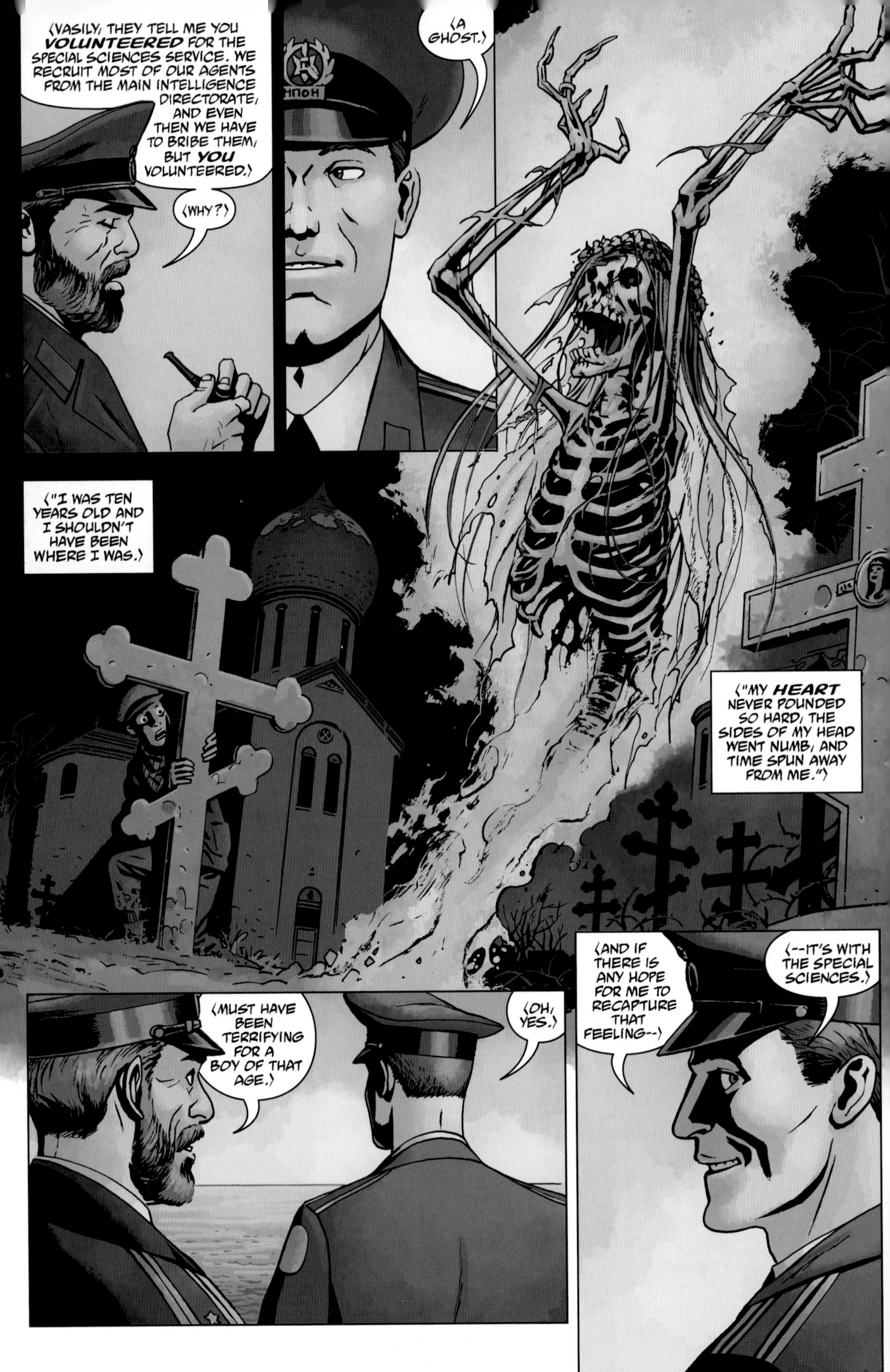

⟨VASILY, THEY TELL ME YOU VOLUNTEERED FOR THE SPECIAL SCIENCES SERVICE. WE RECRUIT MOST OF OUR AGENTS FROM THE MAIN INTELLIGENCE DIRECTORATE, AND EVEN THEN WE HAVE TO BRIBE THEM, BUT YOU VOLUNTEERED.⟩
⟨WHY?⟩
⟨A GHOST.⟩
⟨"I WAS TEN YEARS OLD AND I SHOULDN'T HAVE BEEN WHERE I WAS.⟩
⟨"MY HEART NEVER POUNDED SO HARD, THE SIDES OF MY HEAD WENT NUMB, AND TIME SPUN AWAY FROM ME."⟩
⟨MUST HAVE BEEN TERRIFYING FOR A BOY OF THAT AGE.⟩
⟨OH, YES.⟩
⟨AND IF THERE IS ANY HOPE FOR ME TO RECAPTURE THAT FEELING--⟩
⟨--IT'S WITH THE SPECIAL SCIENCES.⟩

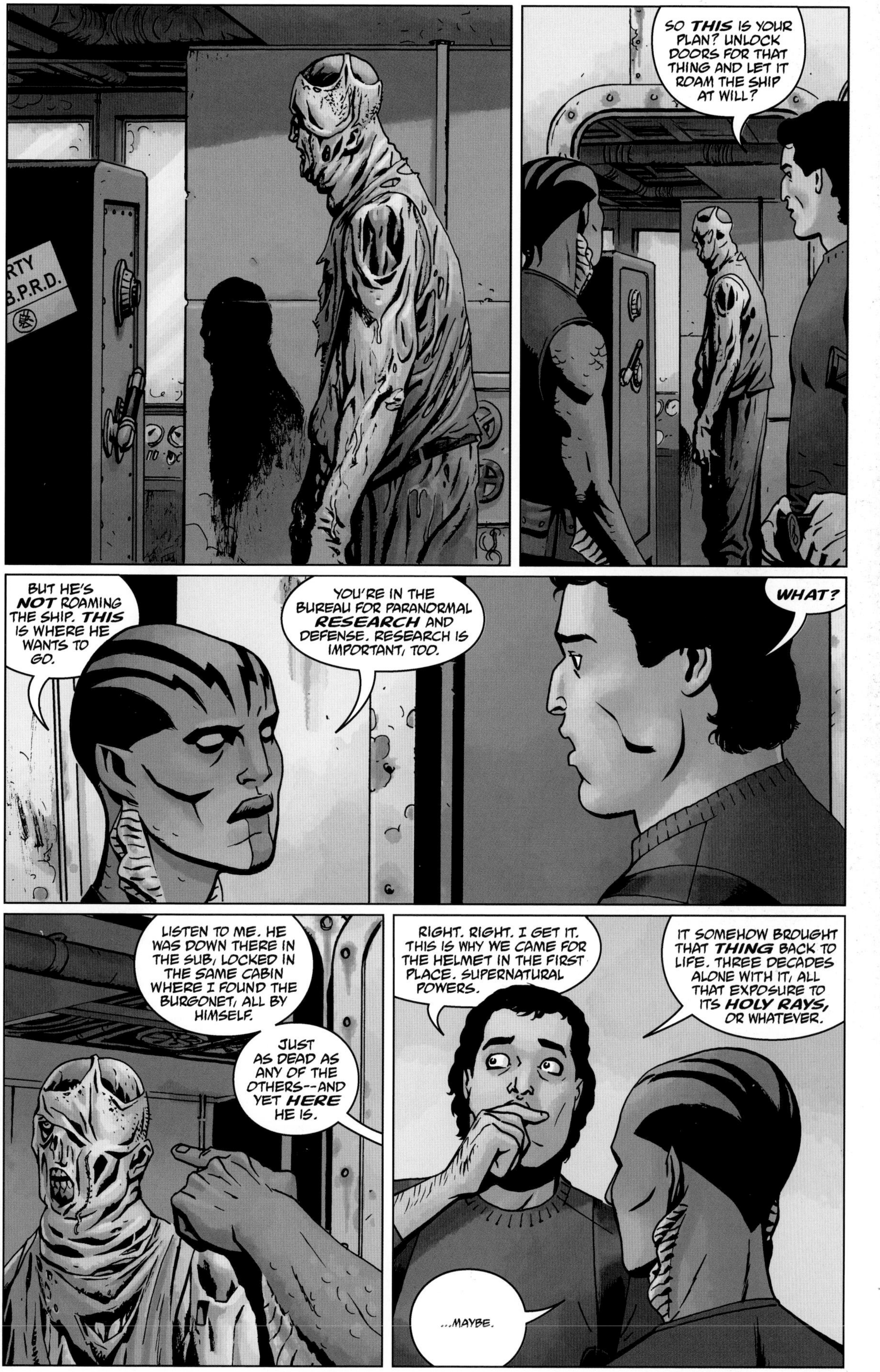
SO THIS IS YOUR PLAN? UNLOCK DOORS FOR THAT THING AND LET IT ROAM THE SHIP AT WILL?
BUT HE'S NOT ROAMING THE SHIP. THIS IS WHERE HE WANTS TO GO.
YOU'RE IN THE BUREAU FOR PARANORMAL RESEARCH AND DEFENSE. RESEARCH IS IMPORTANT, TOO.
WHAT?
LISTEN TO ME. HE WAS DOWN THERE IN THE SUB, LOCKED IN THE SAME CABIN WHERE I FOUND THE BURGONET, ALL BY HIMSELF.
JUST AS DEAD AS ANY OF THE OTHERS--AND YET HERE HE IS.
RIGHT. RIGHT. I GET IT. THIS IS WHY WE CAME FOR THE HELMET IN THE FIRST PLACE. SUPERNATURAL POWERS.
IT SOMEHOW BROUGHT THAT THING BACK TO LIFE. THREE DECADES ALONE WITH IT, ALL THAT EXPOSURE TO ITS HOLY RAYS, OR WHATEVER.
...MAYBE.

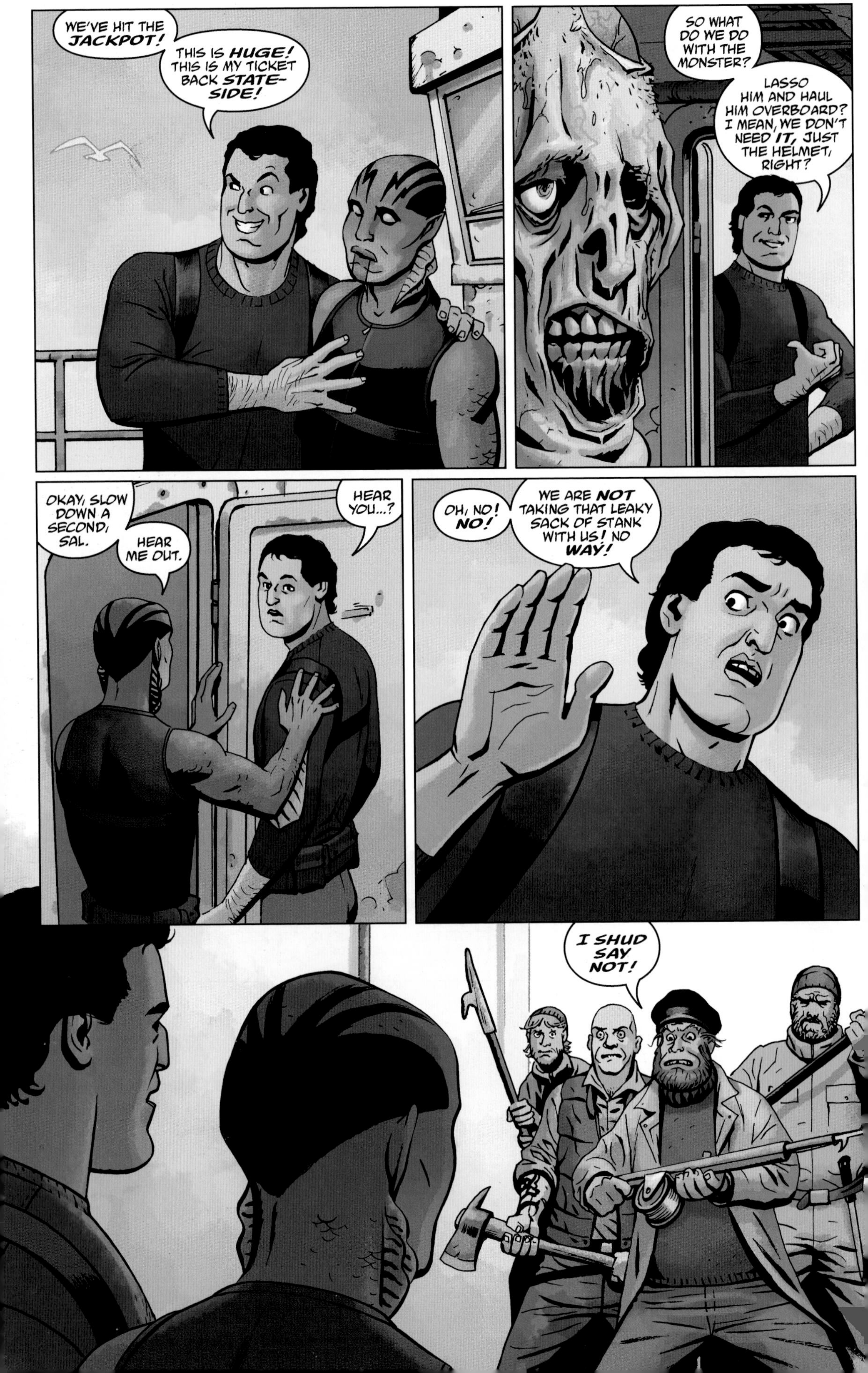
WE'VE HIT THE **JACKPOT!**
THIS IS **HUGE!** THIS IS MY TICKET BACK **STATE-SIDE!**
SO WHAT DO WE DO WITH THE MONSTER?
LASSO HIM AND HAUL HIM OVERBOARD? I MEAN, WE DON'T NEED **IT,** JUST THE HELMET, RIGHT?
OKAY, SLOW DOWN A SECOND, SAL.
HEAR ME OUT.
HEAR YOU...?
OH, NO! **NO!**
WE ARE **NOT** TAKING THAT LEAKY SACK OF STANK WITH US! NO **WAY!**
I SHUD SAY NOT!

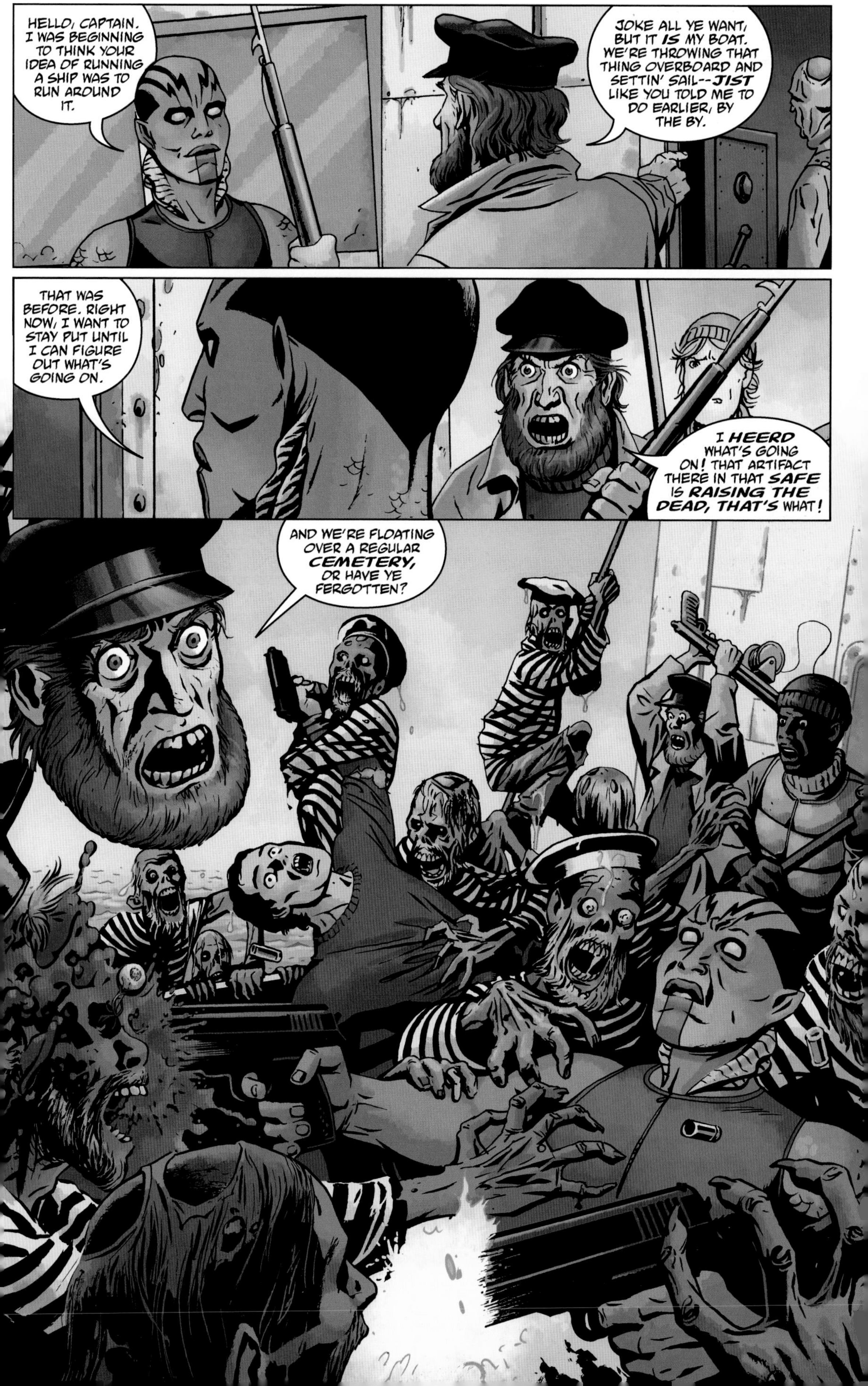
HELLO, CAPTAIN. I WAS BEGINNING TO THINK YOUR IDEA OF RUNNING A SHIP WAS TO RUN AROUND IT.
JOKE ALL YE WANT, BUT IT IS MY BOAT. WE'RE THROWING THAT THING OVERBOARD AND SETTIN' SAIL--JIST LIKE YOU TOLD ME TO DO EARLIER, BY THE BY.
THAT WAS BEFORE. RIGHT NOW, I WANT TO STAY PUT UNTIL I CAN FIGURE OUT WHAT'S GOING ON.
I HEERD WHAT'S GOING ON! THAT ARTIFACT THERE IN THAT SAFE IS RAISING THE DEAD, THAT'S WHAT!
AND WE'RE FLOATING OVER A REGULAR CEMETERY, OR HAVE YE FERGOTTEN?

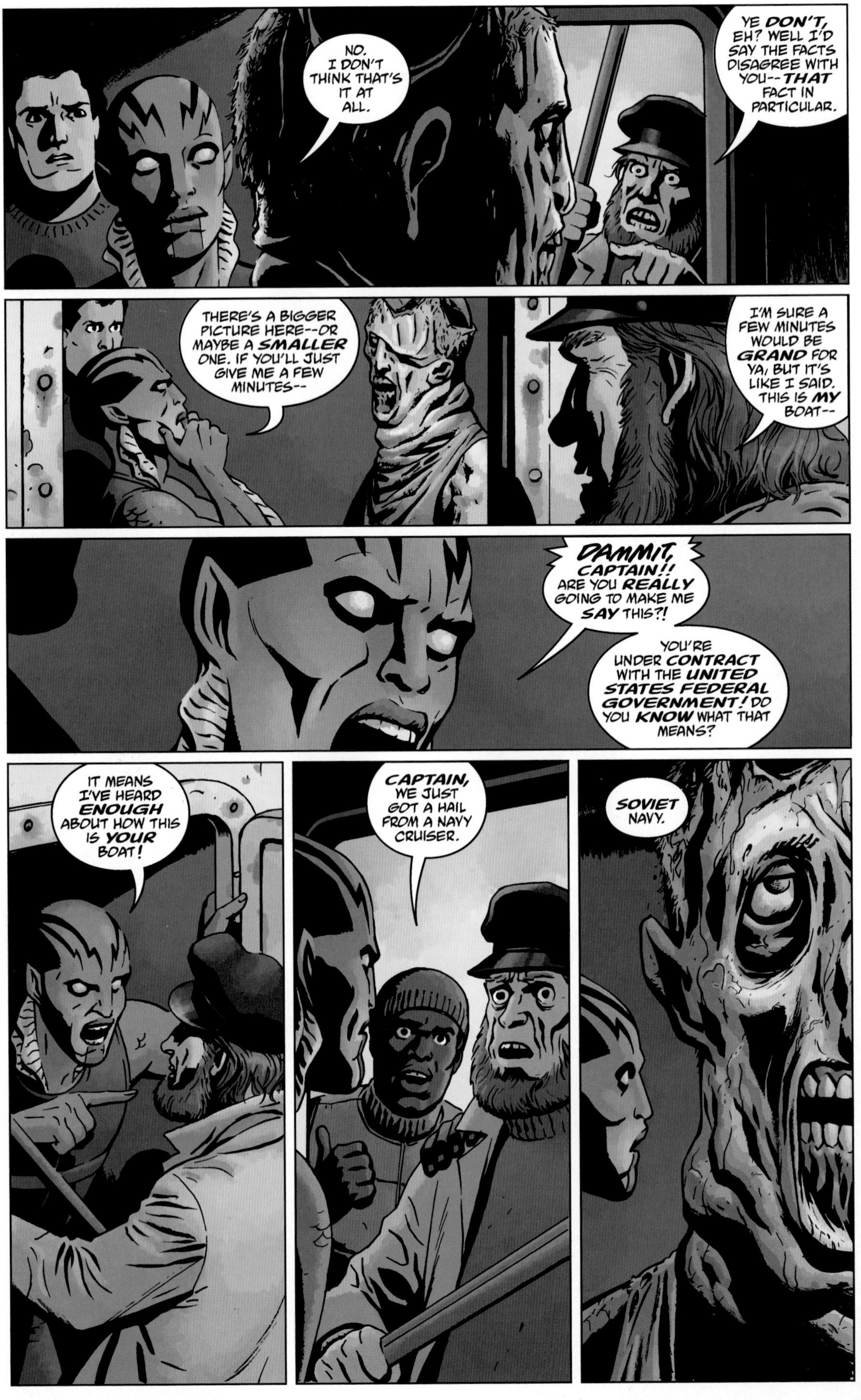
NO. I DON'T THINK THAT'S IT AT ALL.
YE DON'T, EH? WELL I'D SAY THE FACTS DISAGREE WITH YOU--THAT FACT IN PARTICULAR.
THERE'S A BIGGER PICTURE HERE--OR MAYBE A SMALLER ONE. IF YOU'LL JUST GIVE ME A FEW MINUTES--
I'M SURE A FEW MINUTES WOULD BE GRAND FOR YA, BUT IT'S LIKE I SAID. THIS IS MY BOAT--
DAMMIT, CAPTAIN!! ARE YOU REALLY GOING TO MAKE ME SAY THIS?!
YOU'RE UNDER CONTRACT WITH THE UNITED STATES FEDERAL GOVERNMENT! DO YOU KNOW WHAT THAT MEANS?
IT MEANS I'VE HEARD ENOUGH ABOUT HOW THIS IS YOUR BOAT!
CAPTAIN, WE JUST GOT A HAIL FROM A NAVY CRUISER.
SOVIET NAVY.

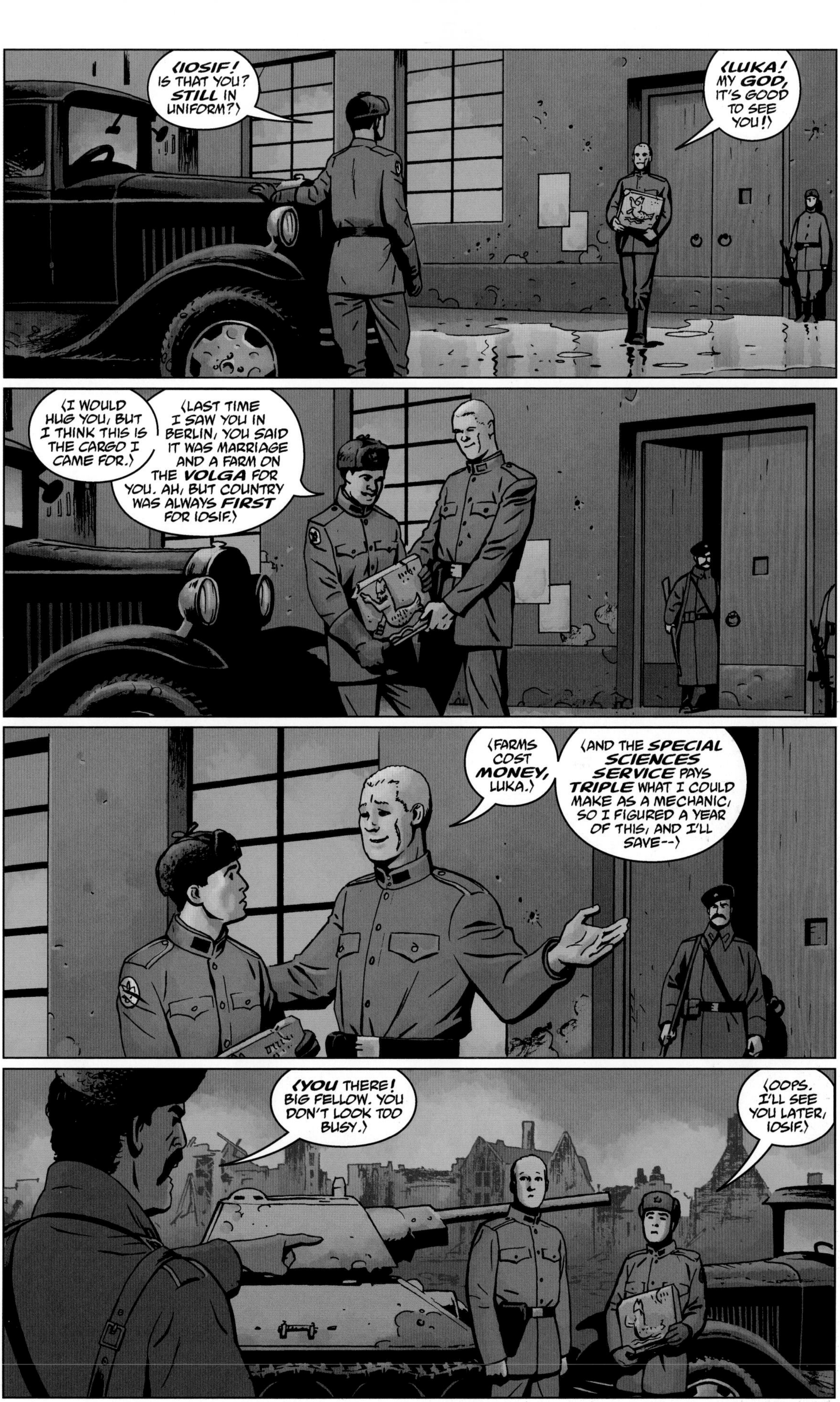
⟨IOSIF! IS THAT YOU? STILL IN UNIFORM?⟩
⟨LUKA! MY GOD, IT'S GOOD TO SEE YOU!⟩
⟨I WOULD HUG YOU, BUT I THINK THIS IS THE CARGO I CAME FOR.⟩
⟨LAST TIME I SAW YOU IN BERLIN, YOU SAID IT WAS MARRIAGE AND A FARM ON THE VOLGA FOR YOU. AH, BUT COUNTRY WAS ALWAYS FIRST FOR IOSIF.⟩
⟨FARMS COST MONEY, LUKA.⟩
⟨AND THE SPECIAL SCIENCES SERVICE PAYS TRIPLE WHAT I COULD MAKE AS A MECHANIC, SO I FIGURED A YEAR OF THIS, AND I'LL SAVE--⟩
⟨YOU THERE! BIG FELLOW. YOU DON'T LOOK TOO BUSY.⟩
⟨OOPS. I'LL SEE YOU LATER, IOSIF.⟩

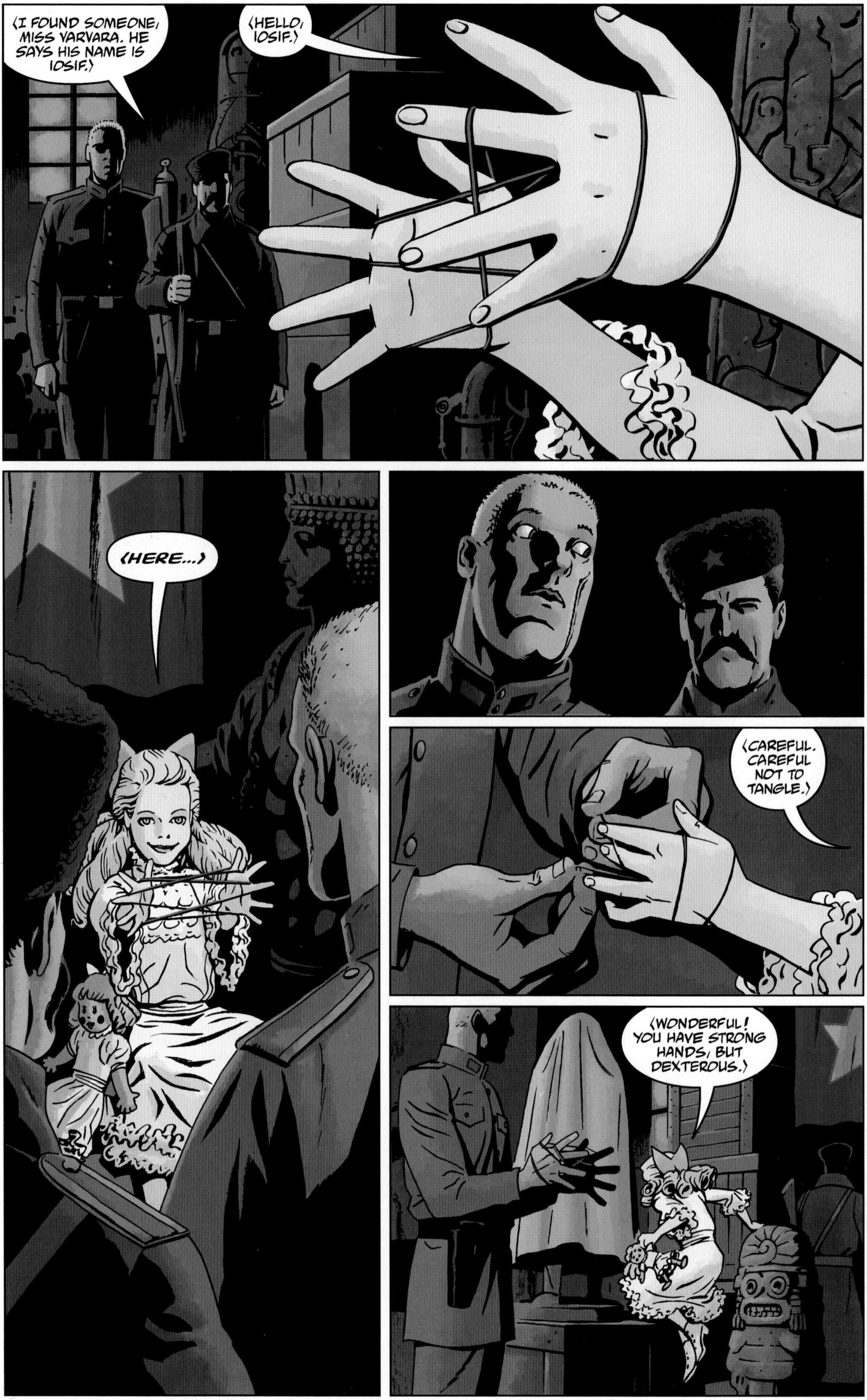
⟨I FOUND SOMEONE, MISS VARVARA. HE SAYS HIS NAME IS IOSIF.⟩
⟨HELLO, IOSIF.⟩
⟨HERE...⟩
⟨CAREFUL. CAREFUL NOT TO TANGLE.⟩
⟨WONDERFUL! YOU HAVE STRONG HANDS, BUT DEXTEROUS.⟩

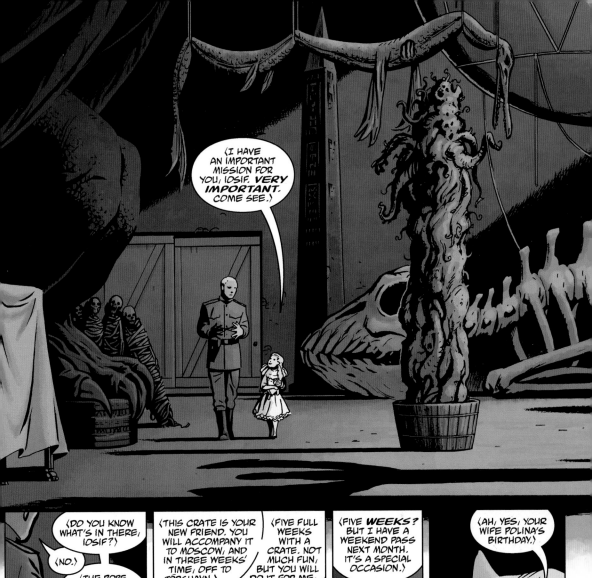

⟨I HAVE AN IMPORTANT MISSION FOR YOU, IOSIF. **VERY IMPORTANT.** COME SEE.⟩

⟨DO YOU KNOW WHAT'S IN THERE, IOSIF?⟩

⟨NO.⟩

⟨THE POPE WANTS IT, BUT ONLY TO LOOK AT. THAT'S ALL. **WE** HAVE BETTER IDEAS.⟩

⟨THIS CRATE IS YOUR NEW FRIEND. YOU WILL ACCOMPANY IT TO MOSCOW, AND IN THREE WEEKS' TIME, OFF TO TÓRSHAVN.⟩

⟨FIVE FULL WEEKS WITH A CRATE. NOT MUCH FUN, BUT YOU WILL DO IT FOR ME, **YES?**⟩

⟨FIVE **WEEKS?** BUT I HAVE A WEEKEND PASS NEXT MONTH. IT'S A SPECIAL OCCASION.⟩

⟨AH, YES, YOUR WIFE POLINA'S BIRTHDAY.⟩

⟨DON'T WORRY. SHE CAN CELEBRATE WITH HER FATHER AND BROTHERS. I WILL SEND A BOX OF CHUCHKELLA.⟩

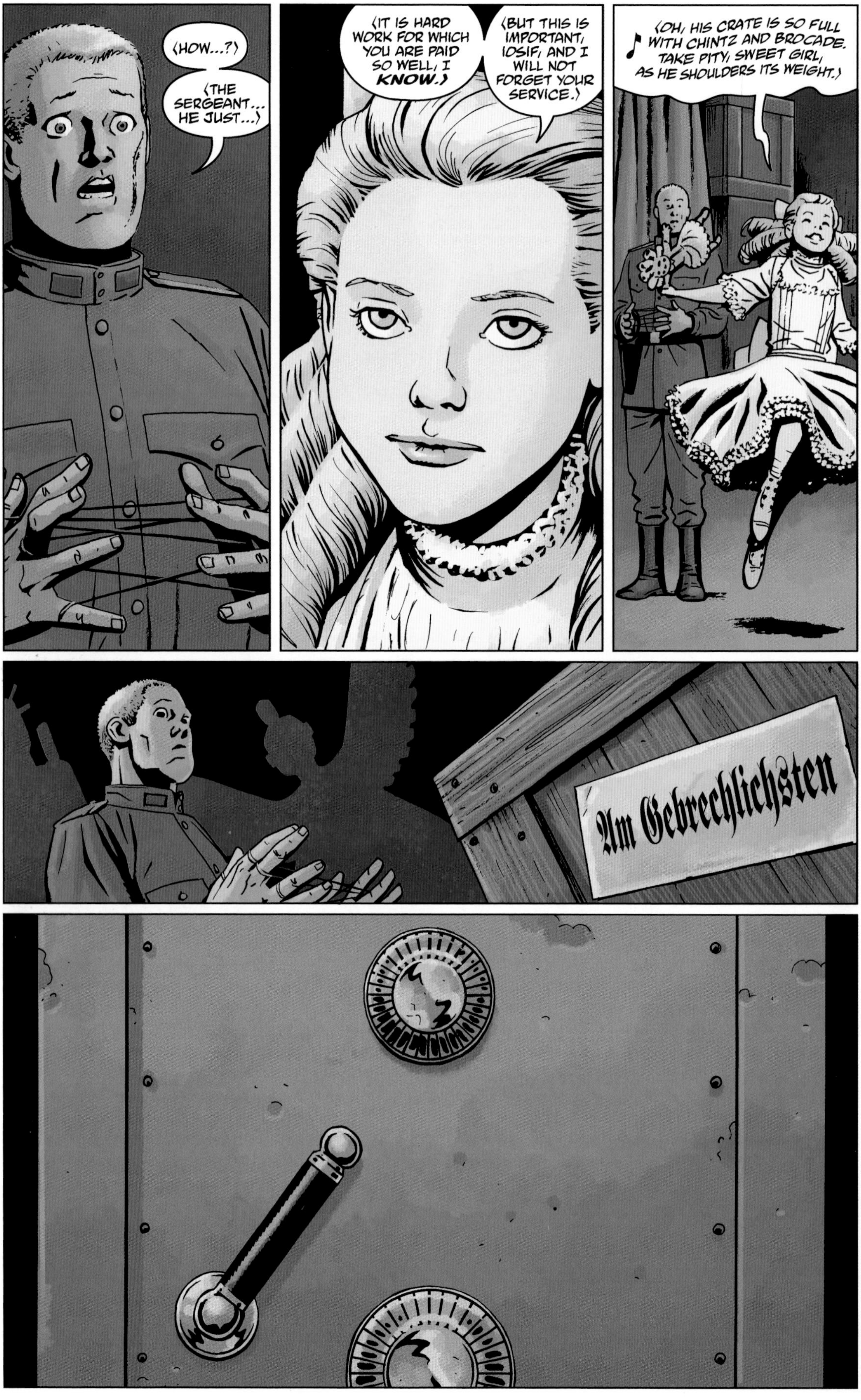
⟨HOW...?⟩
⟨THE SERGEANT... HE JUST...⟩
⟨IT IS HARD WORK FOR WHICH YOU ARE PAID SO WELL, I **KNOW.**⟩
⟨BUT THIS IS IMPORTANT, IOSIF, AND I WILL NOT FORGET YOUR SERVICE.⟩
♪ ⟨OH, HIS CRATE IS SO FULL WITH CHINTZ AND BROCADE. TAKE PITY, SWEET GIRL, AS HE SHOULDERS ITS WEIGHT.⟩
Am Gebrechlichsten

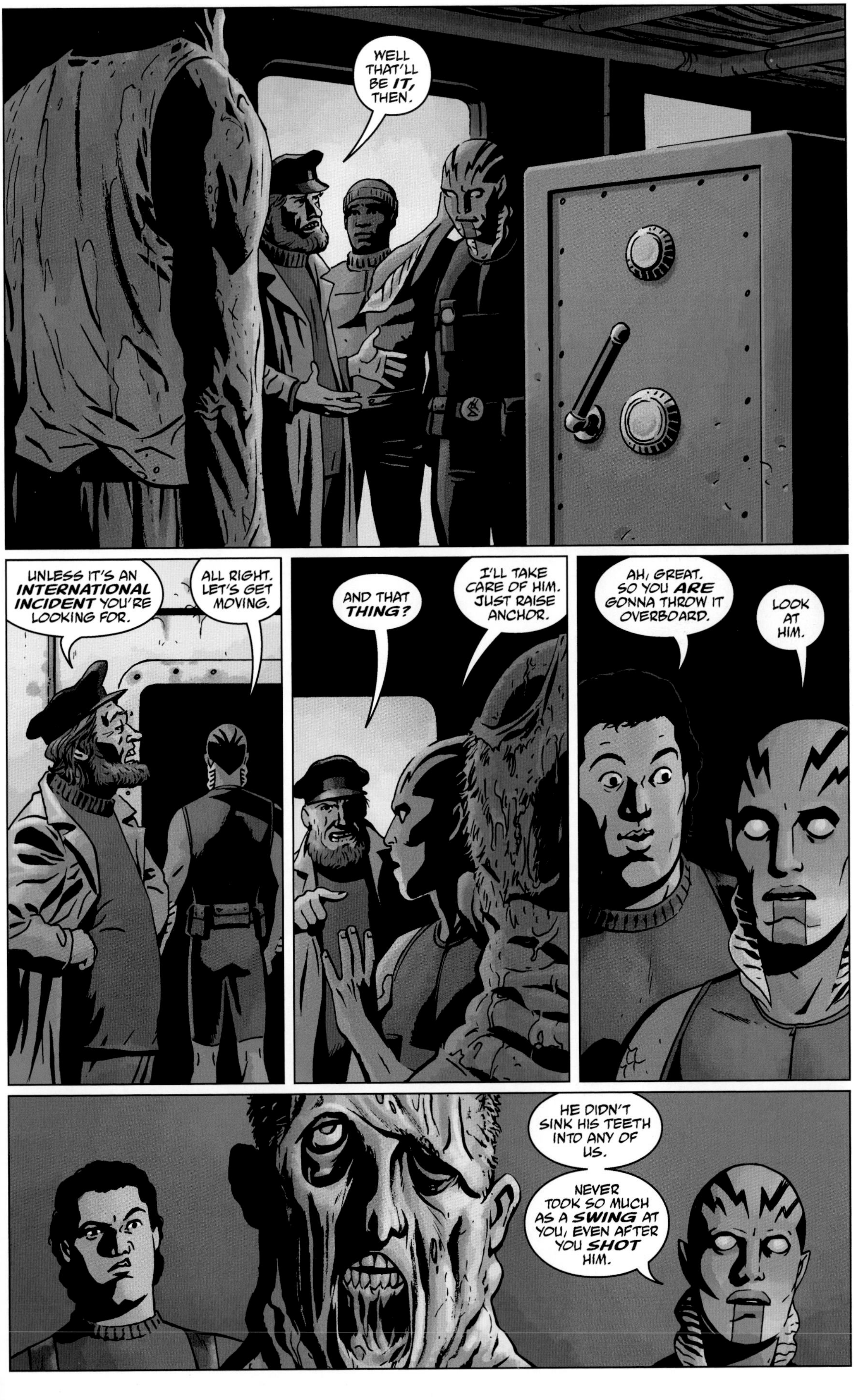
WELL THAT'LL BE *IT*, THEN.
UNLESS IT'S AN *INTERNATIONAL INCIDENT* YOU'RE LOOKING FOR.
ALL RIGHT. LET'S GET MOVING.
AND THAT *THING?*
I'LL TAKE CARE OF HIM. JUST RAISE ANCHOR.
AH, GREAT. SO YOU *ARE* GONNA THROW IT OVERBOARD.
LOOK AT HIM.
HE DIDN'T SINK HIS TEETH INTO ANY OF US.
NEVER TOOK SO MUCH AS A *SWING* AT YOU, EVEN AFTER YOU *SHOT* HIM.

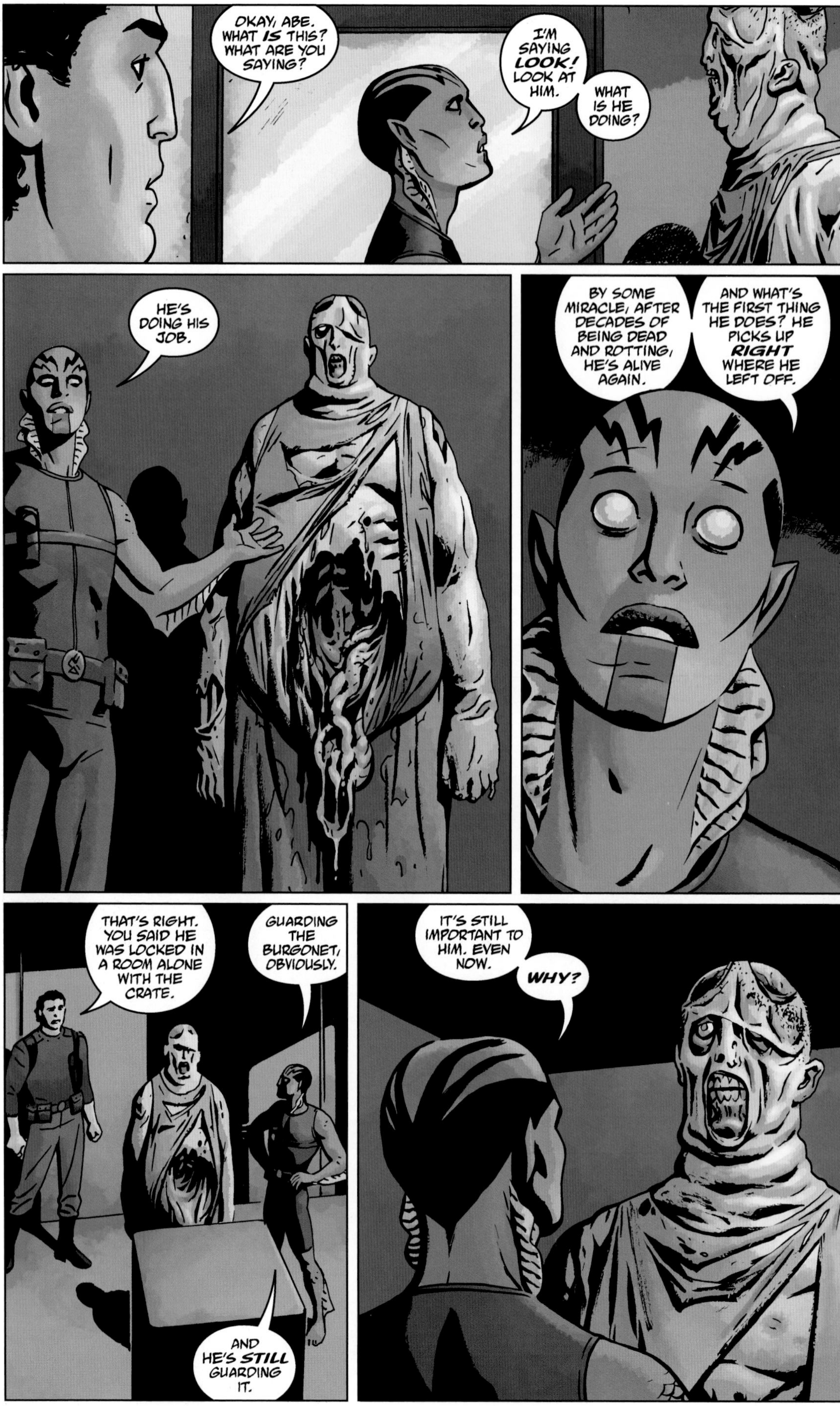
OKAY, ABE. WHAT IS THIS? WHAT ARE YOU SAYING?
I'M SAYING LOOK! LOOK AT HIM.
WHAT IS HE DOING?
HE'S DOING HIS JOB.
BY SOME MIRACLE, AFTER DECADES OF BEING DEAD AND ROTTING, HE'S ALIVE AGAIN.
AND WHAT'S THE FIRST THING HE DOES? HE PICKS UP RIGHT WHERE HE LEFT OFF.
THAT'S RIGHT. YOU SAID HE WAS LOCKED IN A ROOM ALONE WITH THE CRATE.
GUARDING THE BURGONET, OBVIOUSLY.
AND HE'S STILL GUARDING IT.
IT'S STILL IMPORTANT TO HIM. EVEN NOW.
WHY?

WHAT ARE YOU DOING?!

JESUS! JESUS, YOU'RE GIVING IT BACK? BUT THE RUSSIANS--

--WILL PROBABLY CHASE US AS SOON AS THEY FIND IT'S MISSING.

AND IN A CRUISER, THEY'LL CATCH US, TOO.

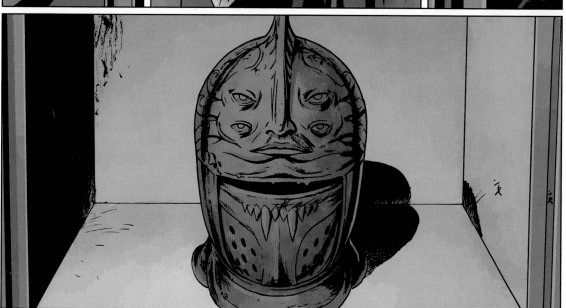

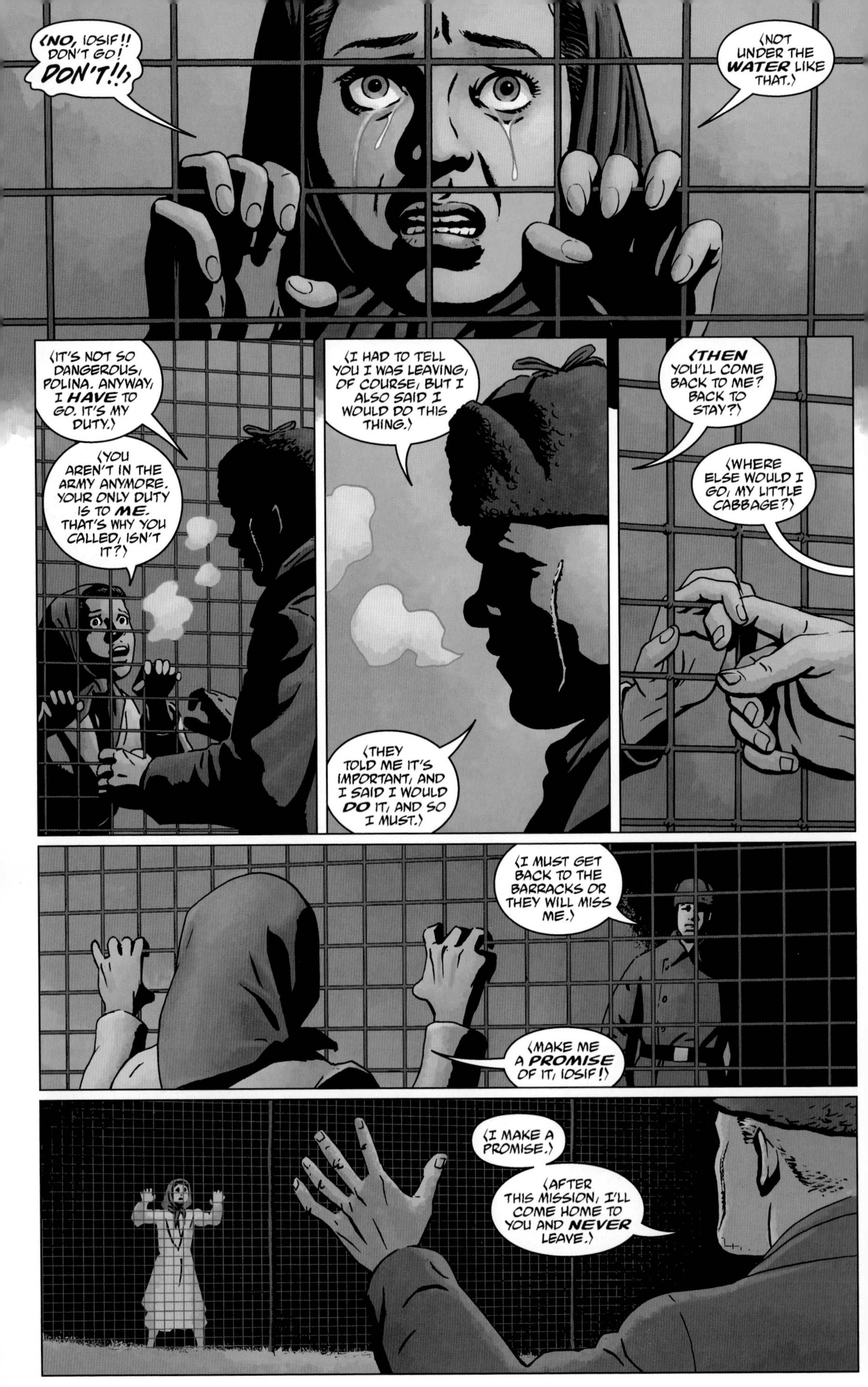
⟨NO, IOSIF!! DON'T GO! DON'T!!⟩
⟨NOT UNDER THE WATER LIKE THAT.⟩
⟨IT'S NOT SO DANGEROUS, POLINA. ANYWAY, I HAVE TO GO. IT'S MY DUTY.⟩
⟨YOU AREN'T IN THE ARMY ANYMORE. YOUR ONLY DUTY IS TO ME. THAT'S WHY YOU CALLED, ISN'T IT?⟩
⟨I HAD TO TELL YOU I WAS LEAVING, OF COURSE, BUT I ALSO SAID I WOULD DO THIS THING.⟩
⟨THEY TOLD ME IT'S IMPORTANT, AND I SAID I WOULD DO IT, AND SO I MUST.⟩
⟨THEN YOU'LL COME BACK TO ME? BACK TO STAY?⟩
⟨WHERE ELSE WOULD I GO, MY LITTLE CABBAGE?⟩
⟨I MUST GET BACK TO THE BARRACKS OR THEY WILL MISS ME.⟩
⟨MAKE ME A PROMISE OF IT, IOSIF!⟩
⟨I MAKE A PROMISE.⟩
⟨AFTER THIS MISSION, I'LL COME HOME TO YOU AND NEVER LEAVE.⟩

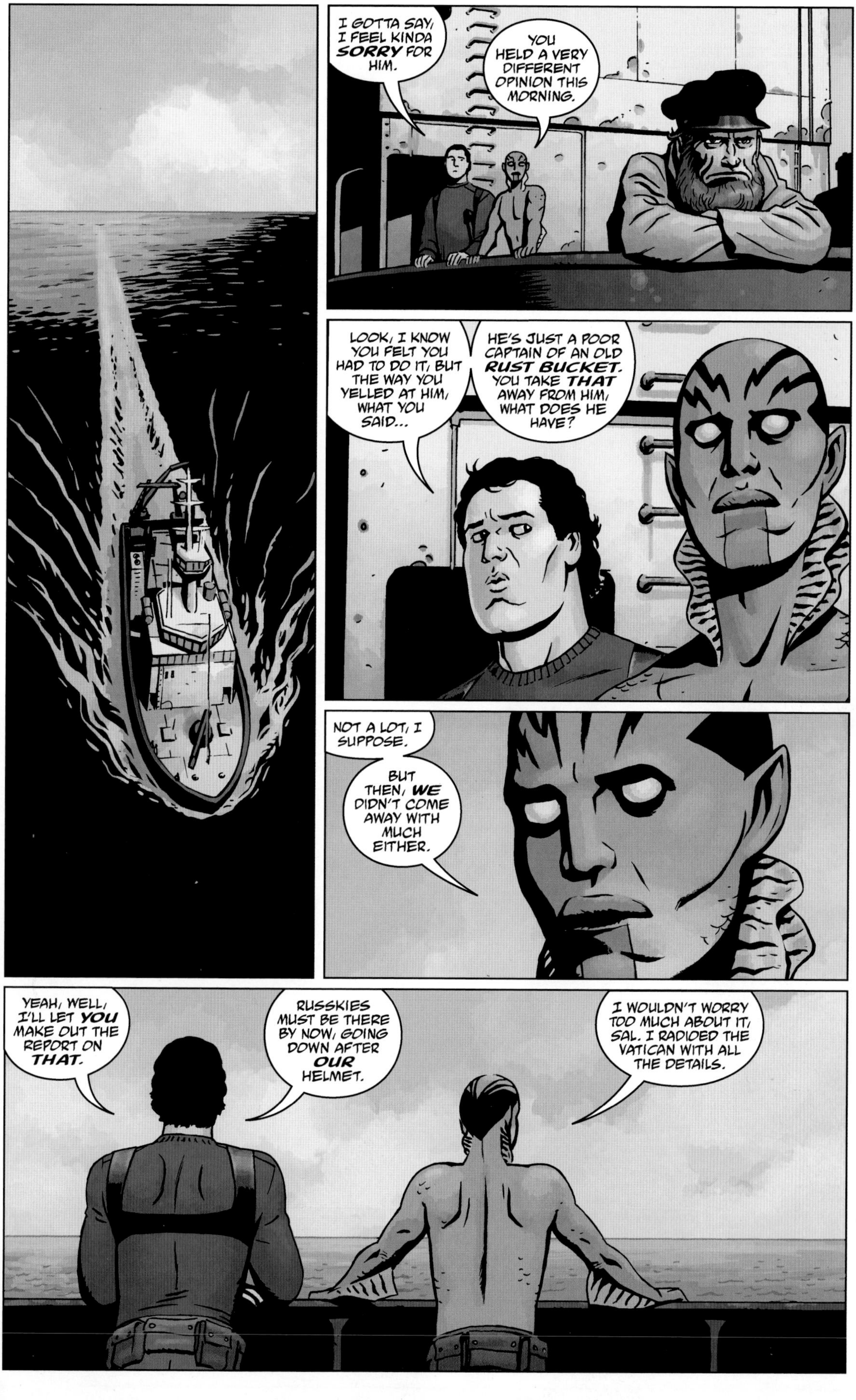

I GOTTA SAY, I FEEL KINDA SORRY FOR HIM.
YOU HELD A VERY DIFFERENT OPINION THIS MORNING.
LOOK, I KNOW YOU FELT YOU HAD TO DO IT, BUT THE WAY YOU YELLED AT HIM, WHAT YOU SAID...
HE'S JUST A POOR CAPTAIN OF AN OLD RUST BUCKET. YOU TAKE THAT AWAY FROM HIM, WHAT DOES HE HAVE?
NOT A LOT, I SUPPOSE.
BUT THEN, WE DIDN'T COME AWAY WITH MUCH EITHER.
YEAH, WELL, I'LL LET YOU MAKE OUT THE REPORT ON THAT.
RUSSKIES MUST BE THERE BY NOW, GOING DOWN AFTER OUR HELMET.
I WOULDN'T WORRY TOO MUCH ABOUT IT, SAL. I RADIOED THE VATICAN WITH ALL THE DETAILS.

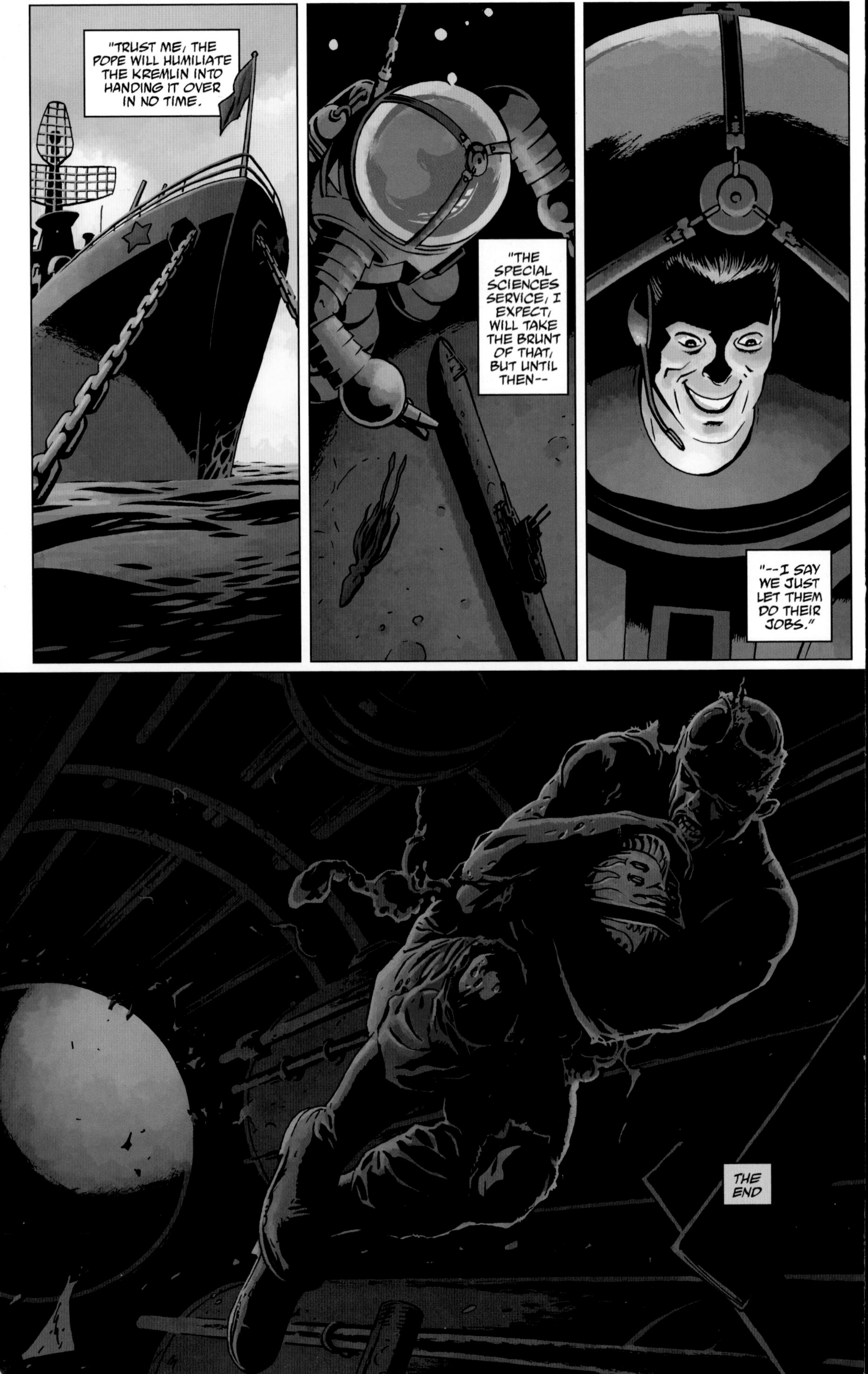
"TRUST ME, THE POPE WILL HUMILIATE THE KREMLIN INTO HANDING IT OVER IN NO TIME.
"THE SPECIAL SCIENCES SERVICE, I EXPECT, WILL TAKE THE BRUNT OF THAT, BUT UNTIL THEN--
"--I SAY WE JUST LET THEM DO THEIR JOBS."
THE END

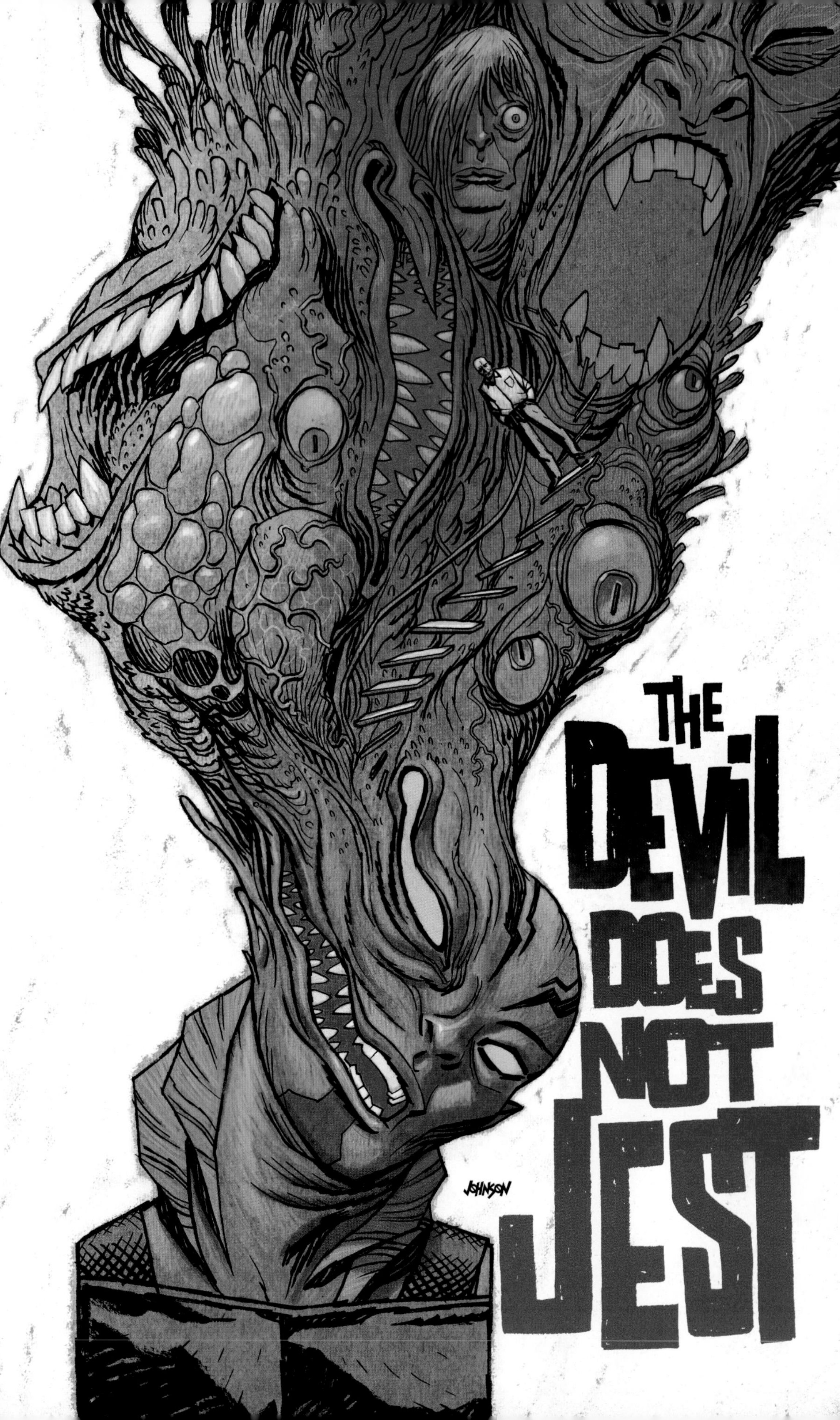
THE DEVIL DOES NOT JEST
JOHNSON

ART BY
**James Harren**

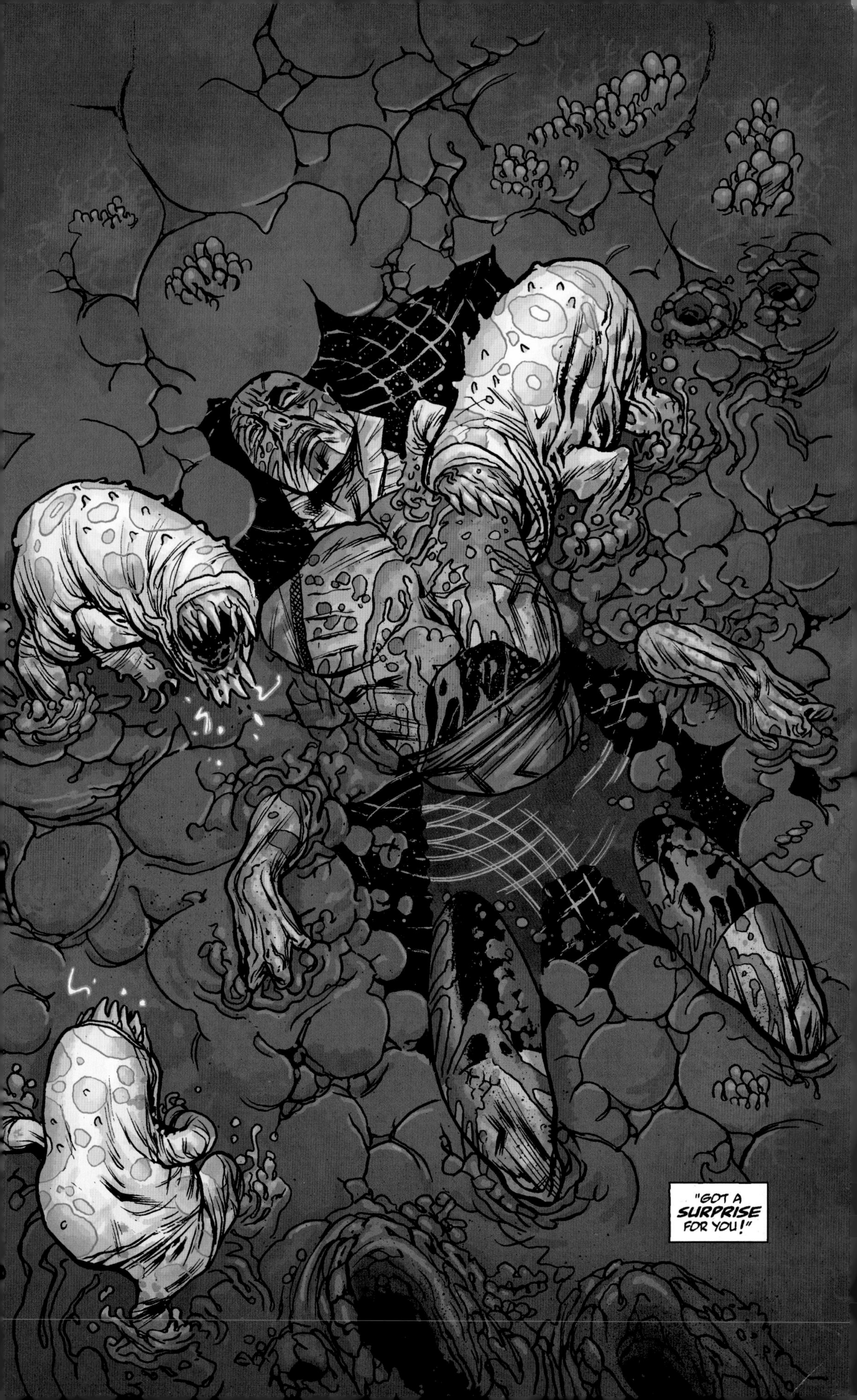
"GOT A SURPRISE FOR YOU!"

WHAT MAKES YOU THINK I LIKE SURPRISES?

CIRCUMNAVIGATI HELL

GARVER VAN LAER

GOETIA ICONOGRAPHY —A HISTORY—

YOU'LL LIKE *THIS* ONE. CONSIDER IT ANOTHER INSTALLMENT OF MY THANKS FOR GETTING ME THE HELL OUT OF *SCOTLAND*.

COME ON.

BUT ARE YOU SURE IT'S THE SAME *VAN LAER*?

ABSOLUTELY. THE ONE WHO WROTE ALL THOSE BOOKS YOU'VE BEEN READING. *THIS* GUY'S HIS GRANDSON.

HIYA, SALVATORE. HOW'VE YOU BEEN?

ABE.

HEY, SHERMAN.

AND WHAT IS IT--EXACTLY-- THAT HE WANTS FROM US?

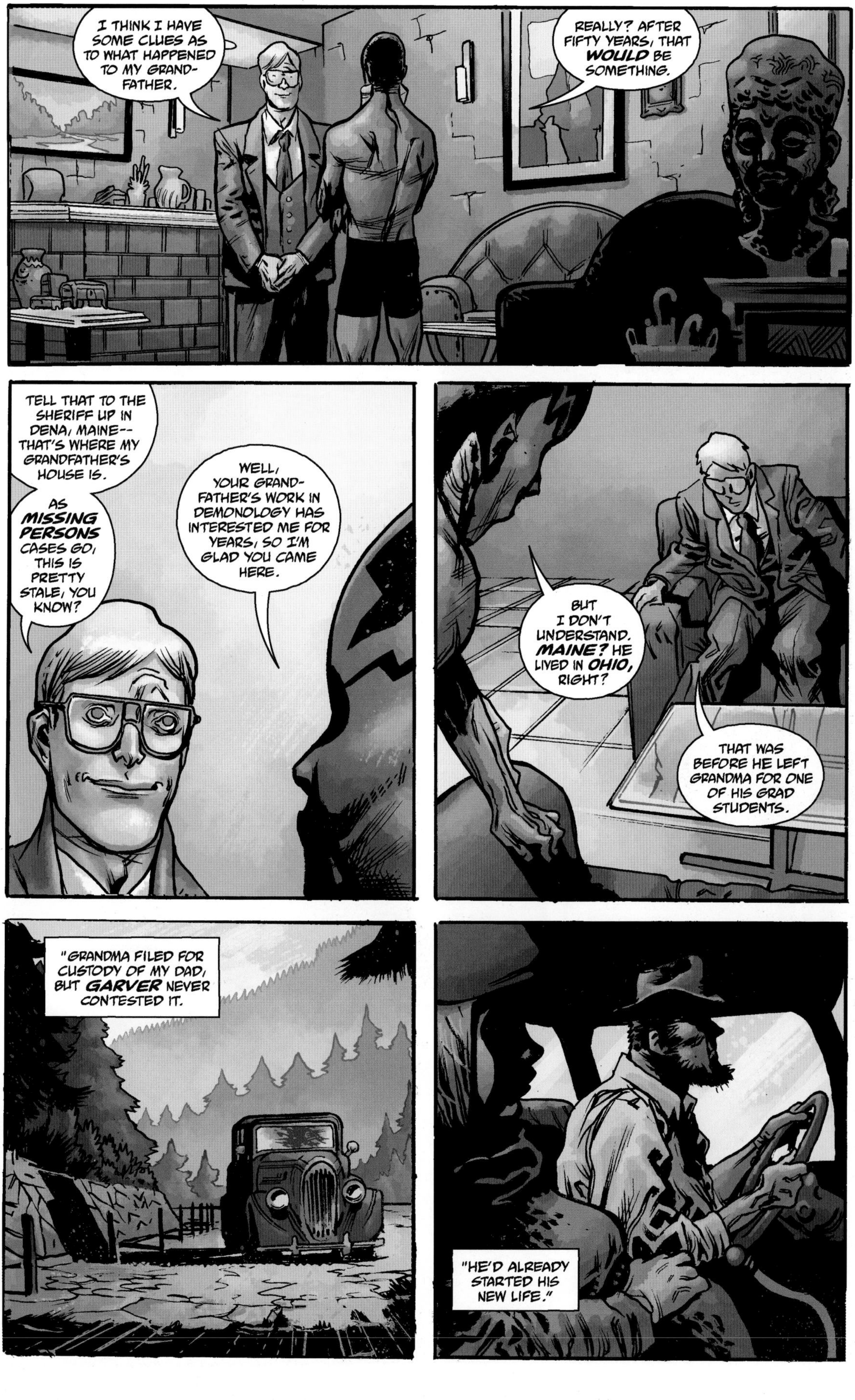
I THINK I HAVE SOME CLUES AS TO WHAT HAPPENED TO MY GRAND-FATHER.
REALLY? AFTER FIFTY YEARS, THAT WOULD BE SOMETHING.
TELL THAT TO THE SHERIFF UP IN DENA, MAINE-- THAT'S WHERE MY GRANDFATHER'S HOUSE IS.
AS MISSING PERSONS CASES GO, THIS IS PRETTY STALE, YOU KNOW?
WELL, YOUR GRAND-FATHER'S WORK IN DEMONOLOGY HAS INTERESTED ME FOR YEARS, SO I'M GLAD YOU CAME HERE.
BUT I DON'T UNDERSTAND. MAINE? HE LIVED IN OHIO, RIGHT?
THAT WAS BEFORE HE LEFT GRANDMA FOR ONE OF HIS GRAD STUDENTS.
"GRANDMA FILED FOR CUSTODY OF MY DAD, BUT GARVER NEVER CONTESTED IT.
"HE'D ALREADY STARTED HIS NEW LIFE."

SO **THAT'S** WHY HE LEFT VANDRIST UNIVERSITY.

THAT, AND HIS RESEARCH THAT LED HIM TO START SERIOUSLY PRACTICING **THEURGY.**

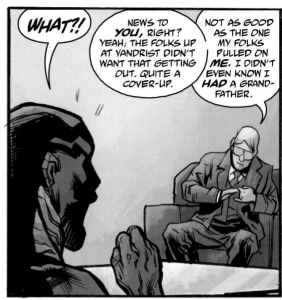

**WHAT?!**

NEWS TO **YOU**, RIGHT? YEAH, THE FOLKS UP AT VANDRIST DIDN'T WANT THAT GETTING OUT. QUITE A COVER-UP.

NOT AS GOOD AS THE ONE MY FOLKS PULLED ON **ME.** I DIDN'T EVEN KNOW I **HAD** A GRAND-FATHER.

UNTIL I FOUND THIS.

1937

GARVER MAILED IT BACK IN 1937 TO TELL MY DAD THAT HE HAD A LITTLE BROTHER.

AS FAR AS **I** KNOW, IT'S THE ONLY COMMUNICATION BETWEEN THEM AFTER THE SPLIT.

I LOST MY FATHER IN MARCH TO CANCER, BUT I FOUND AN UNCLE.

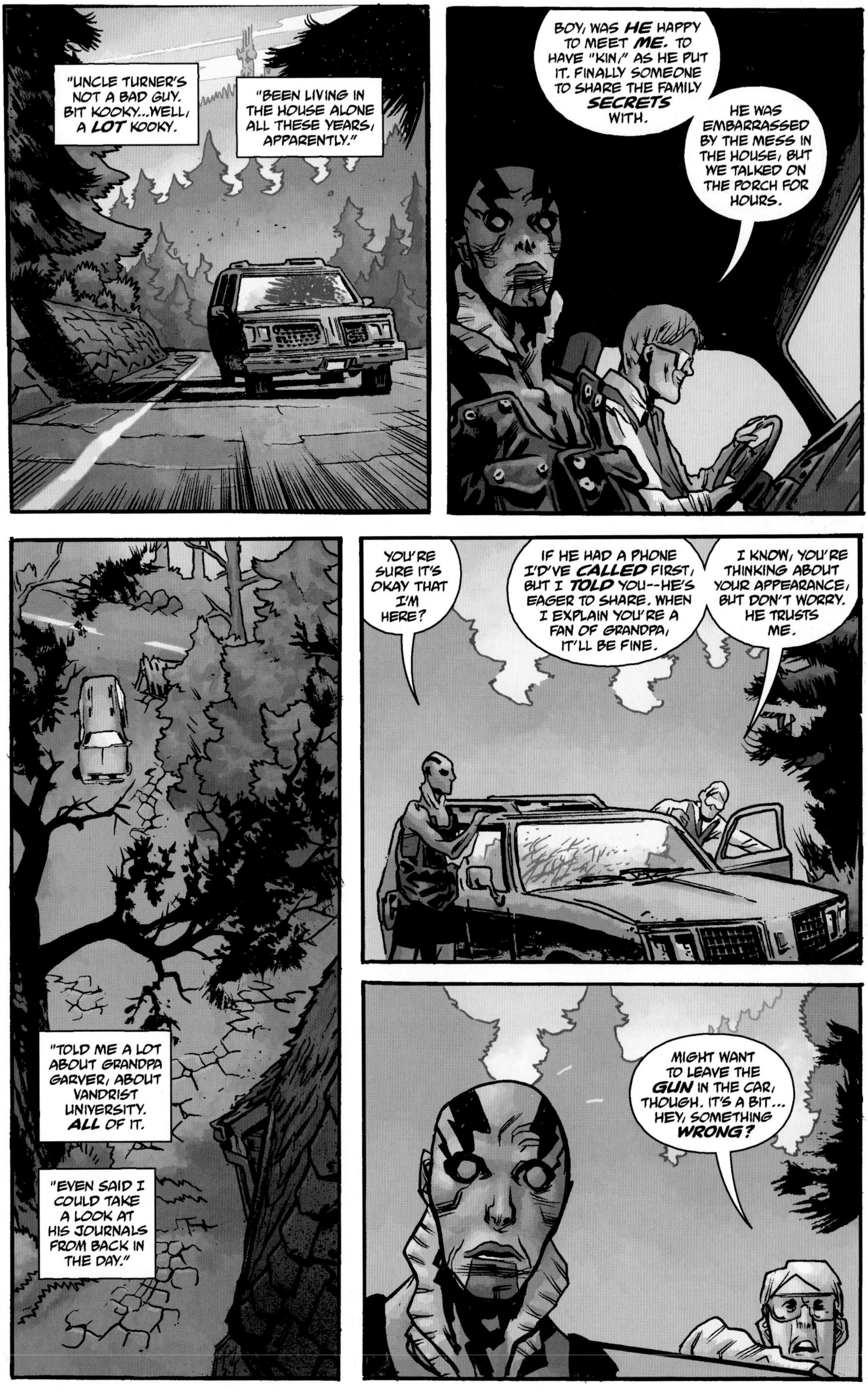

"UNCLE TURNER'S NOT A BAD GUY. BIT KOOKY...WELL, A LOT KOOKY.
"BEEN LIVING IN THE HOUSE ALONE ALL THESE YEARS, APPARENTLY."
BOY, WAS HE HAPPY TO MEET ME. TO HAVE "KIN," AS HE PUT IT. FINALLY SOMEONE TO SHARE THE FAMILY SECRETS WITH.
HE WAS EMBARRASSED BY THE MESS IN THE HOUSE, BUT WE TALKED ON THE PORCH FOR HOURS.
"TOLD ME A LOT ABOUT GRANDPA GARVER, ABOUT VANDRIST UNIVERSITY. ALL OF IT.
"EVEN SAID I COULD TAKE A LOOK AT HIS JOURNALS FROM BACK IN THE DAY."
YOU'RE SURE IT'S OKAY THAT I'M HERE?
IF HE HAD A PHONE I'D'VE CALLED FIRST, BUT I TOLD YOU--HE'S EAGER TO SHARE. WHEN I EXPLAIN YOU'RE A FAN OF GRANDPA, IT'LL BE FINE.
I KNOW, YOU'RE THINKING ABOUT YOUR APPEARANCE, BUT DON'T WORRY. HE TRUSTS ME.
MIGHT WANT TO LEAVE THE GUN IN THE CAR, THOUGH. IT'S A BIT... HEY, SOMETHING WRONG?

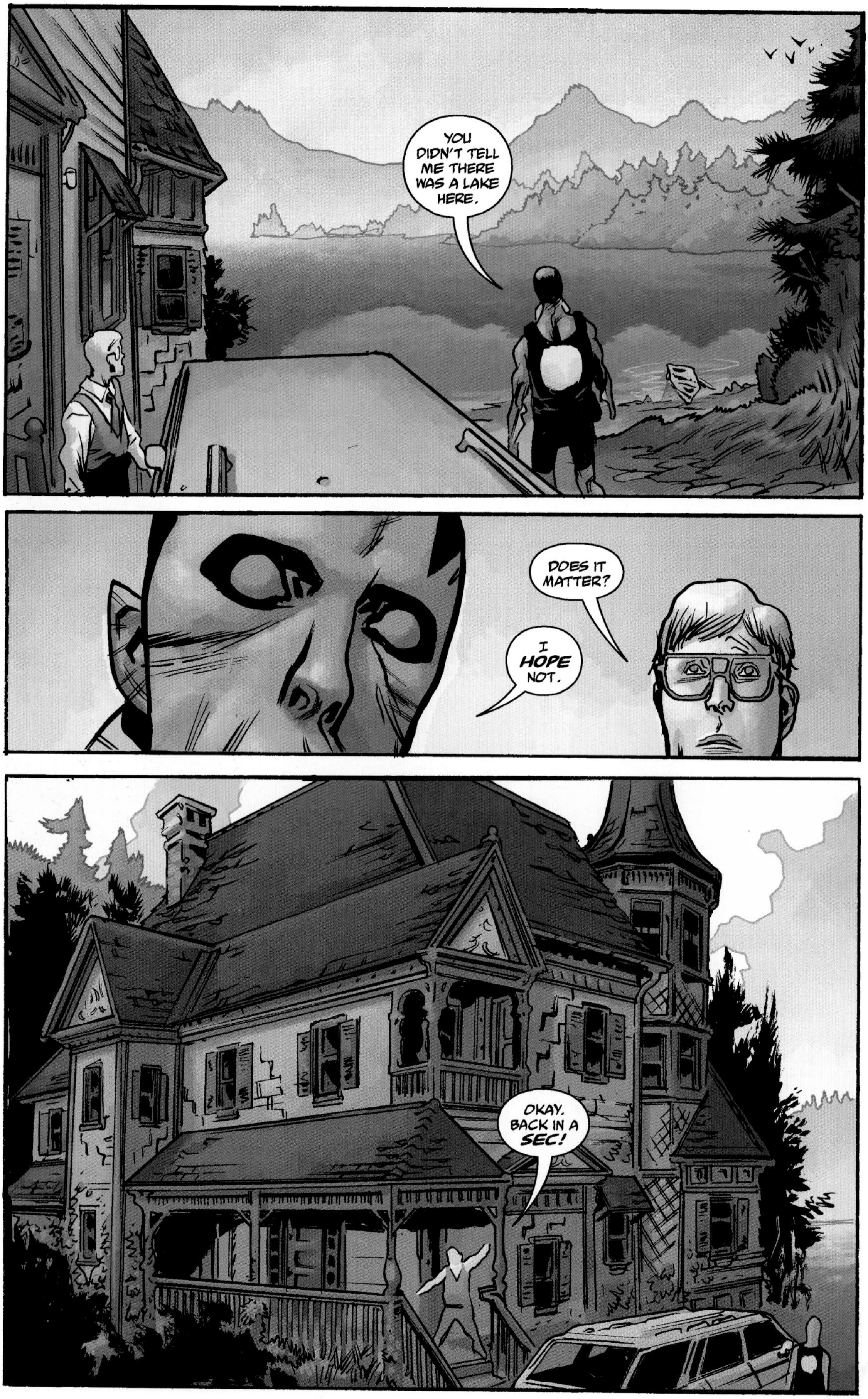
YOU DIDN'T TELL ME THERE WAS A LAKE HERE.
DOES IT MATTER?
I HOPE NOT.
OKAY. BACK IN A SEC!

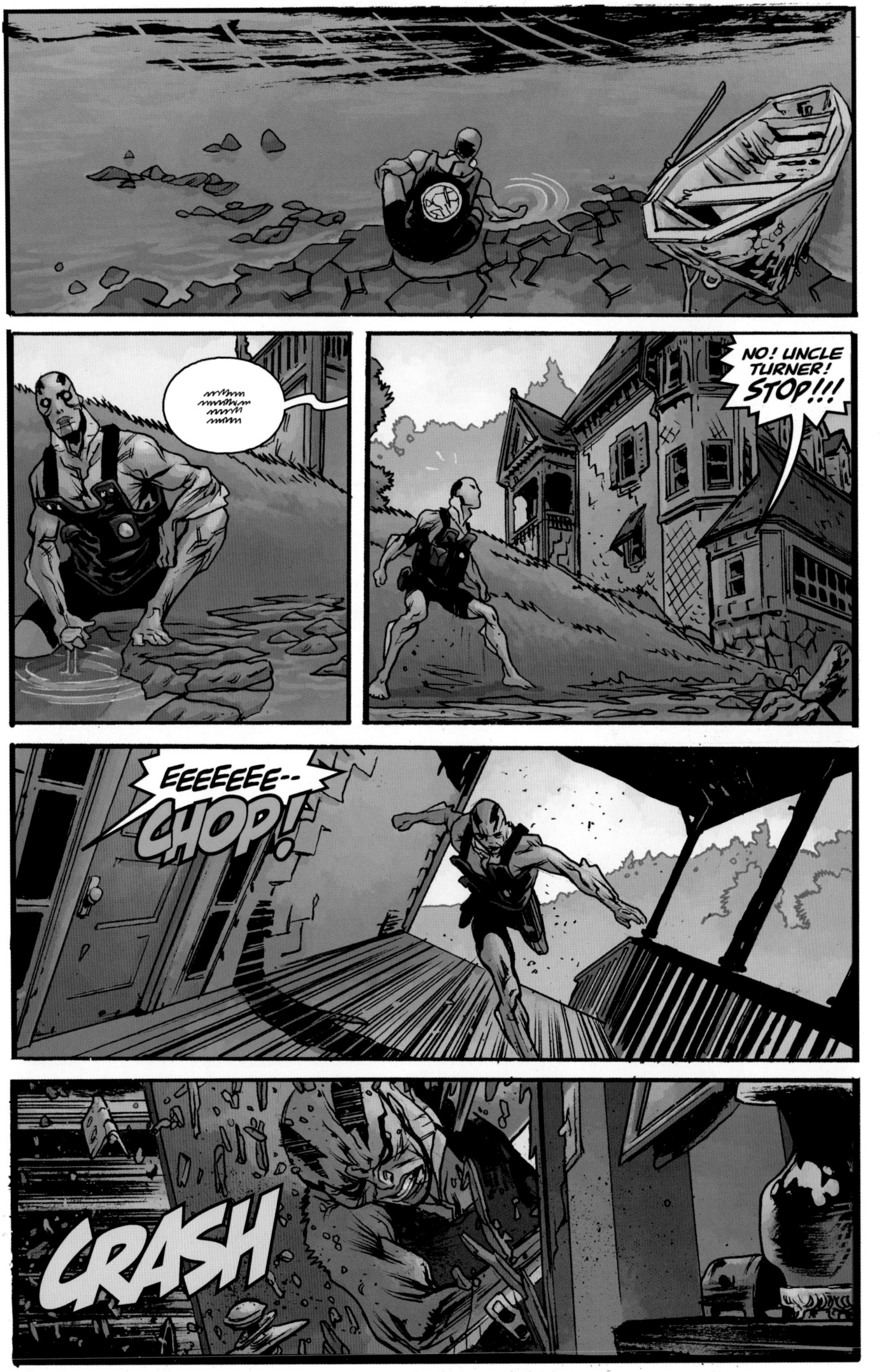

NO! UNCLE TURNER! STOP!!!
EEEEEEE--CHOP!
CRASH

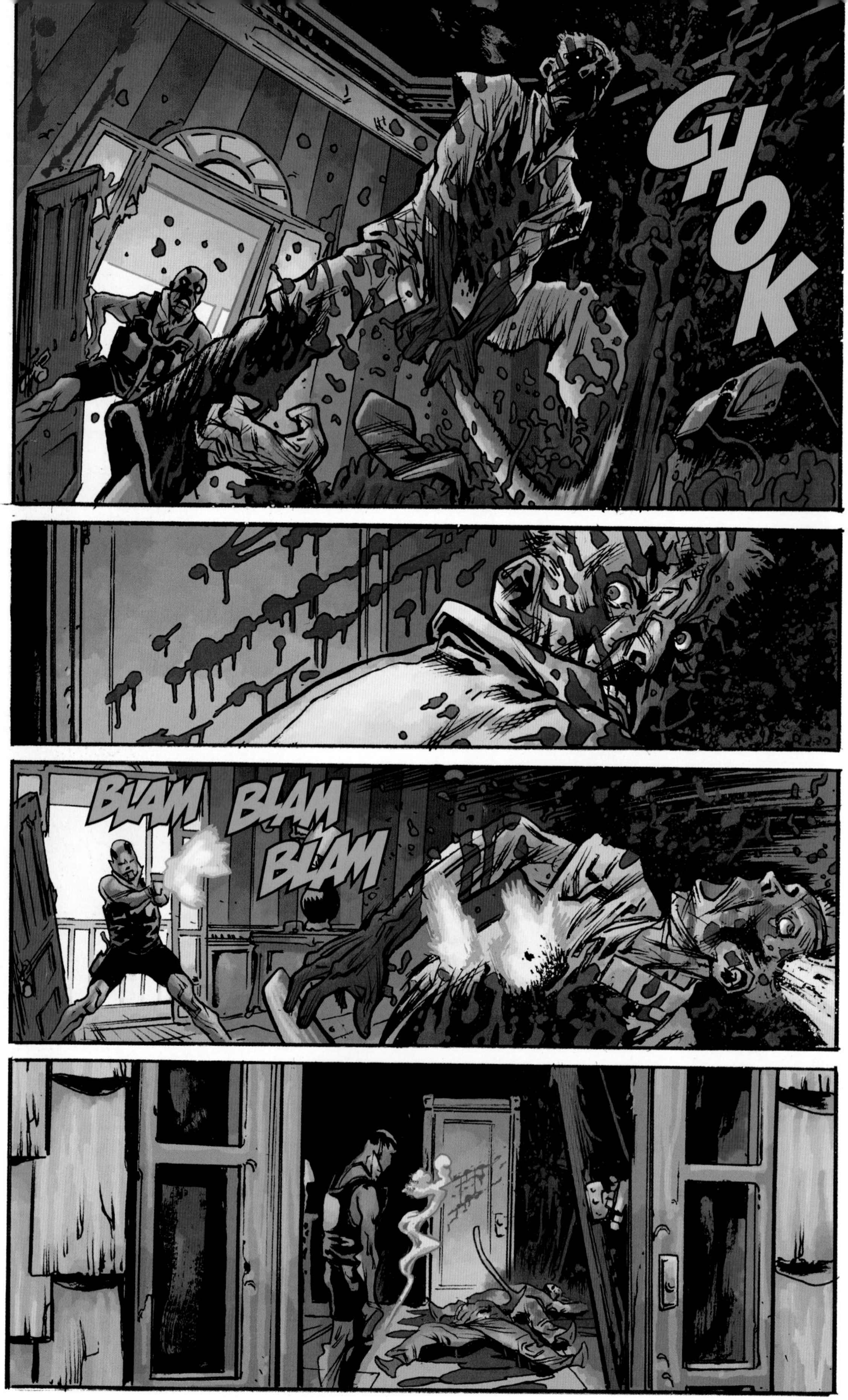
CHOK
BLAM
BLAM
BLAM

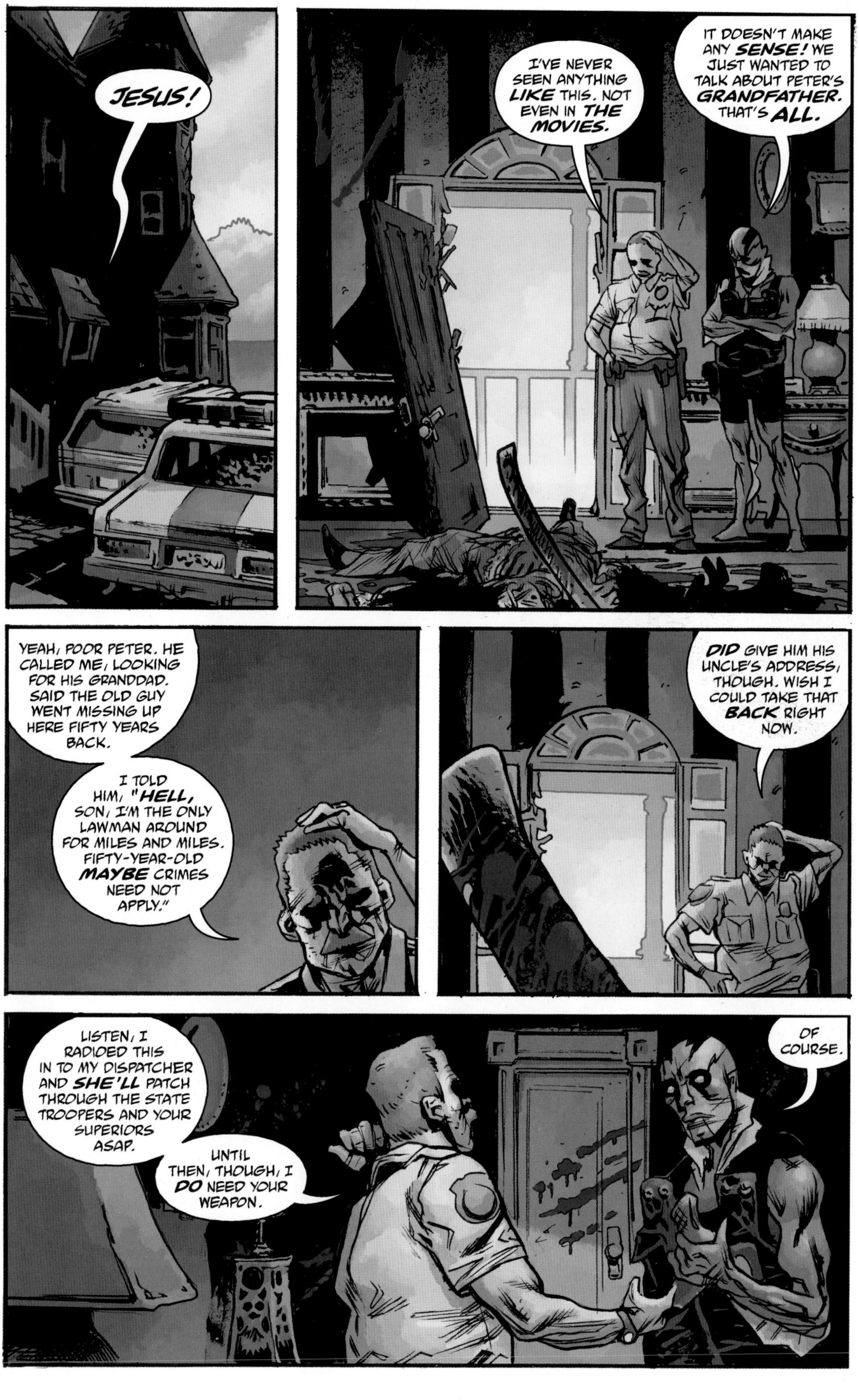
JESUS!
I'VE NEVER SEEN ANYTHING LIKE THIS. NOT EVEN IN THE MOVIES.
IT DOESN'T MAKE ANY SENSE! WE JUST WANTED TO TALK ABOUT PETER'S GRANDFATHER. THAT'S ALL.
YEAH, POOR PETER. HE CALLED ME, LOOKING FOR HIS GRANDDAD. SAID THE OLD GUY WENT MISSING UP HERE FIFTY YEARS BACK.
I TOLD HIM, "HELL, SON, I'M THE ONLY LAWMAN AROUND FOR MILES AND MILES. FIFTY-YEAR-OLD MAYBE CRIMES NEED NOT APPLY."
DID GIVE HIM HIS UNCLE'S ADDRESS, THOUGH. WISH I COULD TAKE THAT BACK RIGHT NOW.
LISTEN, I RADIOED THIS IN TO MY DISPATCHER AND SHE'LL PATCH THROUGH THE STATE TROOPERS AND YOUR SUPERIORS ASAP.
UNTIL THEN, THOUGH, I DO NEED YOUR WEAPON.
OF COURSE.

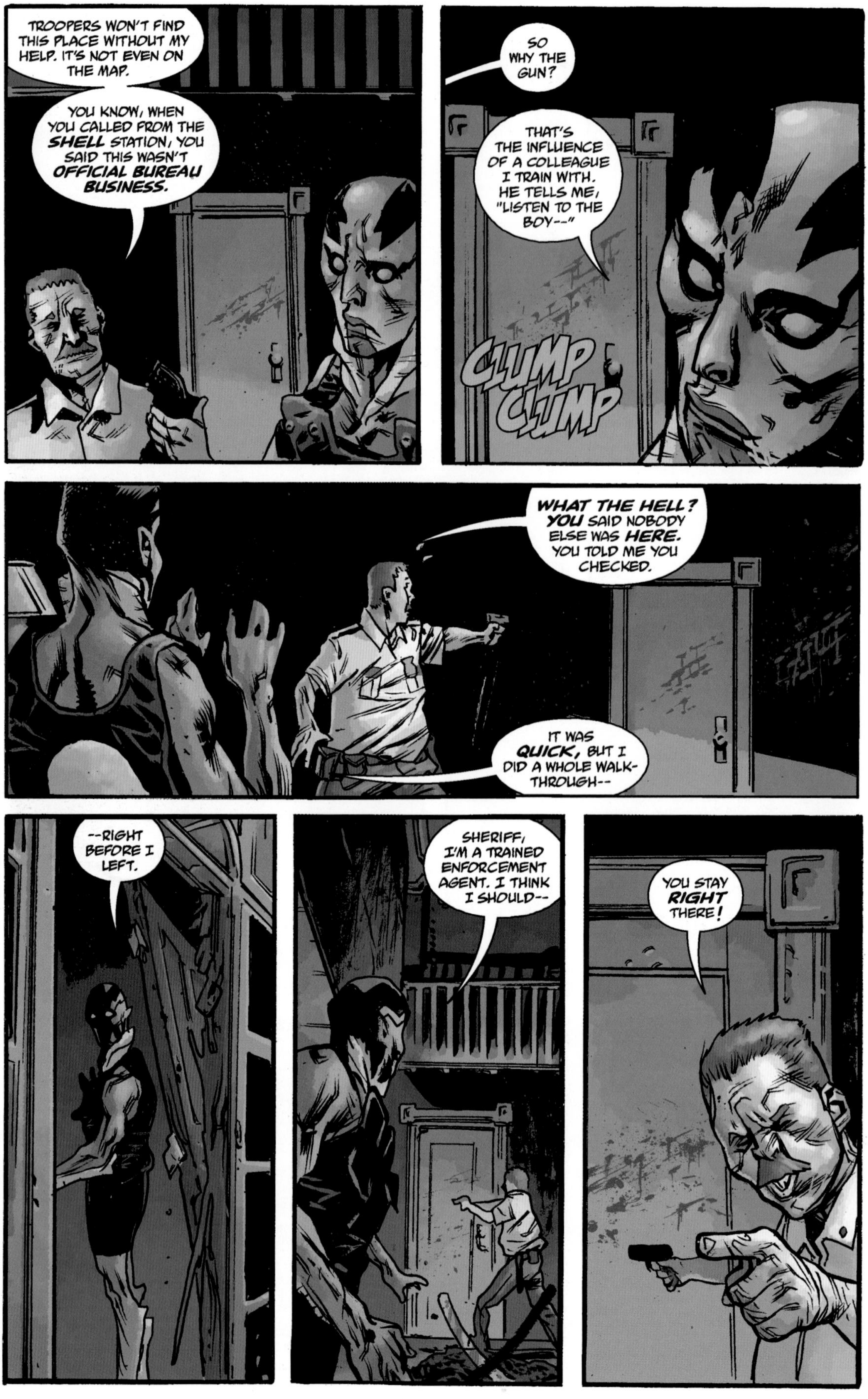

TROOPERS WON'T FIND THIS PLACE WITHOUT MY HELP. IT'S NOT EVEN ON THE MAP.
YOU KNOW, WHEN YOU CALLED FROM THE SHELL STATION, YOU SAID THIS WASN'T OFFICIAL BUREAU BUSINESS.
SO WHY THE GUN?
THAT'S THE INFLUENCE OF A COLLEAGUE I TRAIN WITH. HE TELLS ME, "LISTEN TO THE BOY--"
CLUMP CLUMP
WHAT THE HELL? YOU SAID NOBODY ELSE WAS HERE. YOU TOLD ME YOU CHECKED.
IT WAS QUICK, BUT I DID A WHOLE WALK-THROUGH--
--RIGHT BEFORE I LEFT.
SHERIFF, I'M A TRAINED ENFORCEMENT AGENT. I THINK I SHOULD--
YOU STAY RIGHT THERE!

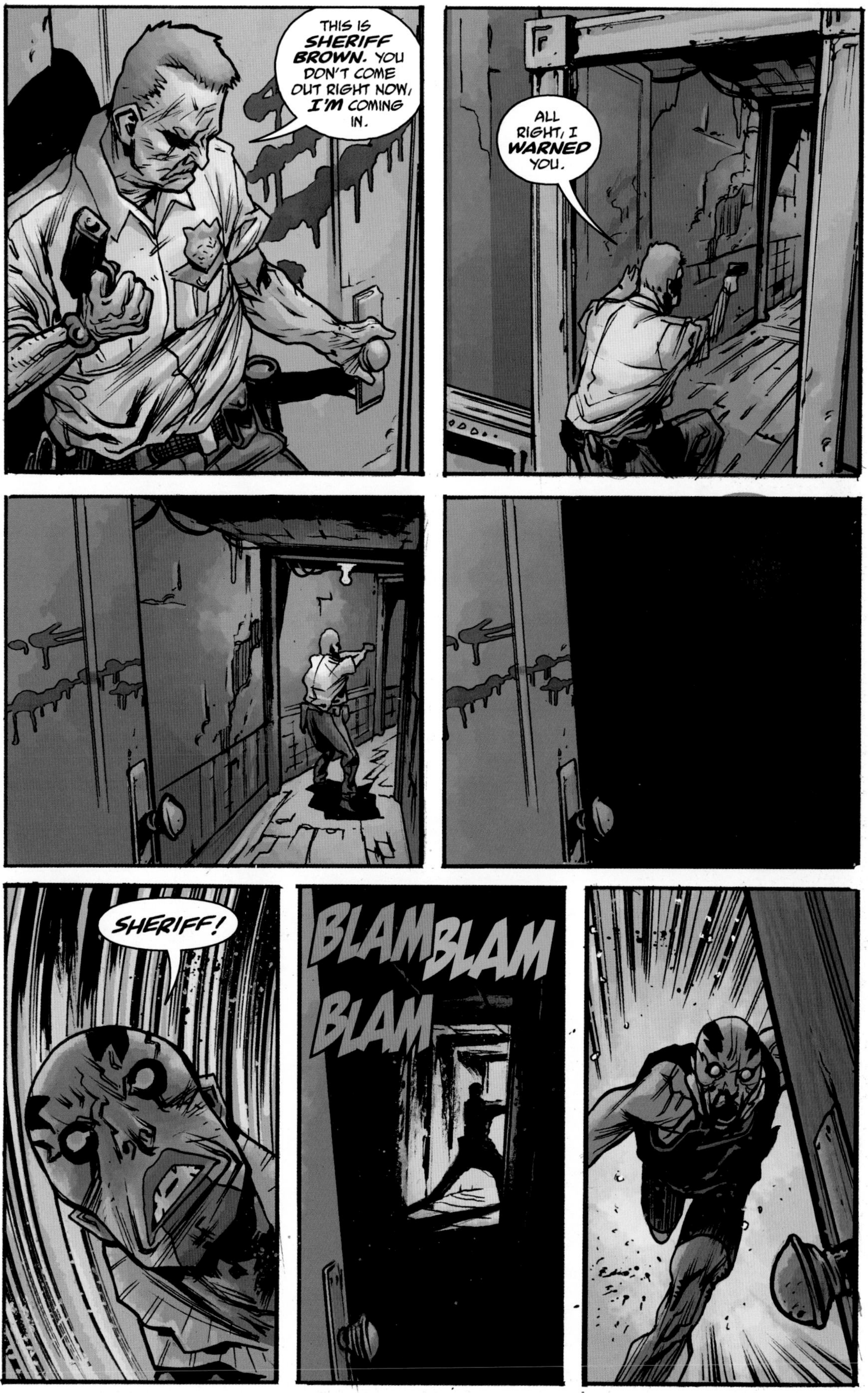
THIS IS SHERIFF BROWN. YOU DON'T COME OUT RIGHT NOW, I'M COMING IN.
ALL RIGHT, I WARNED YOU.
SHERIFF!
BLAM BLAM BLAM

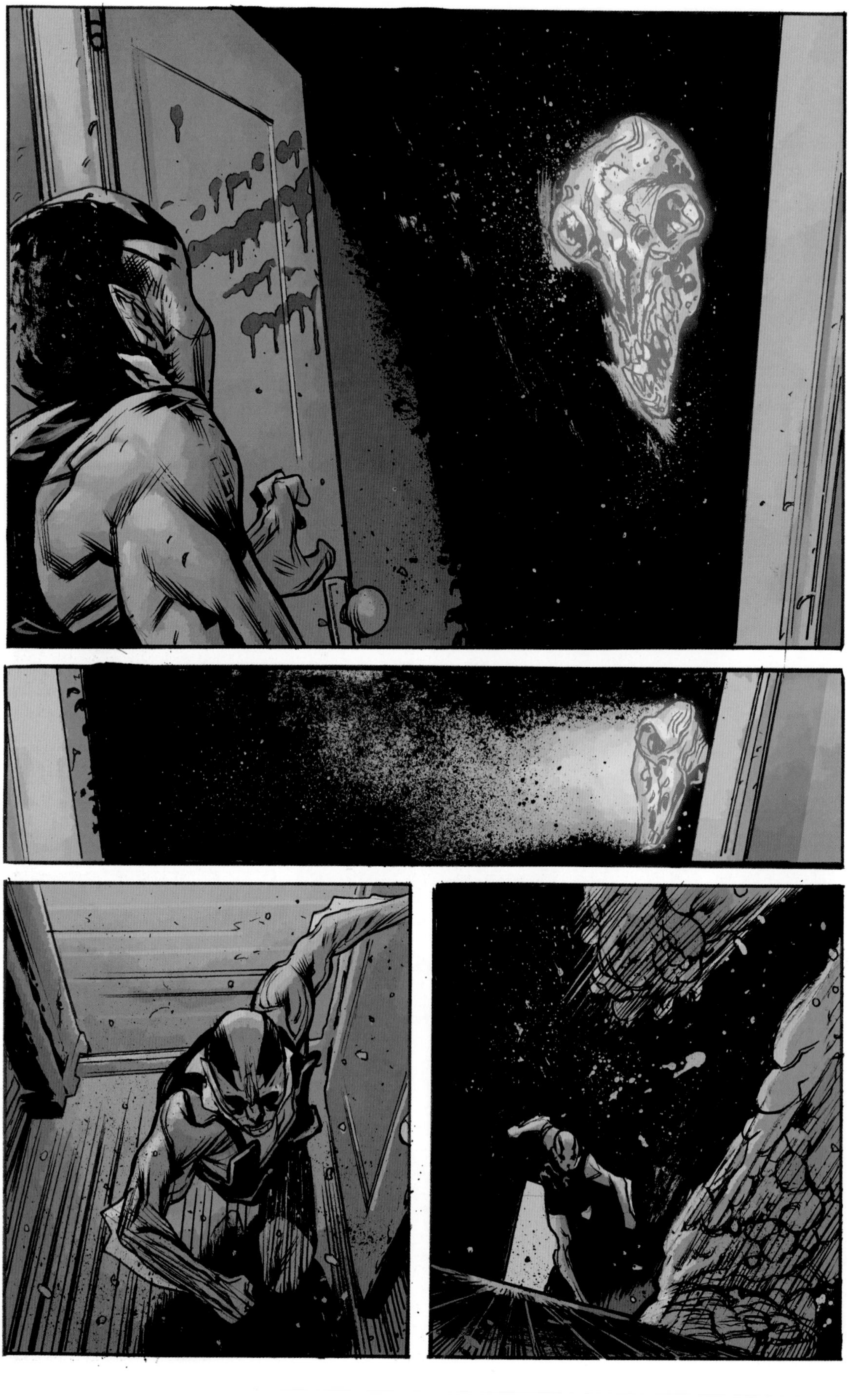

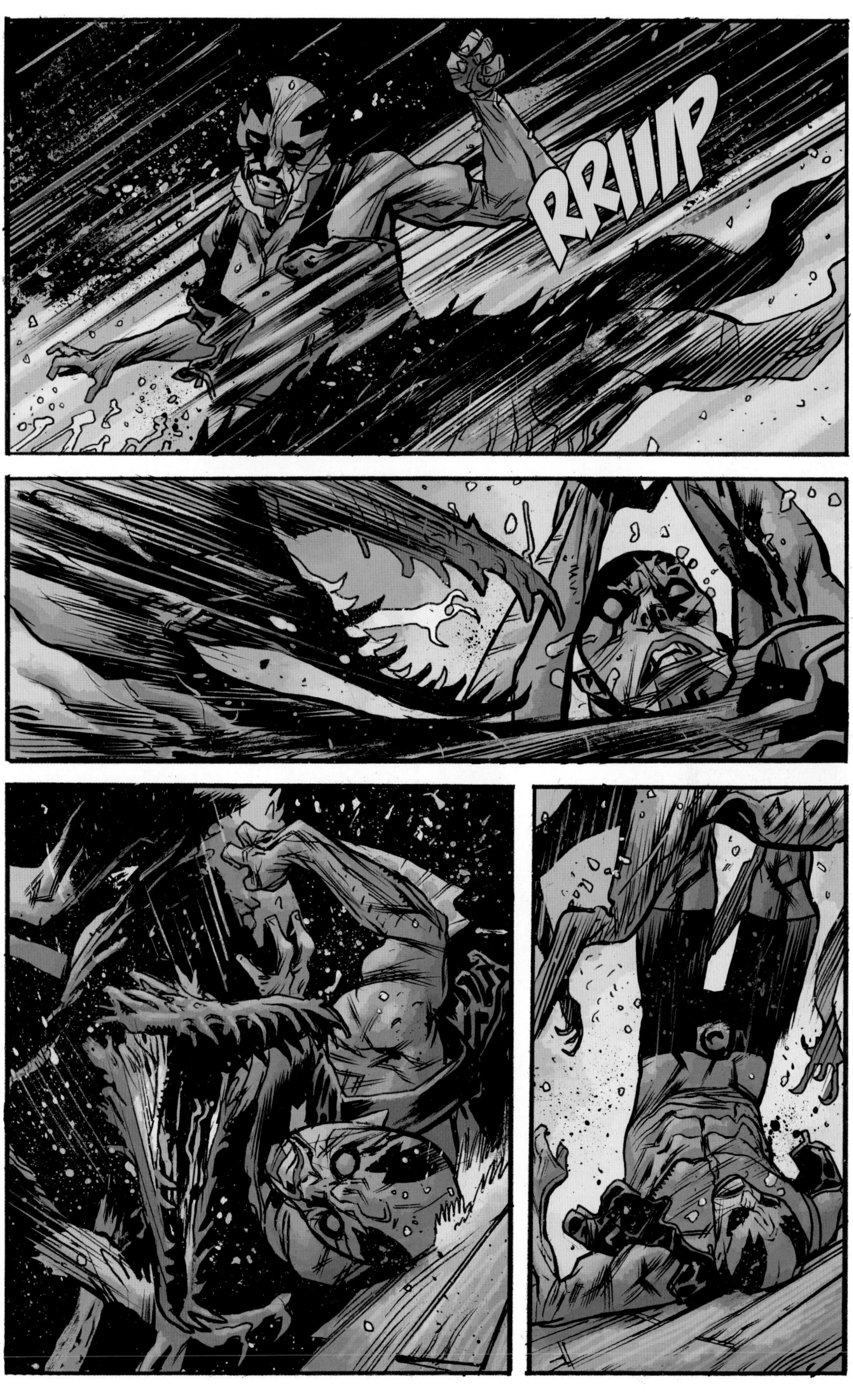
RRIIIP

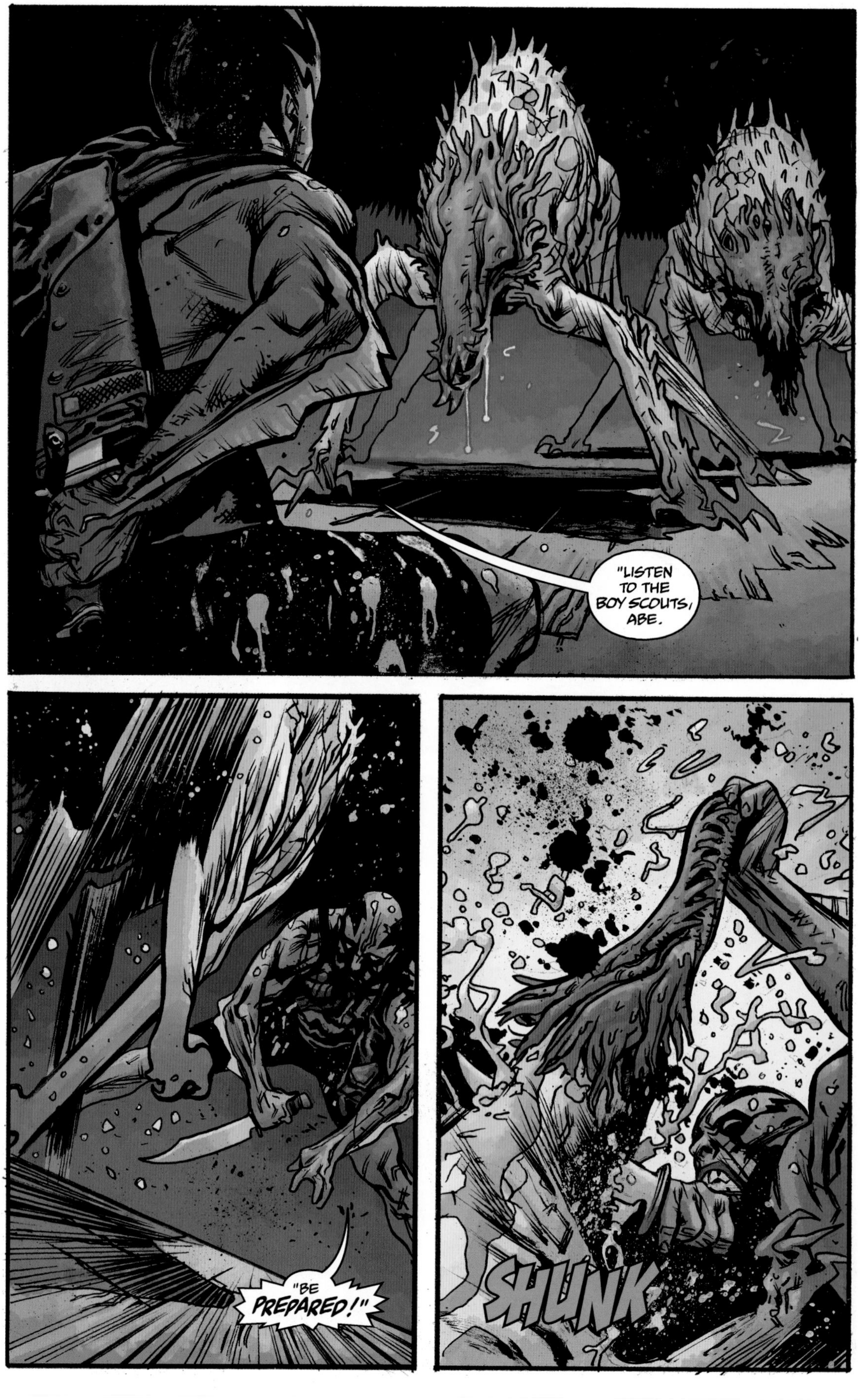
"LISTEN TO THE BOY SCOUTS, ABE.
"BE PREPARED!"
SHUNK

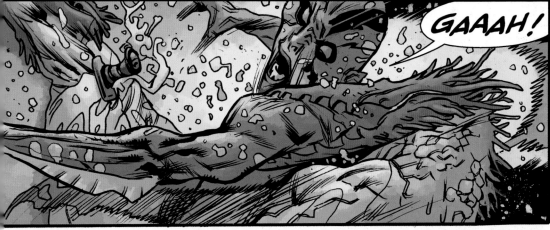

GAAAH!

SSPLITT SPLTT

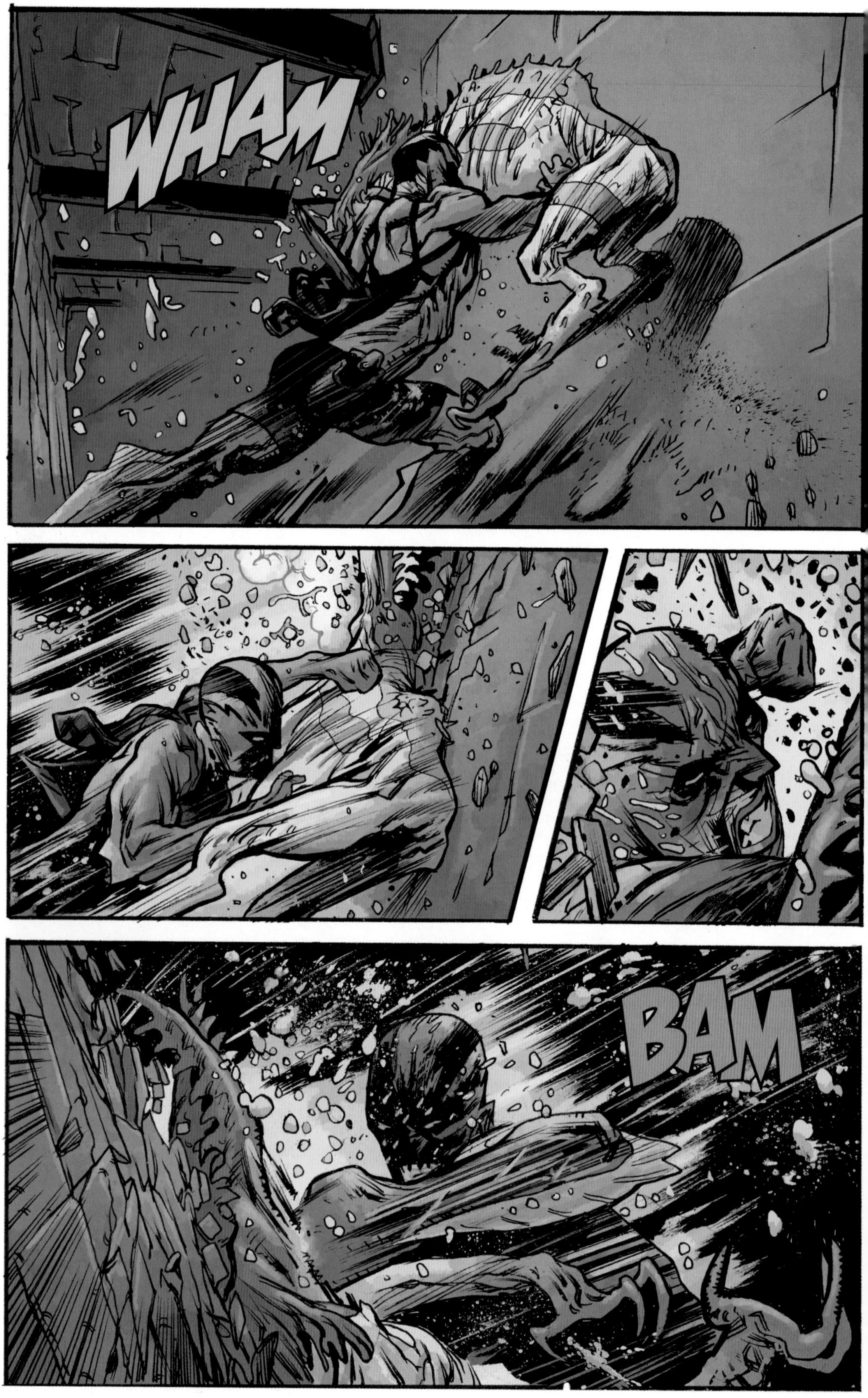
WHAM
BAM

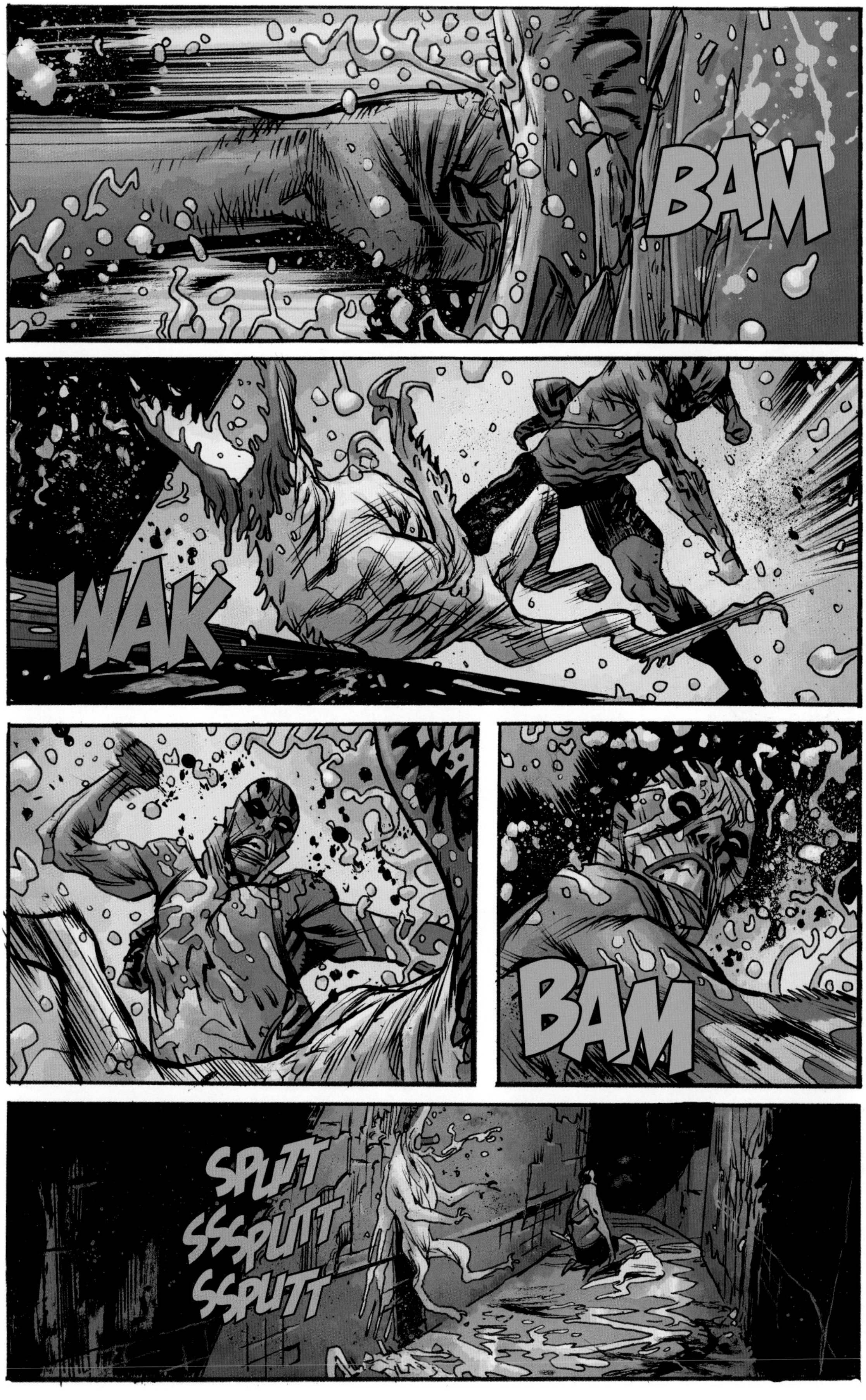
BAM
WAK
BAM
SPUTT
SSSPUTT
SSPUTT

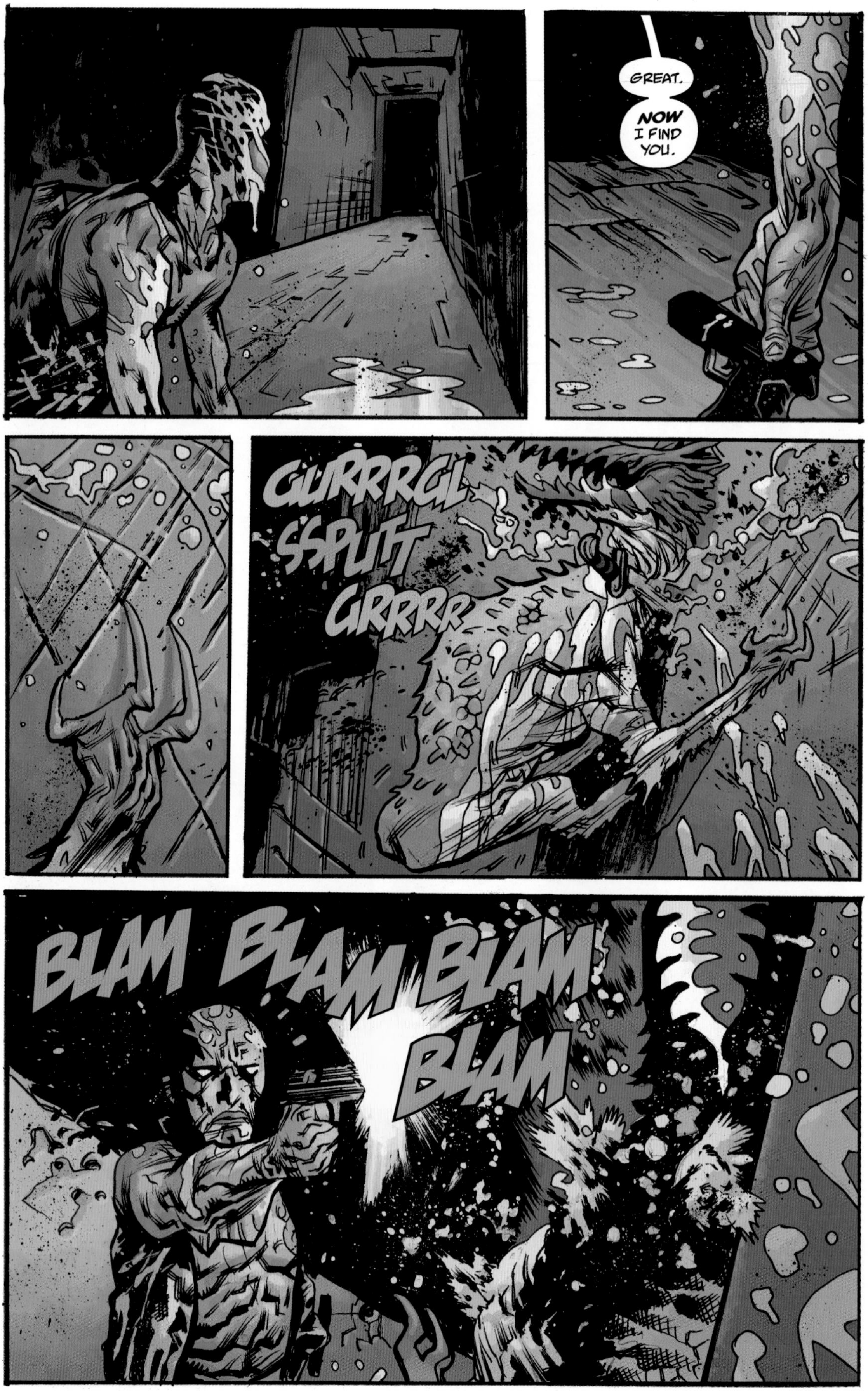
GREAT.
NOW I FIND YOU.
GURRRGL SSPUTT GRRRR
BLAM BLAM BLAM BLAM

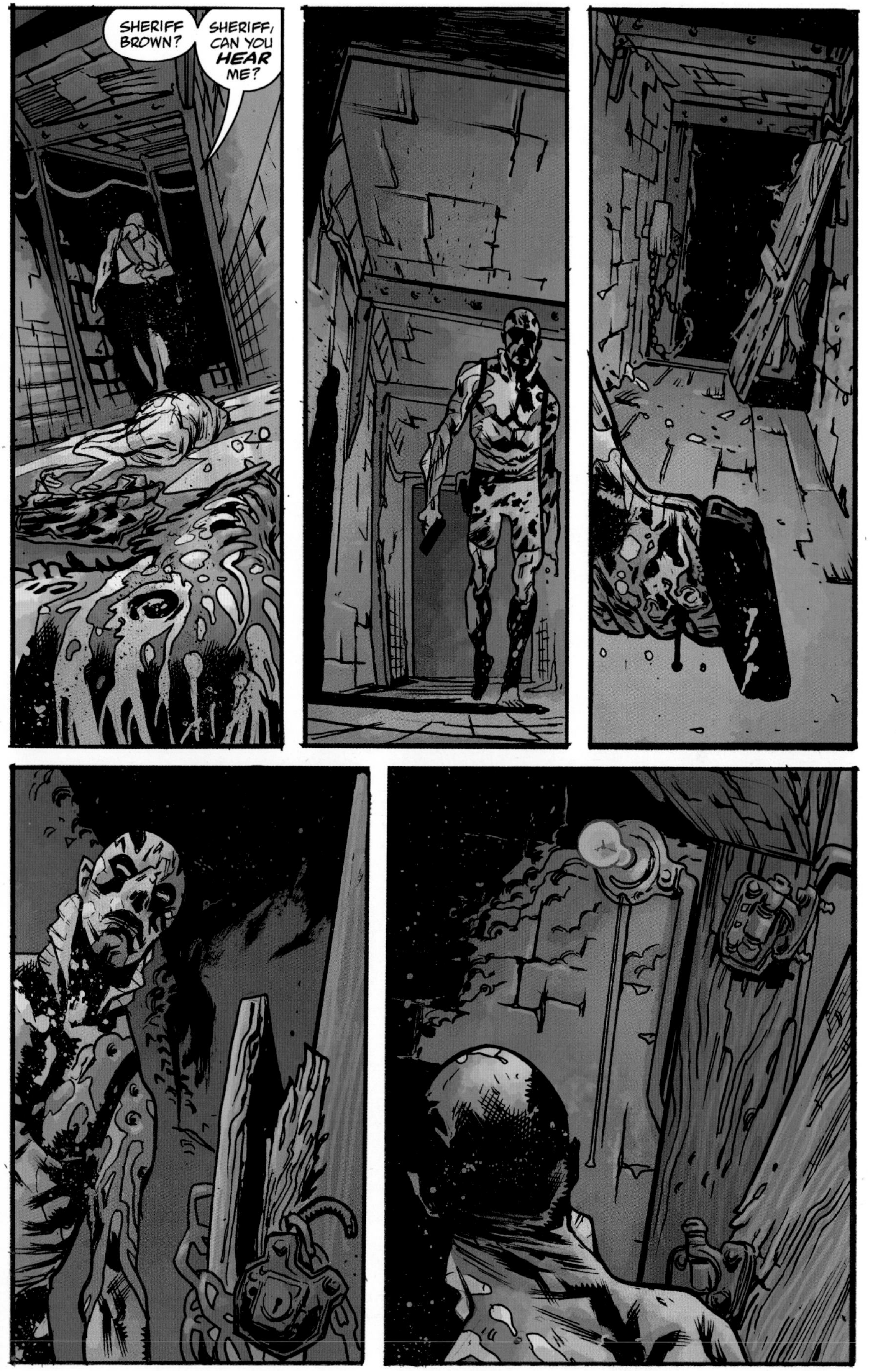
SHERIFF BROWN?
SHERIFF, CAN YOU HEAR ME?

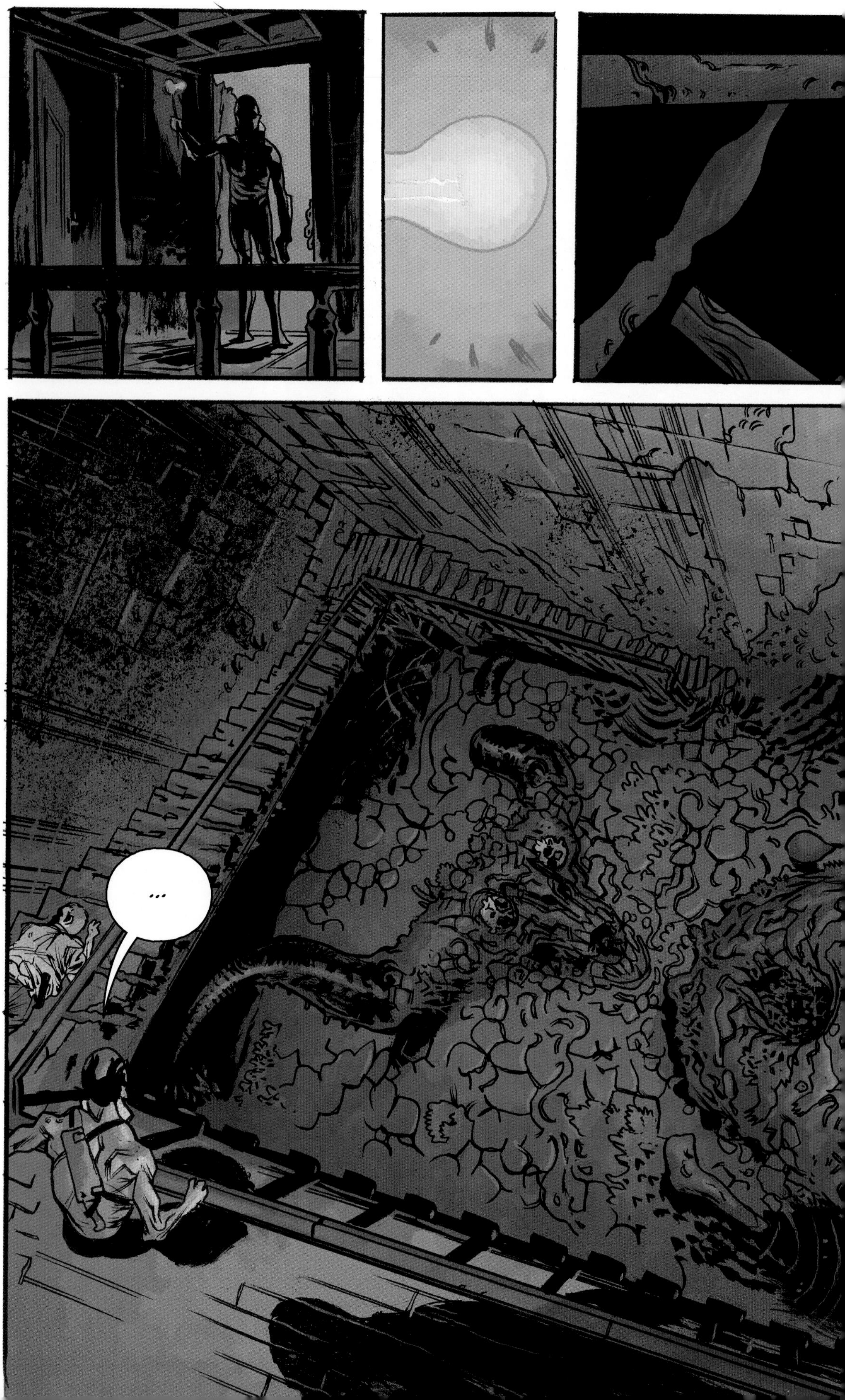
...

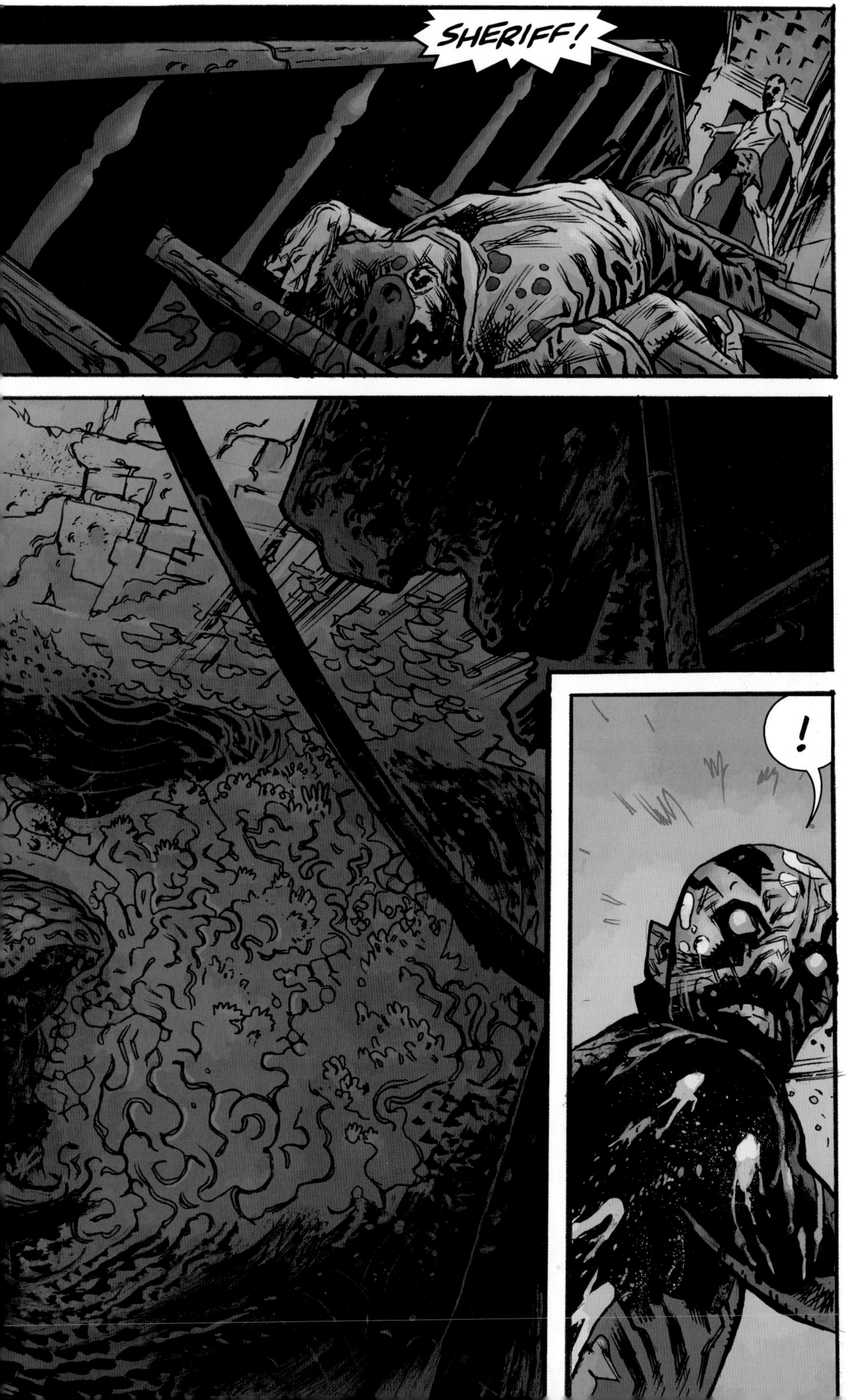
SHERIFF!
!

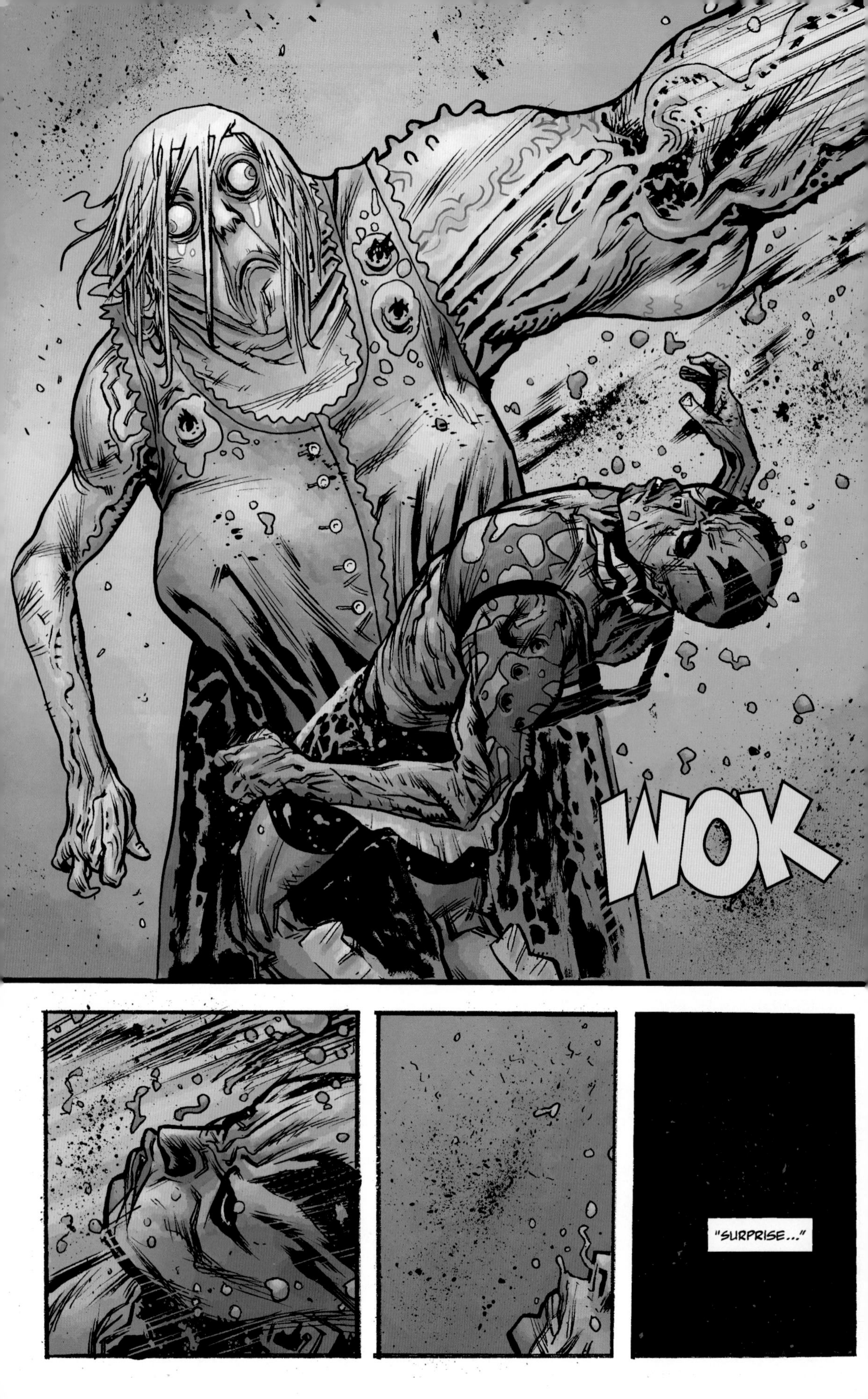
WOK
"SURPRISE..."

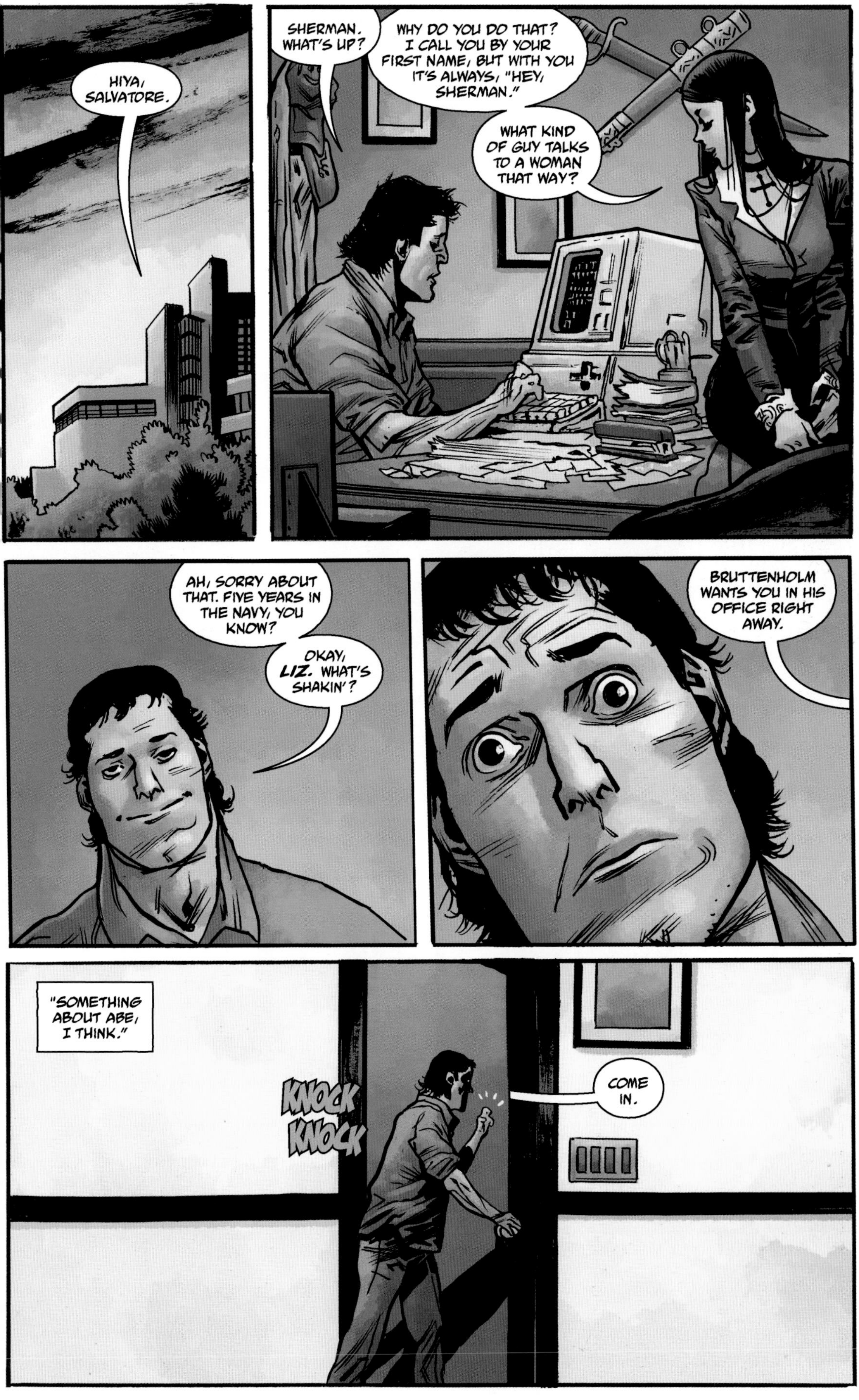
HIYA, SALVATORE.
SHERMAN. WHAT'S UP?
WHY DO YOU DO THAT? I CALL YOU BY YOUR FIRST NAME, BUT WITH YOU IT'S ALWAYS, "HEY, SHERMAN."
WHAT KIND OF GUY TALKS TO A WOMAN THAT WAY?
AH, SORRY ABOUT THAT. FIVE YEARS IN THE NAVY, YOU KNOW?
OKAY, LIZ. WHAT'S SHAKIN'?
BRUTTENHOLM WANTS YOU IN HIS OFFICE RIGHT AWAY.
"SOMETHING ABOUT ABE, I THINK."
KNOCK KNOCK
COME IN.

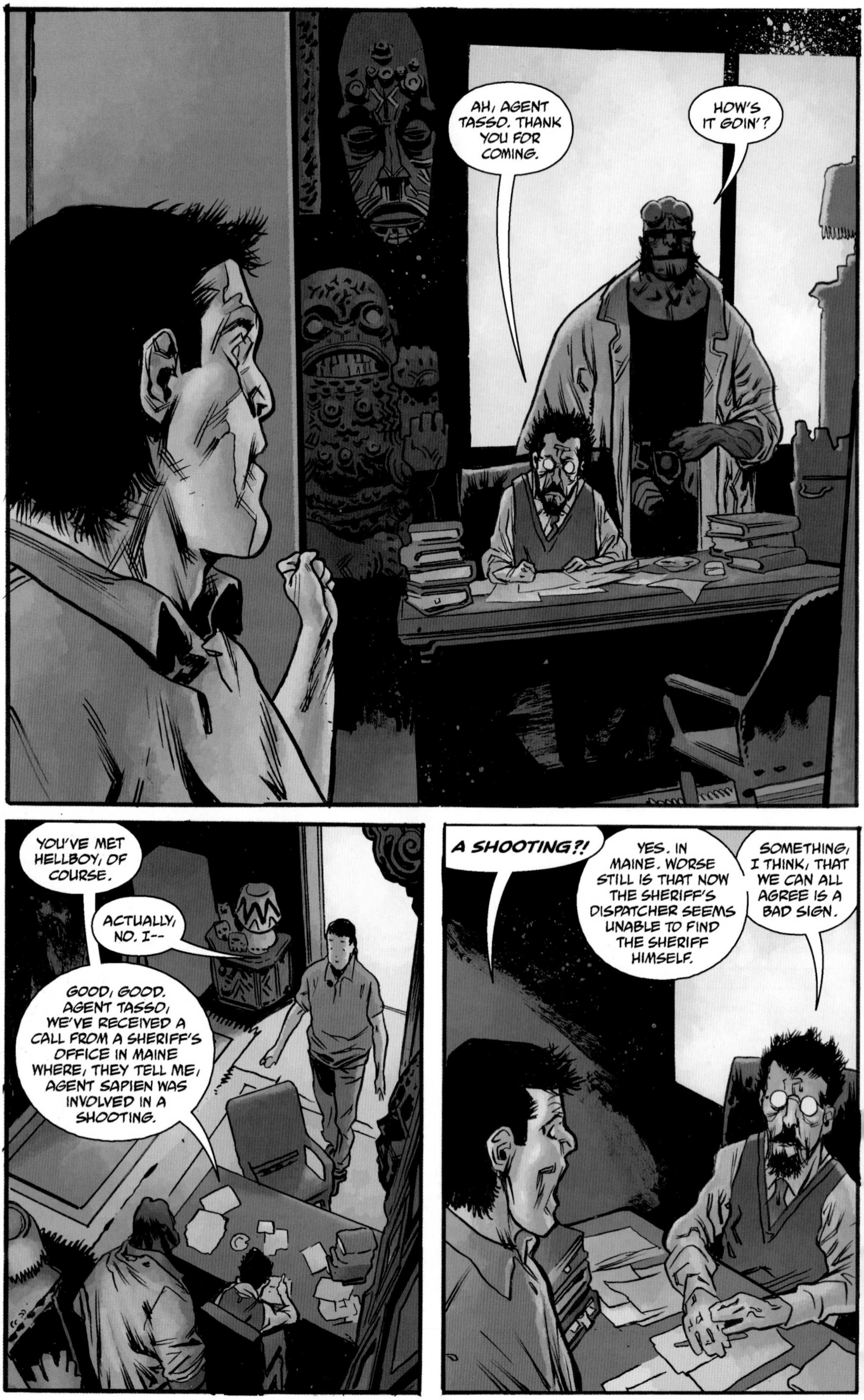
AH, AGENT TASSO. THANK YOU FOR COMING.
HOW'S IT GOIN'?
YOU'VE MET HELLBOY, OF COURSE.
ACTUALLY, NO. I--
GOOD, GOOD. AGENT TASSO, WE'VE RECEIVED A CALL FROM A SHERIFF'S OFFICE IN MAINE WHERE, THEY TELL ME, AGENT SAPIEN WAS INVOLVED IN A SHOOTING.
A SHOOTING?!
YES. IN MAINE. WORSE STILL IS THAT NOW THE SHERIFF'S DISPATCHER SEEMS UNABLE TO FIND THE SHERIFF HIMSELF.
SOMETHING, I THINK, THAT WE CAN ALL AGREE IS A BAD SIGN.

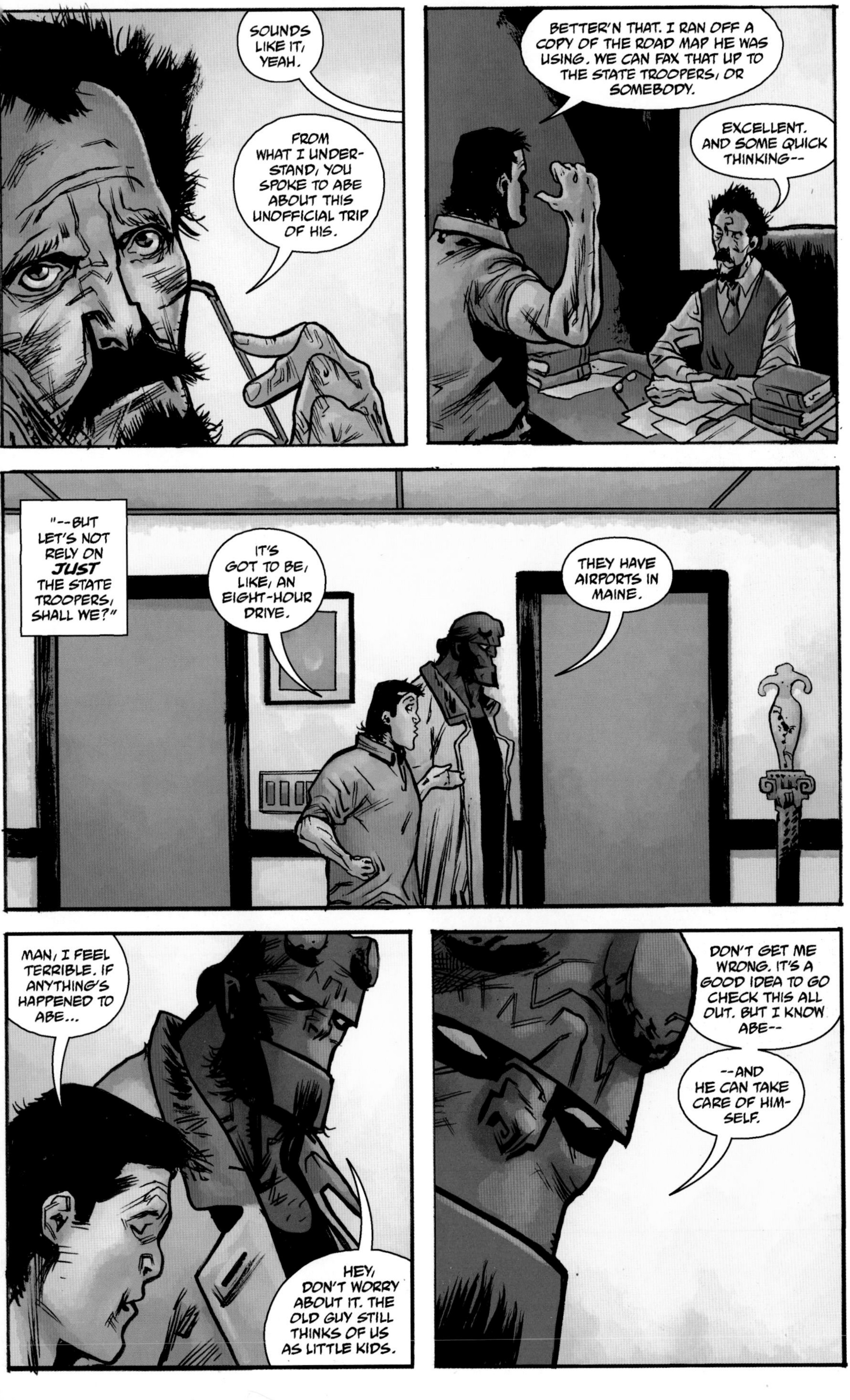
SOUNDS LIKE IT, YEAH.
FROM WHAT I UNDER-STAND, YOU SPOKE TO ABE ABOUT THIS UNOFFICIAL TRIP OF HIS.
BETTER'N THAT. I RAN OFF A COPY OF THE ROAD MAP HE WAS USING. WE CAN FAX THAT UP TO THE STATE TROOPERS, OR SOMEBODY.
EXCELLENT. AND SOME QUICK THINKING--
"--BUT LET'S NOT RELY ON JUST THE STATE TROOPERS, SHALL WE?"
IT'S GOT TO BE, LIKE, AN EIGHT-HOUR DRIVE.
THEY HAVE AIRPORTS IN MAINE.
MAN, I FEEL TERRIBLE. IF ANYTHING'S HAPPENED TO ABE...
HEY, DON'T WORRY ABOUT IT. THE OLD GUY STILL THINKS OF US AS LITTLE KIDS.
DON'T GET ME WRONG. IT'S A GOOD IDEA TO GO CHECK THIS ALL OUT. BUT I KNOW ABE--
--AND HE CAN TAKE CARE OF HIM-SELF.

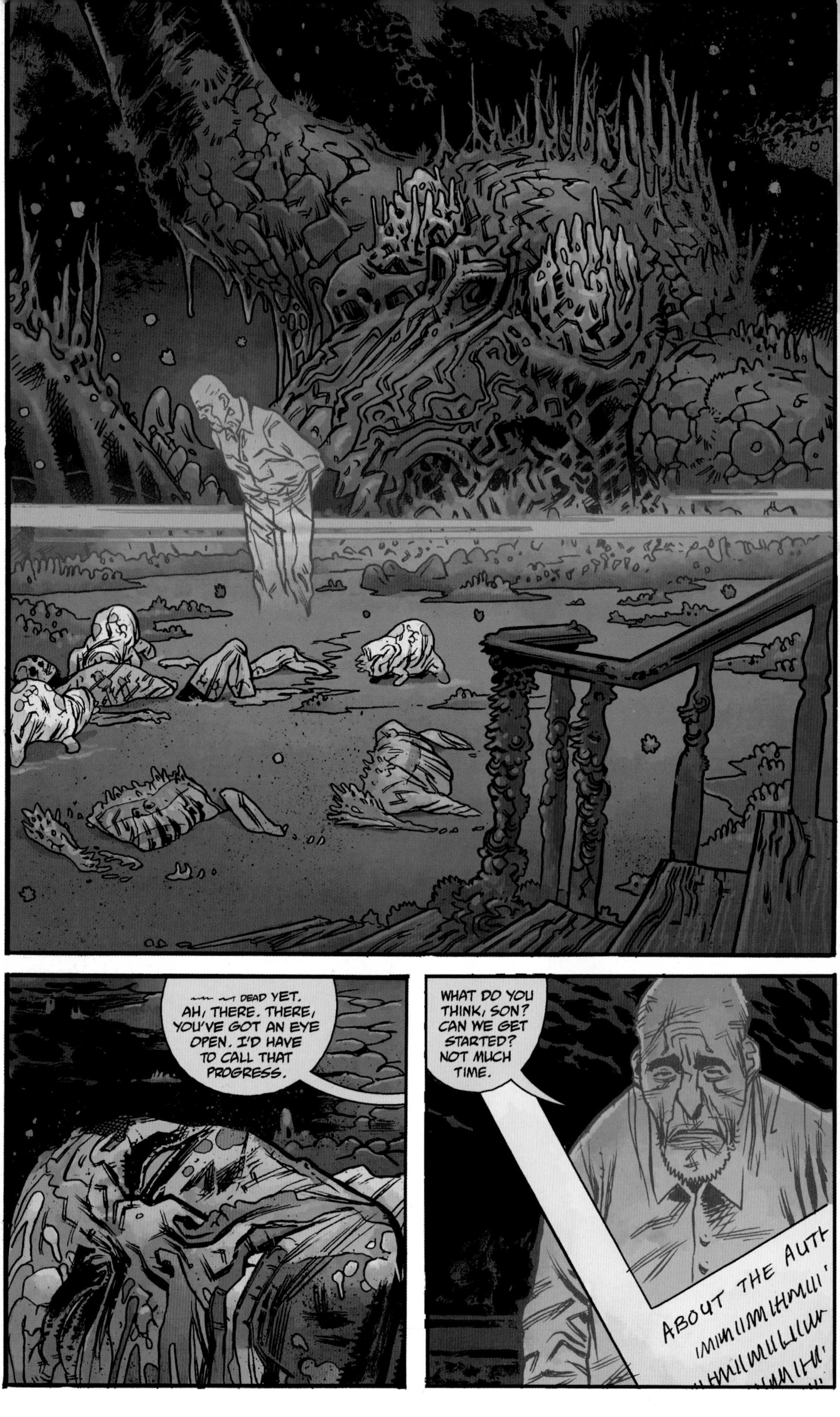
DEAD YET.
AH, THERE. THERE, YOU'VE GOT AN EYE OPEN. I'D HAVE TO CALL THAT PROGRESS.
WHAT DO YOU THINK, SON? CAN WE GET STARTED? NOT MUCH TIME.
ABOUT THE AUTH

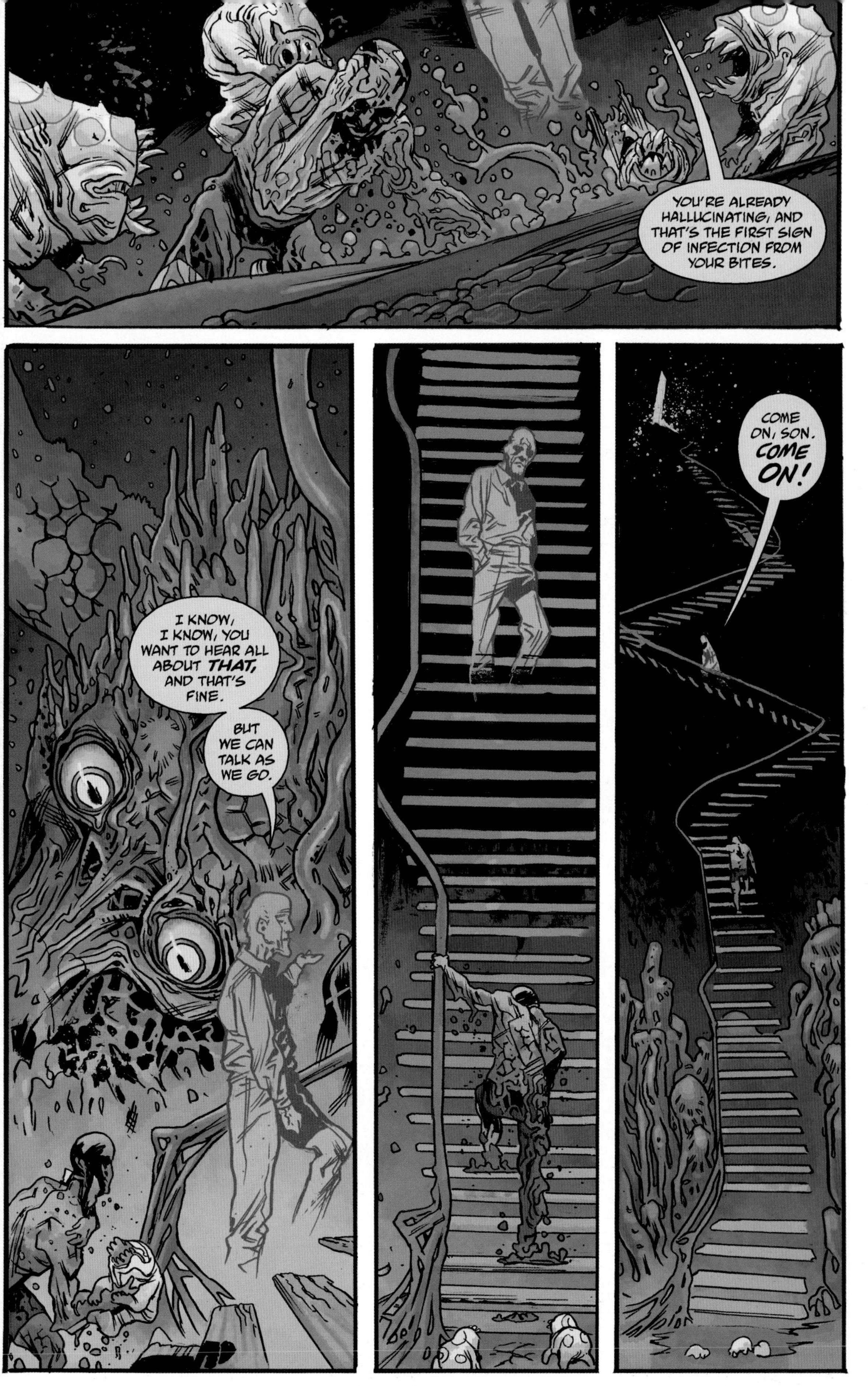
YOU'RE ALREADY HALLUCINATING, AND THAT'S THE FIRST SIGN OF INFECTION FROM YOUR BITES.
I KNOW, I KNOW, YOU WANT TO HEAR ALL ABOUT THAT, AND THAT'S FINE.
BUT WE CAN TALK AS WE GO.
COME ON, SON. COME ON!

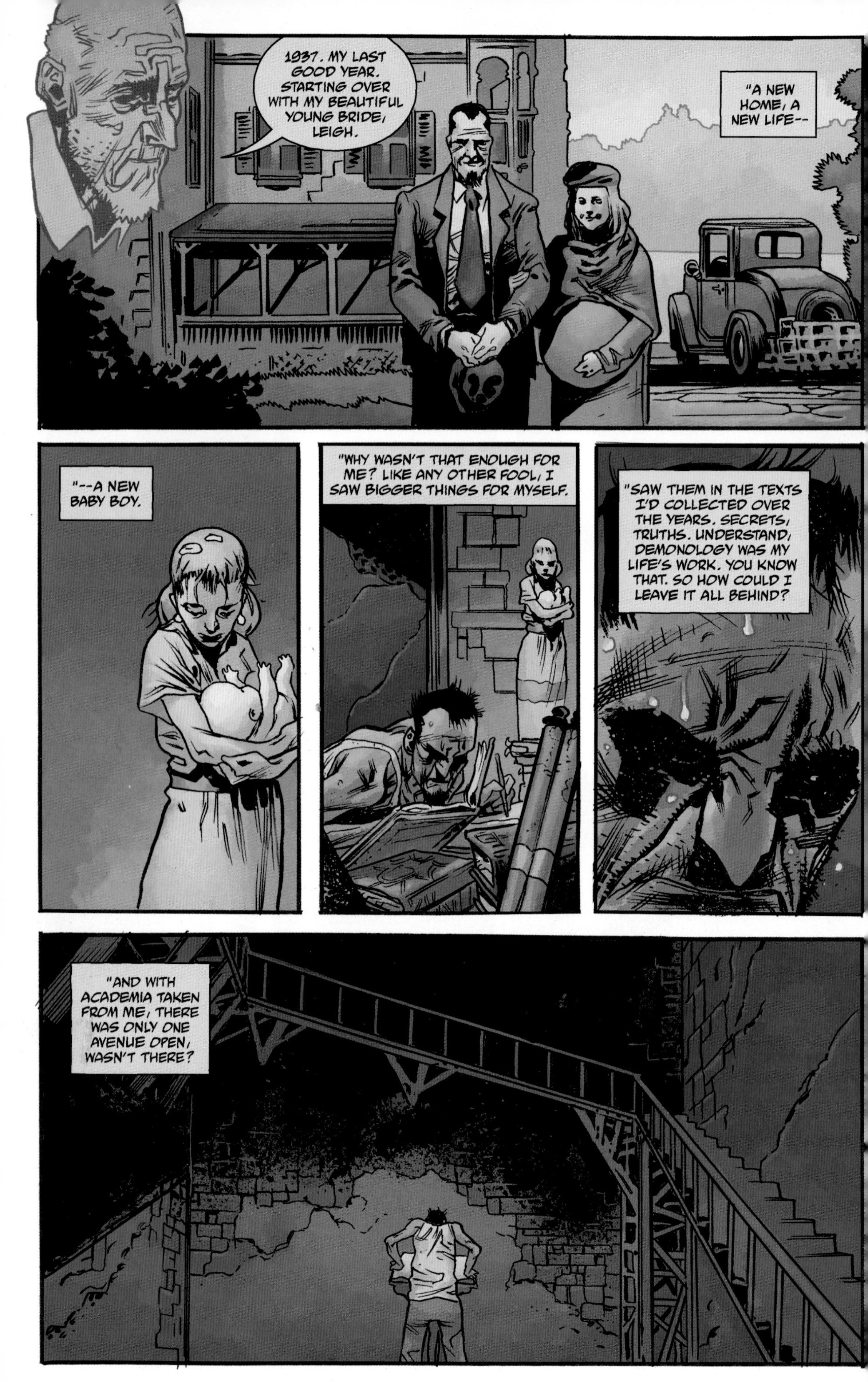
1937. MY LAST GOOD YEAR. STARTING OVER WITH MY BEAUTIFUL YOUNG BRIDE, LEIGH.
"A NEW HOME, A NEW LIFE--
"--A NEW BABY BOY.
"WHY WASN'T THAT ENOUGH FOR ME? LIKE ANY OTHER FOOL, I SAW BIGGER THINGS FOR MYSELF.
"SAW THEM IN THE TEXTS I'D COLLECTED OVER THE YEARS. SECRETS, TRUTHS. UNDERSTAND, DEMONOLOGY WAS MY LIFE'S WORK. YOU KNOW THAT. SO HOW COULD I LEAVE IT ALL BEHIND?
"AND WITH ACADEMIA TAKEN FROM ME, THERE WAS ONLY ONE AVENUE OPEN, WASN'T THERE?

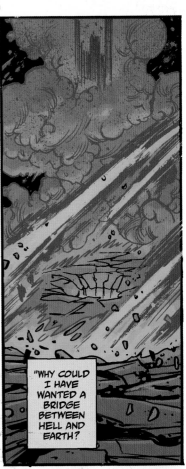

"BUT FOR ALL THAT, I WAS A FOOL.

"WHY COULD I HAVE WANTED A BRIDGE BETWEEN HELL AND EARTH?

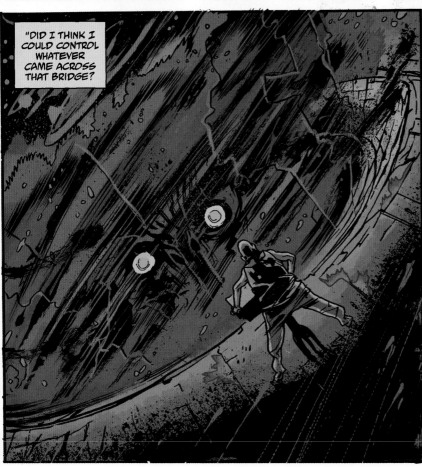

"DID I THINK I COULD CONTROL WHATEVER CAME ACROSS THAT BRIDGE?

"I DON'T KNOW."

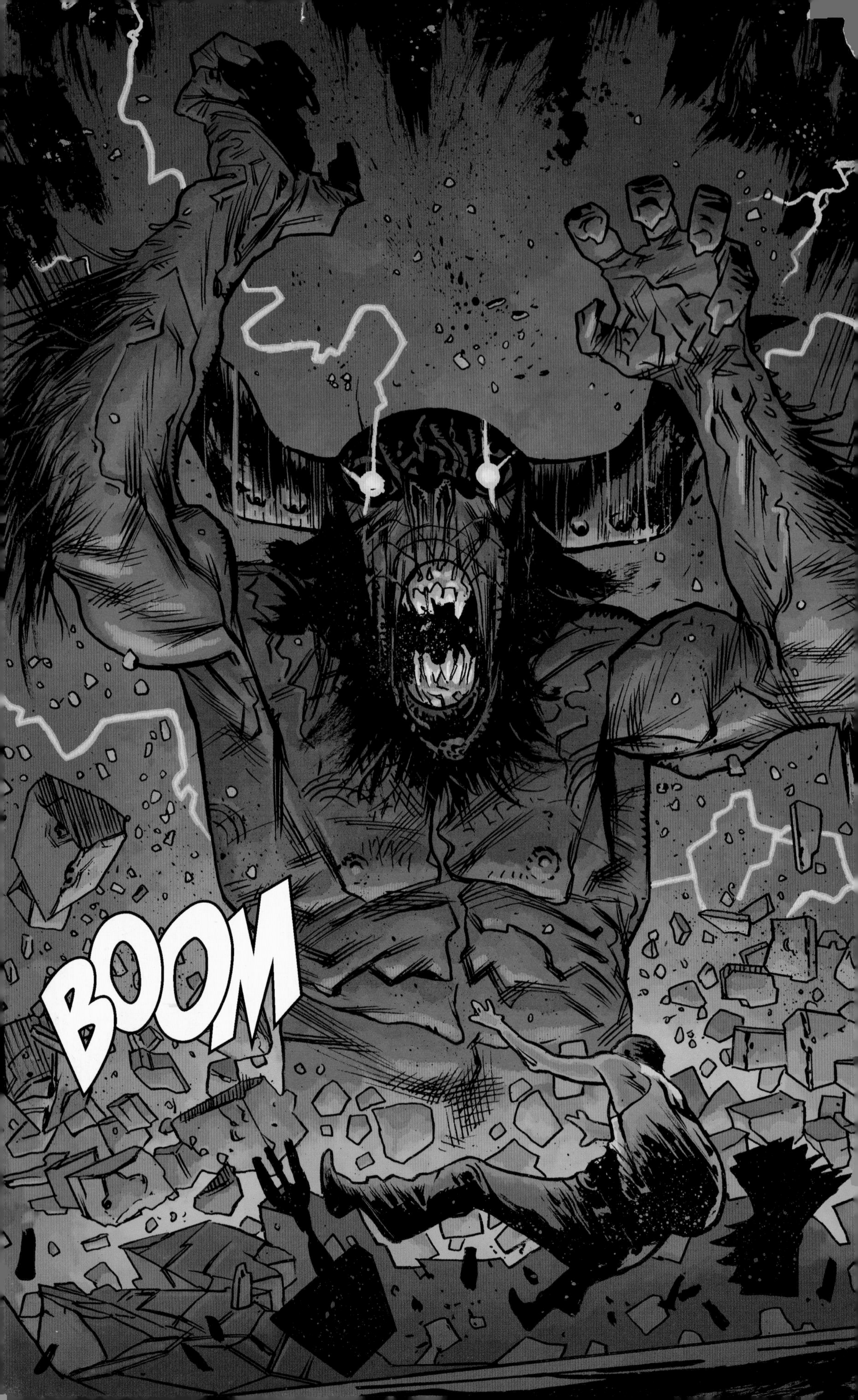
BOOM

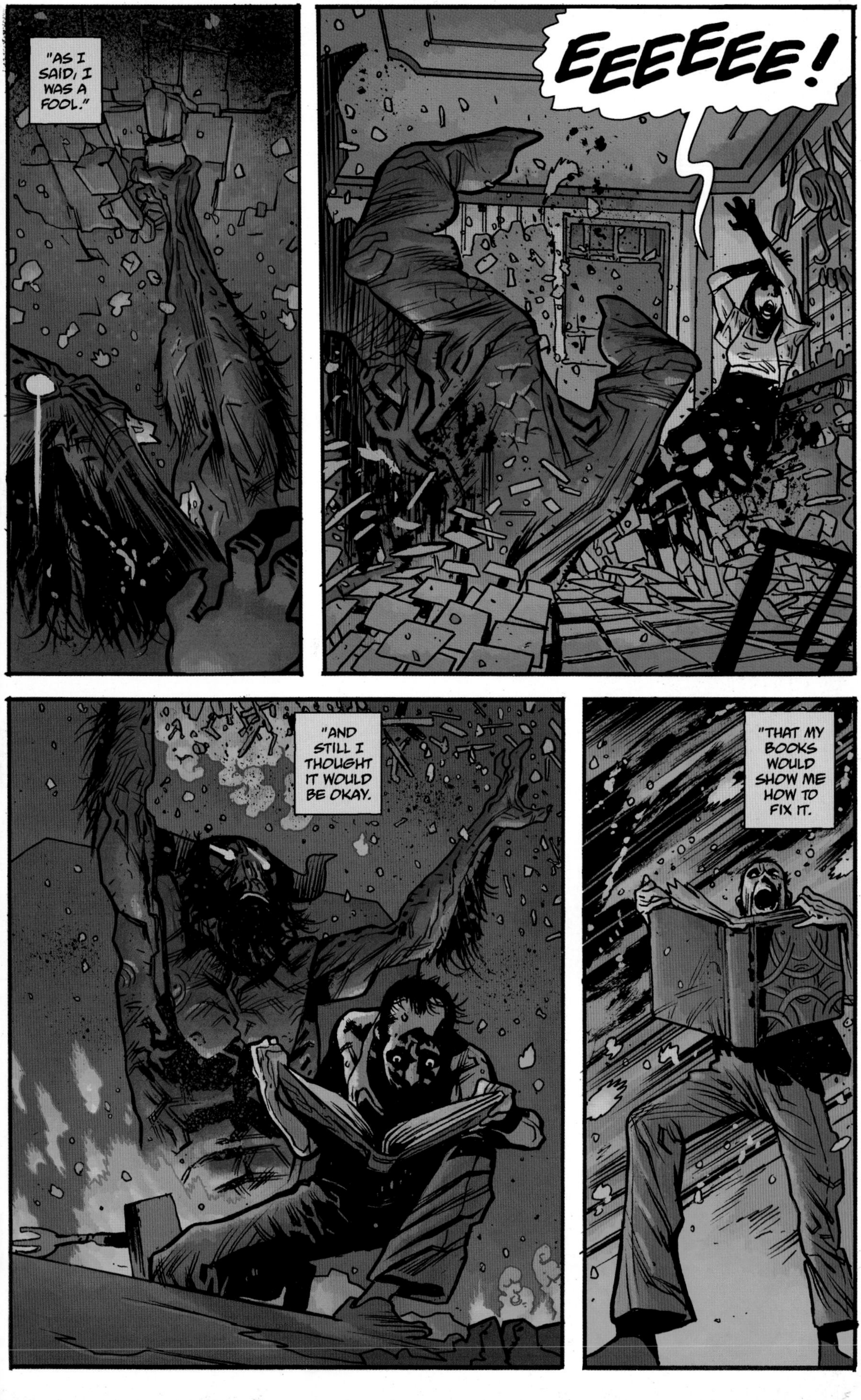
"AS I SAID, I WAS A FOOL."
EEEEEE!
"AND STILL I THOUGHT IT WOULD BE OKAY.
"THAT MY BOOKS WOULD SHOW ME HOW TO FIX IT.

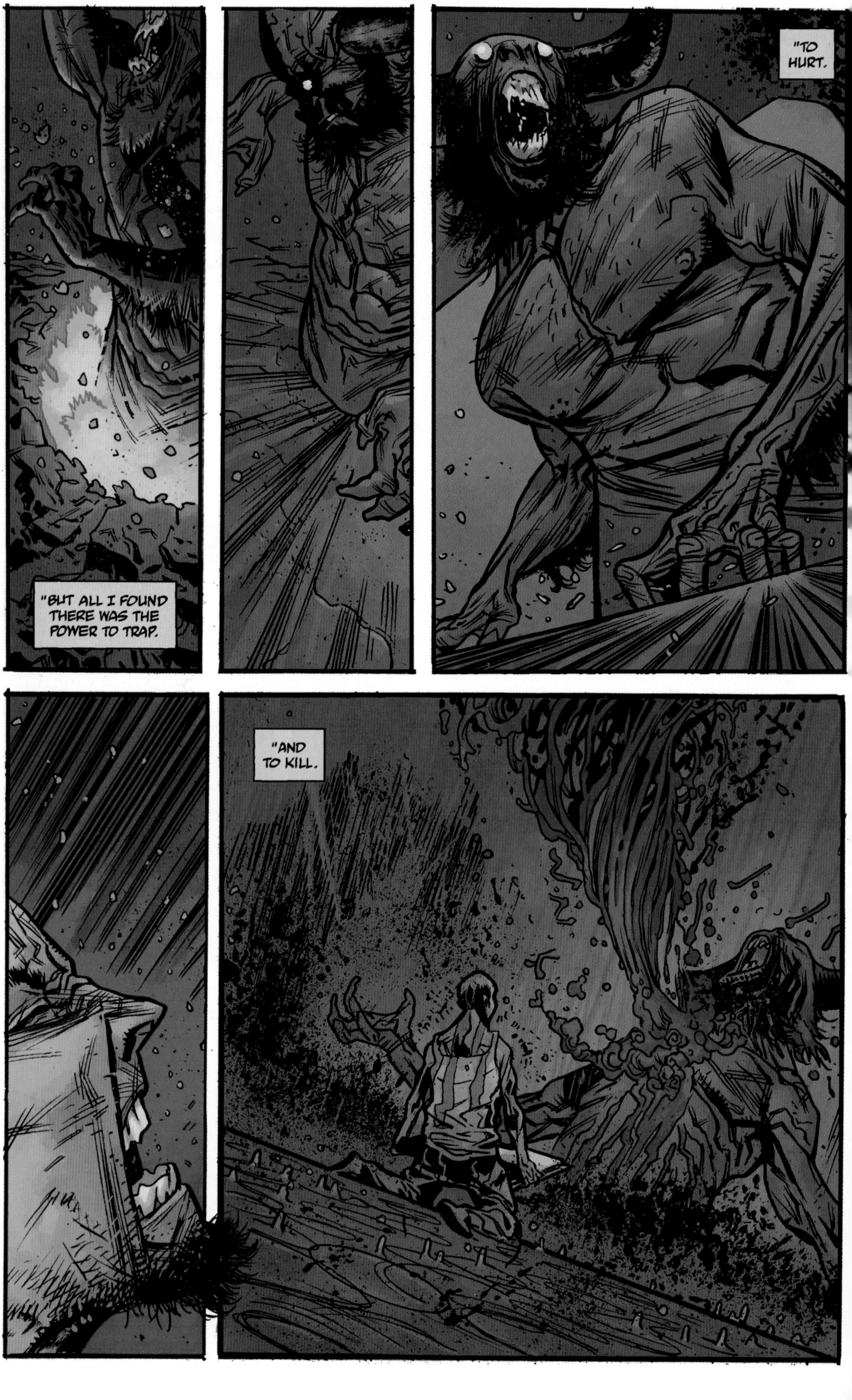
"BUT ALL I FOUND THERE WAS THE POWER TO TRAP.
"TO HURT.
"AND TO KILL.

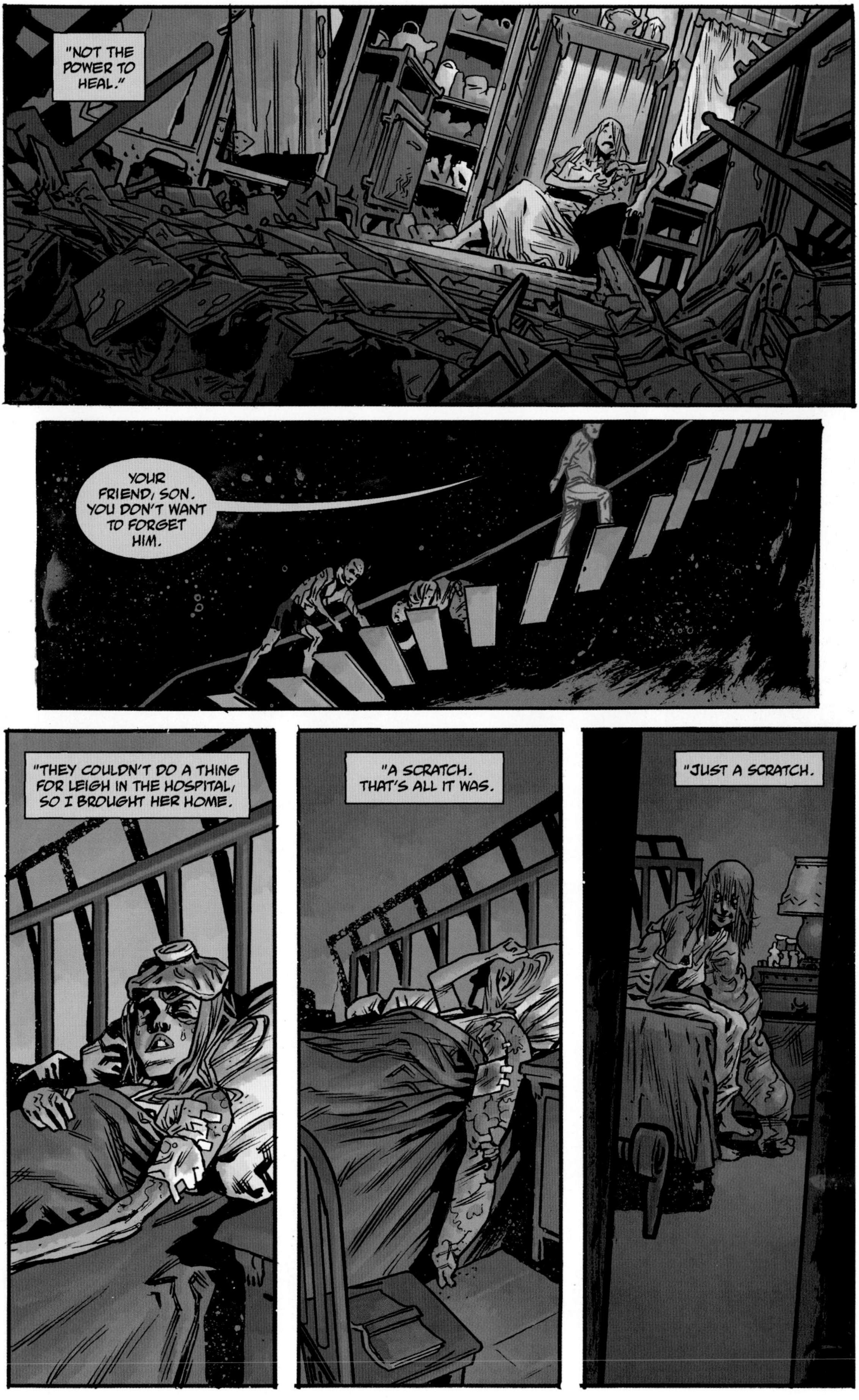
"NOT THE POWER TO HEAL."
YOUR FRIEND, SON. YOU DON'T WANT TO FORGET HIM.
"THEY COULDN'T DO A THING FOR LEIGH IN THE HOSPITAL, SO I BROUGHT HER HOME.
"A SCRATCH. THAT'S ALL IT WAS.
"JUST A SCRATCH.

"FORTUNATELY, LEIGH HERSELF WASN'T SO VIRULENT AS THE MONSTER THAT MARKED HER.

"SULFAMETHIN. IT SAVED TURNER'S LIFE.

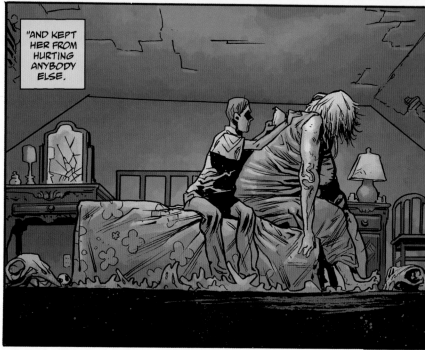

"AND KEPT HER FROM HURTING ANYBODY ELSE.

"WHILE I...I JUST GREW OLD."

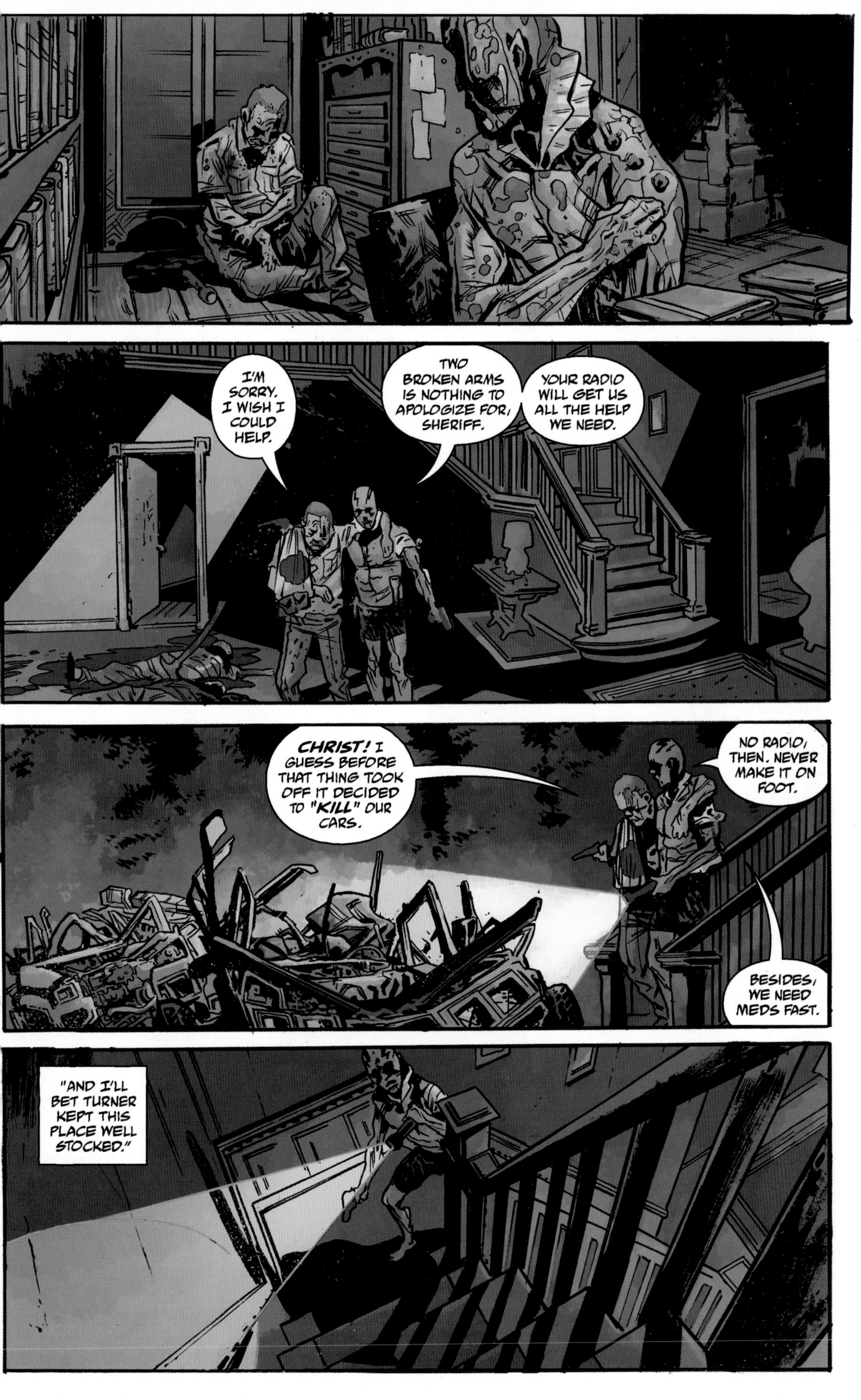
I'M SORRY. I WISH I COULD HELP.
TWO BROKEN ARMS IS NOTHING TO APOLOGIZE FOR, SHERIFF.
YOUR RADIO WILL GET US ALL THE HELP WE NEED.
CHRIST! I GUESS BEFORE THAT THING TOOK OFF IT DECIDED TO "KILL" OUR CARS.
NO RADIO, THEN. NEVER MAKE IT ON FOOT.
BESIDES, WE NEED MEDS FAST.
"AND I'LL BET TURNER KEPT THIS PLACE WELL STOCKED."

WHERE ARE THE LIGHT SWITCHES HERE?

JUST HOPE I CAN KEEP MY HEAD STRAIGHT LONG ENOUGH--

DAMN!!

YOU AGAIN!!

YOU'RE NO HALLUCINATION! BUT WHAT THE HELL ARE YOU?!

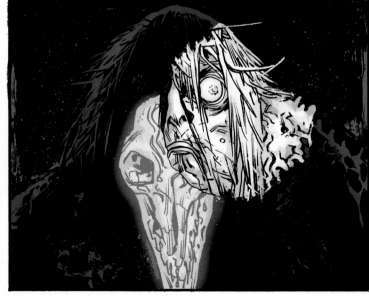

BLAM
BLAM
BLAM
BLAM
BLAM

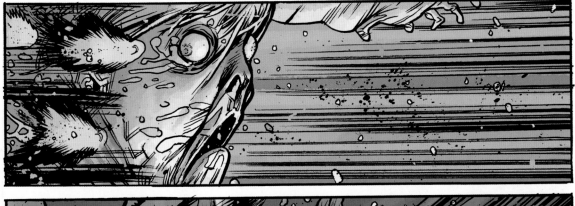

WHACK

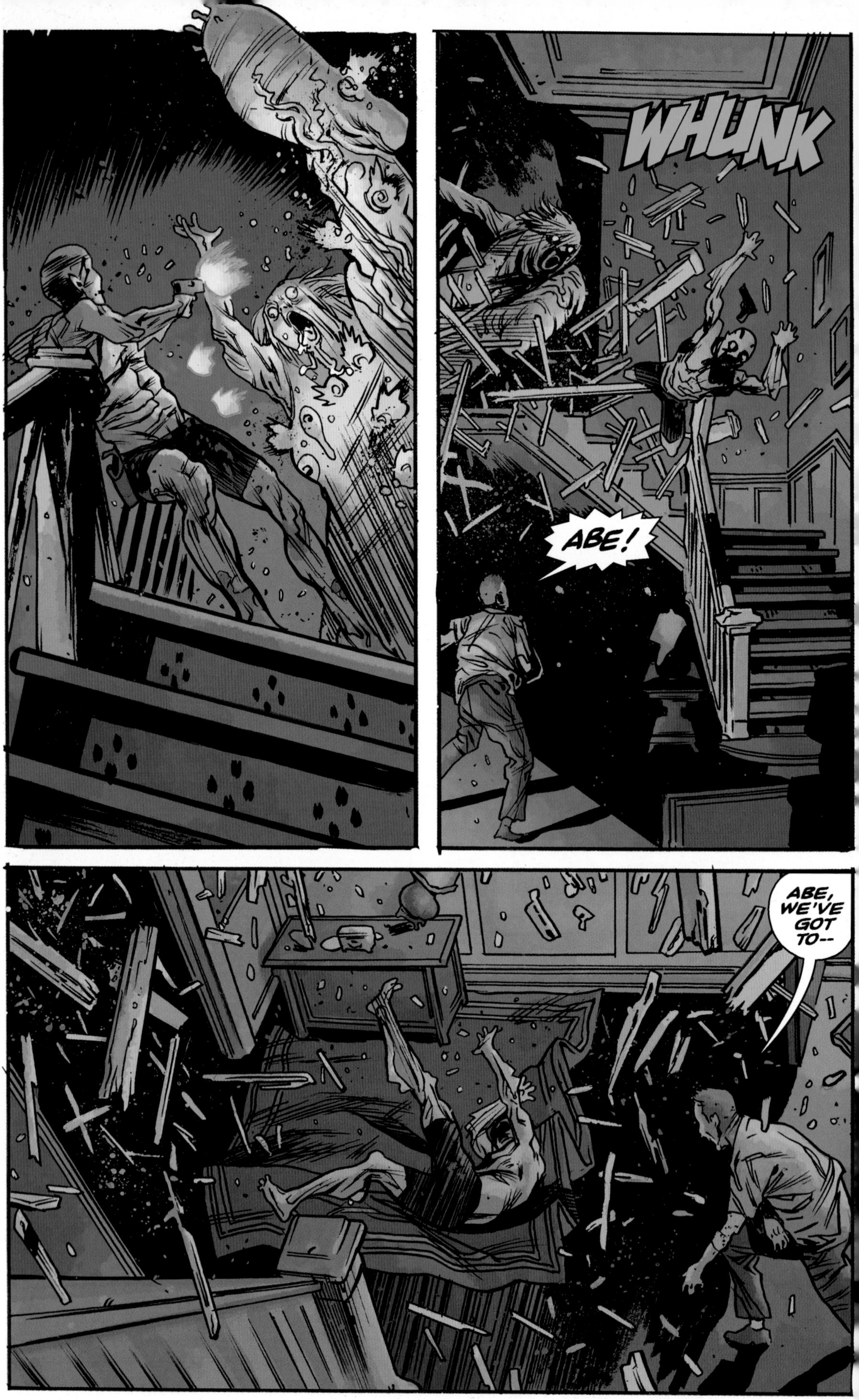
WHUNK
ABE!
ABE, WE'VE GOT TO--

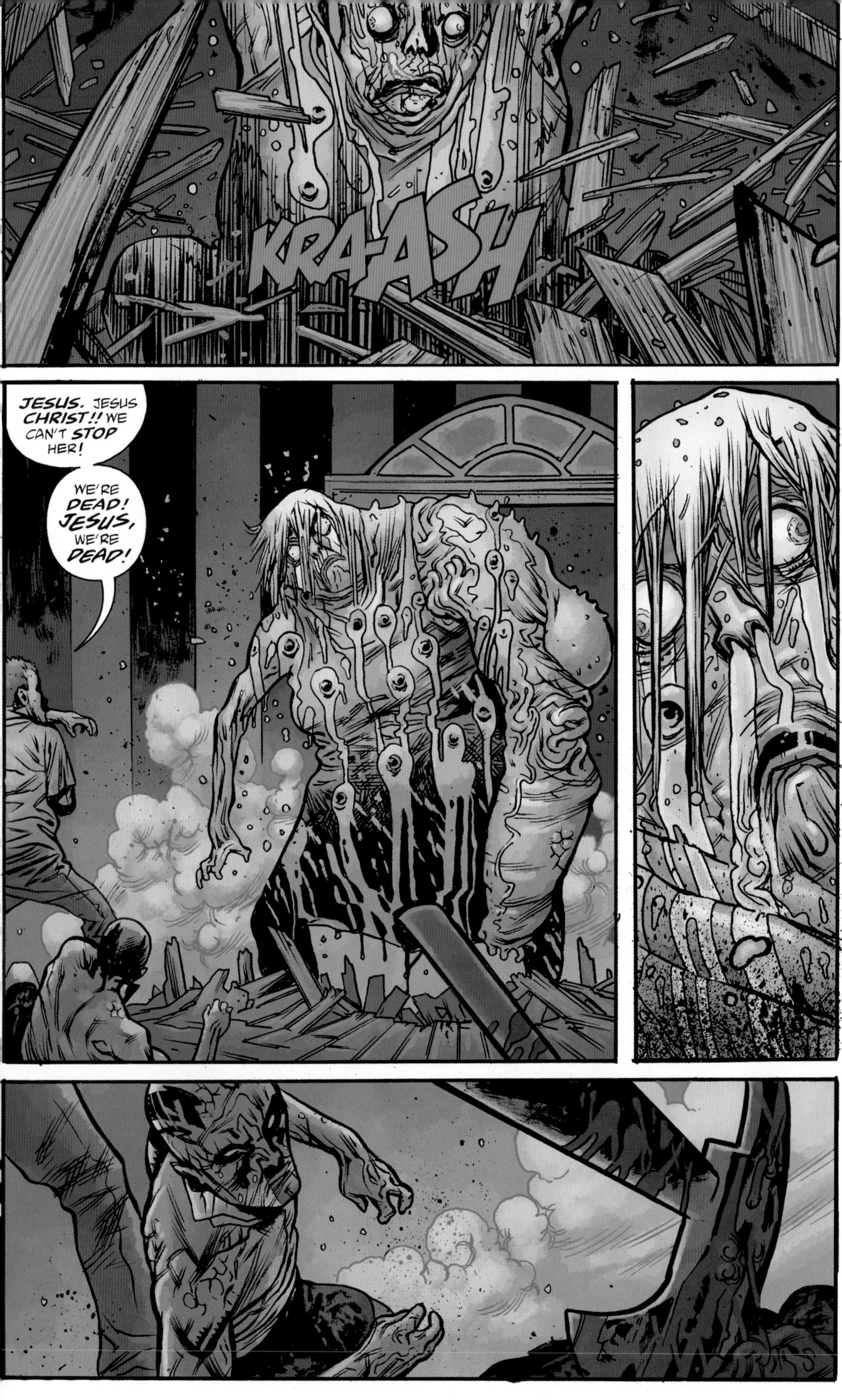
KRAASH
JESUS. JESUS CHRIST!! WE CAN'T STOP HER!
WE'RE DEAD! JESUS, WE'RE DEAD!

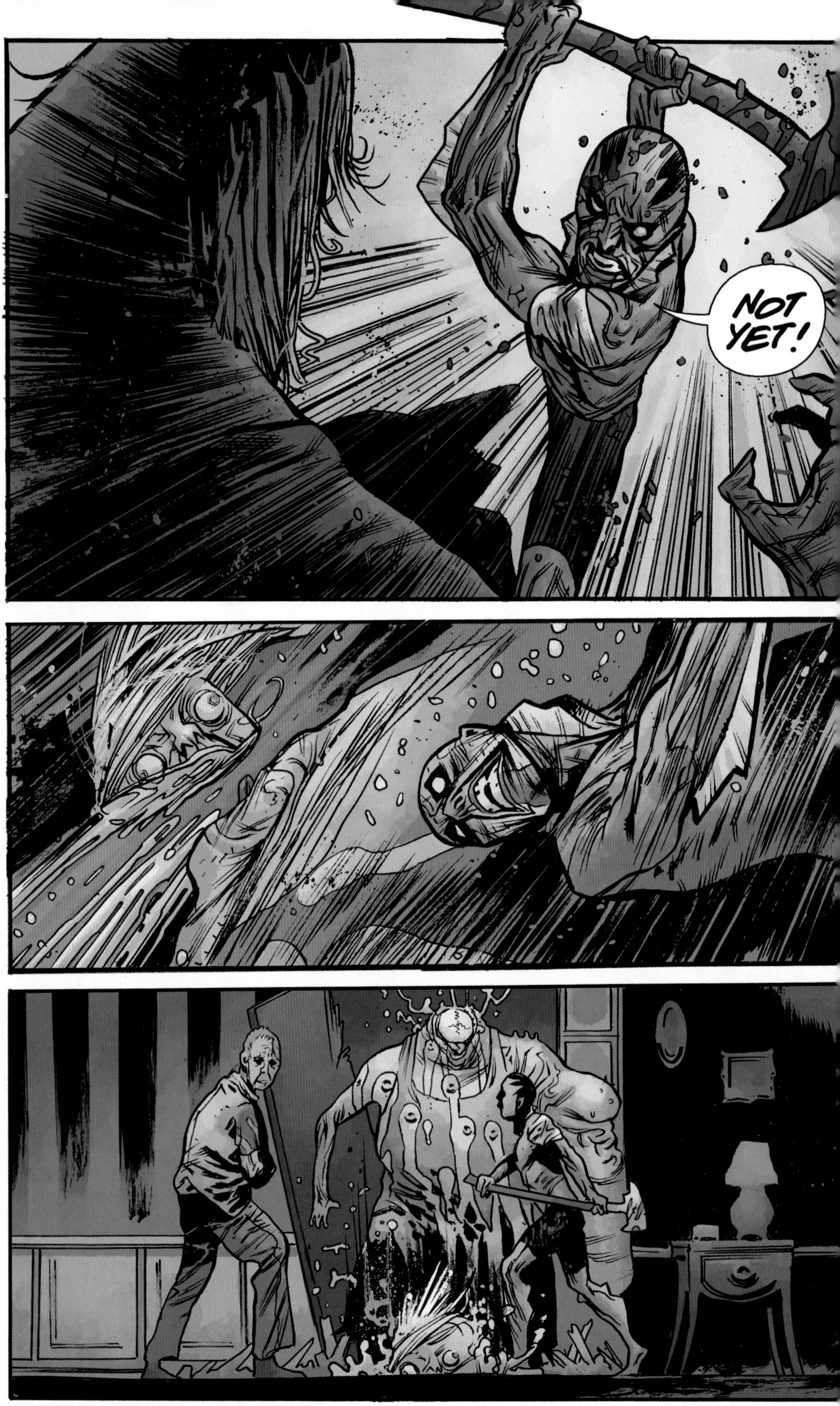
NOT YET!

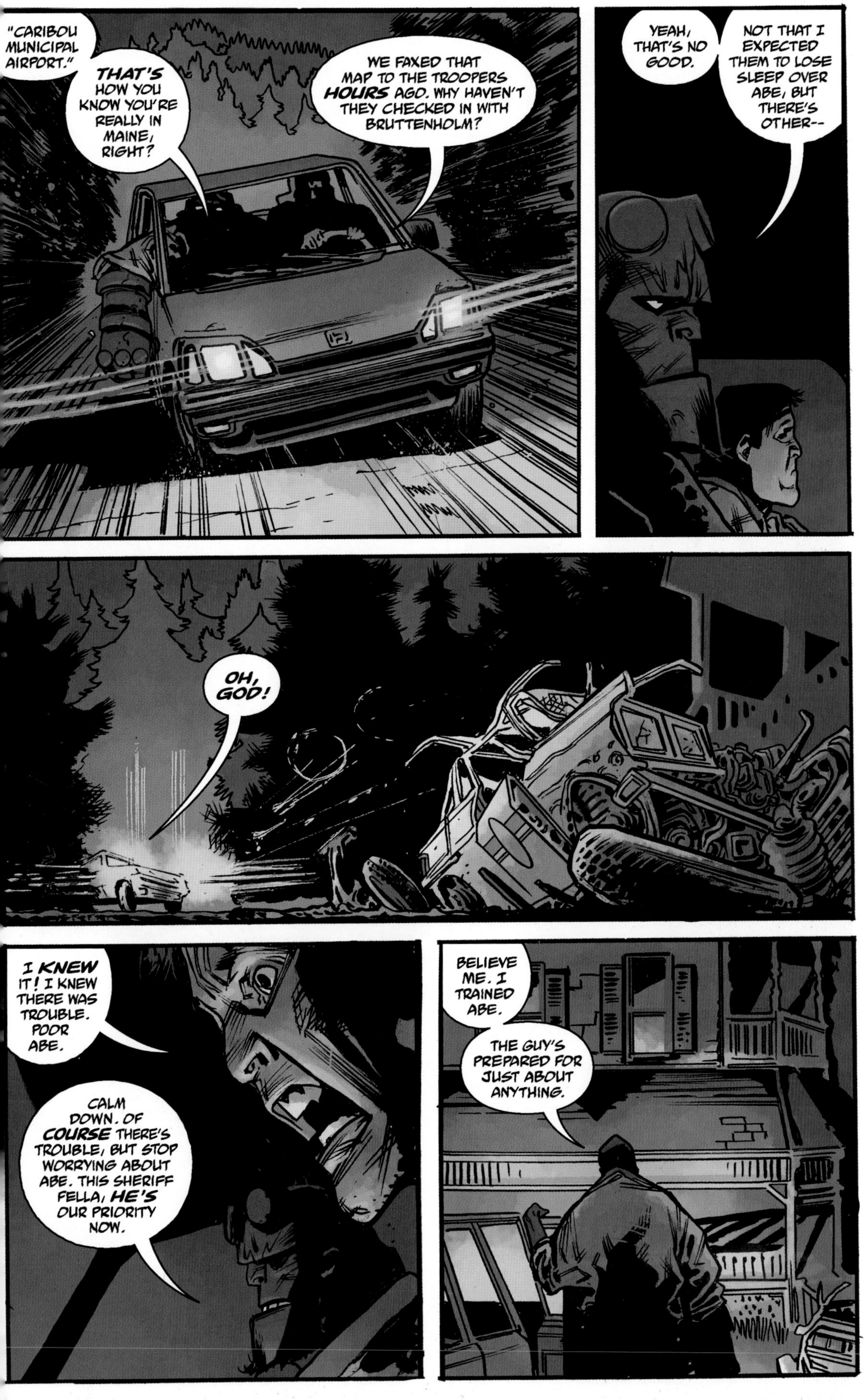
"CARIBOU MUNICIPAL AIRPORT."
THAT'S HOW YOU KNOW YOU'RE REALLY IN MAINE, RIGHT?
WE FAXED THAT MAP TO THE TROOPERS HOURS AGO. WHY HAVEN'T THEY CHECKED IN WITH BRUTTENHOLM?
YEAH, THAT'S NO GOOD.
NOT THAT I EXPECTED THEM TO LOSE SLEEP OVER ABE, BUT THERE'S OTHER--
OH, GOD!
I KNEW IT! I KNEW THERE WAS TROUBLE. POOR ABE.
CALM DOWN. OF COURSE THERE'S TROUBLE, BUT STOP WORRYING ABOUT ABE. THIS SHERIFF FELLA, HE'S OUR PRIORITY NOW.
BELIEVE ME. I TRAINED ABE.
THE GUY'S PREPARED FOR JUST ABOUT ANYTHING.

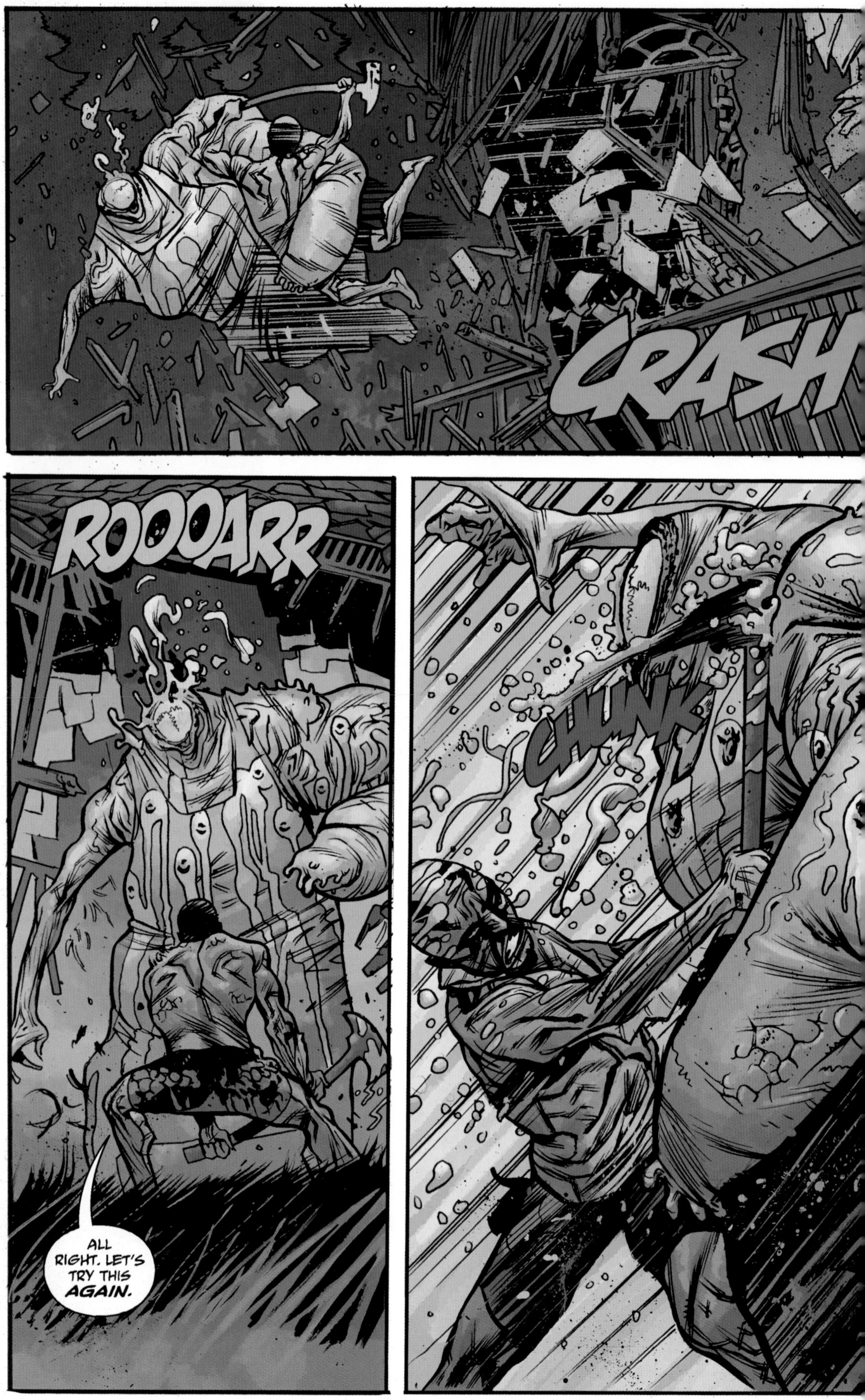
CRASH
ROOOARR
ALL RIGHT. LET'S TRY THIS AGAIN.
CHUNK

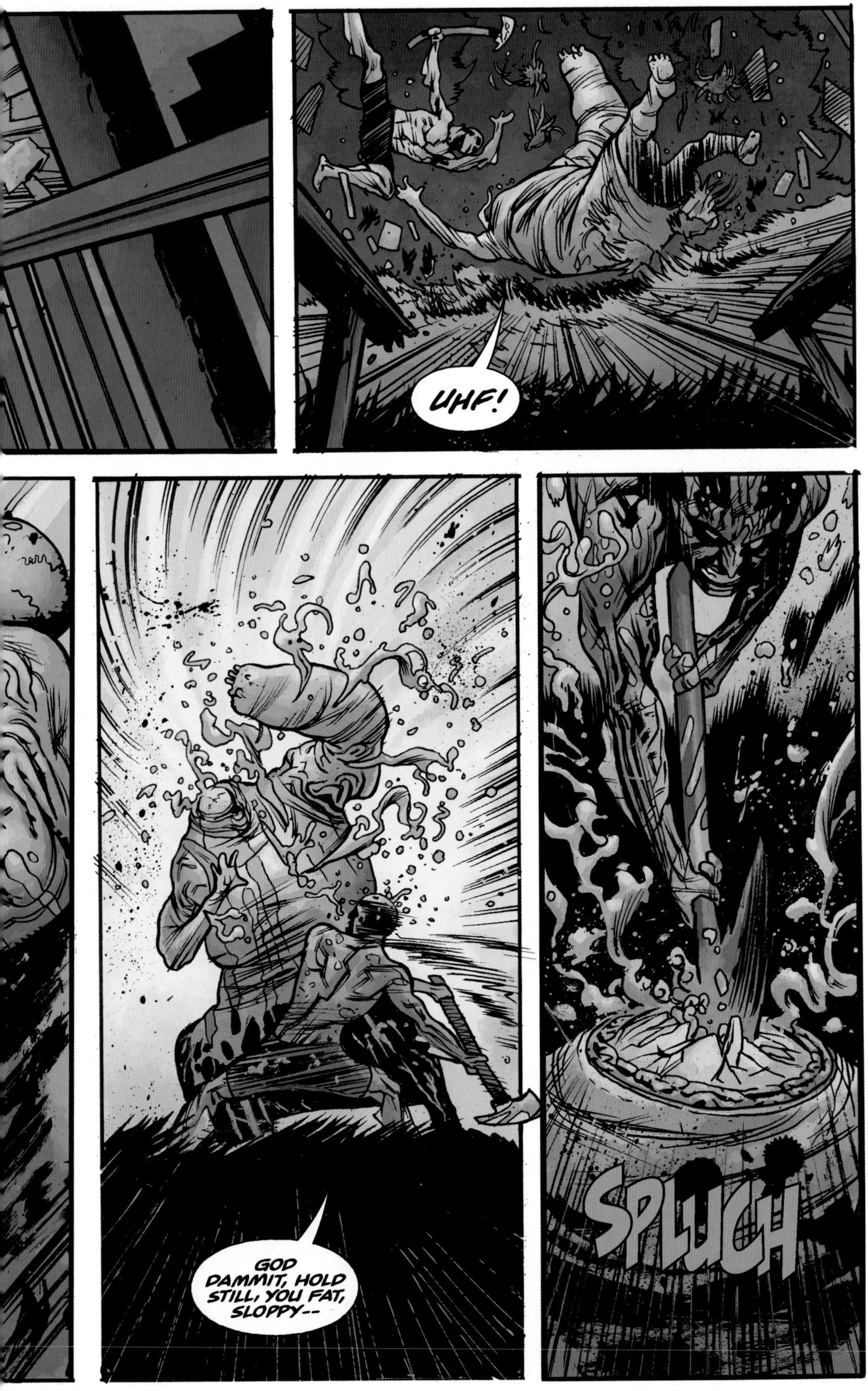
UHF!
GOD DAMMIT, HOLD STILL, YOU FAT, SLOPPY--
SPLUCH

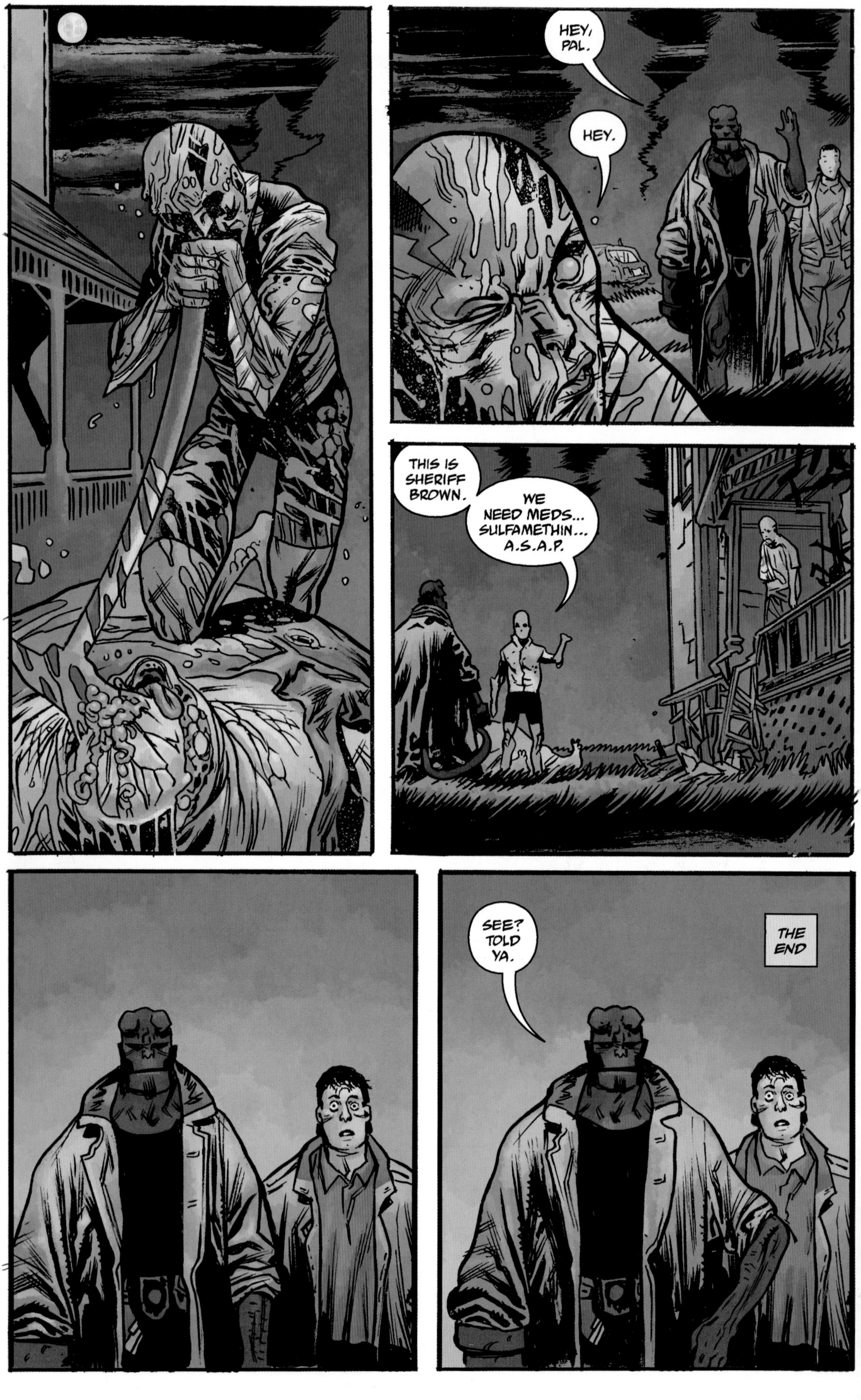
HEY, PAL.
HEY.
THIS IS SHERIFF BROWN.
WE NEED MEDS... SULFAMETHIN... A.S.A.P.
SEE? TOLD YA.
THE END

# ABE SAPIEN™

## SKETCHBOOK

**Notes by Scott Allie**

**Initial Abe studies by Patric Reynolds.**

Patric's designs for the monster in *The Haunted Boy*.

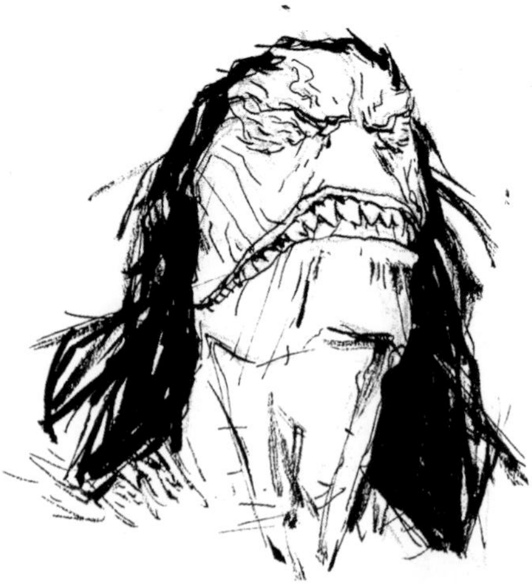

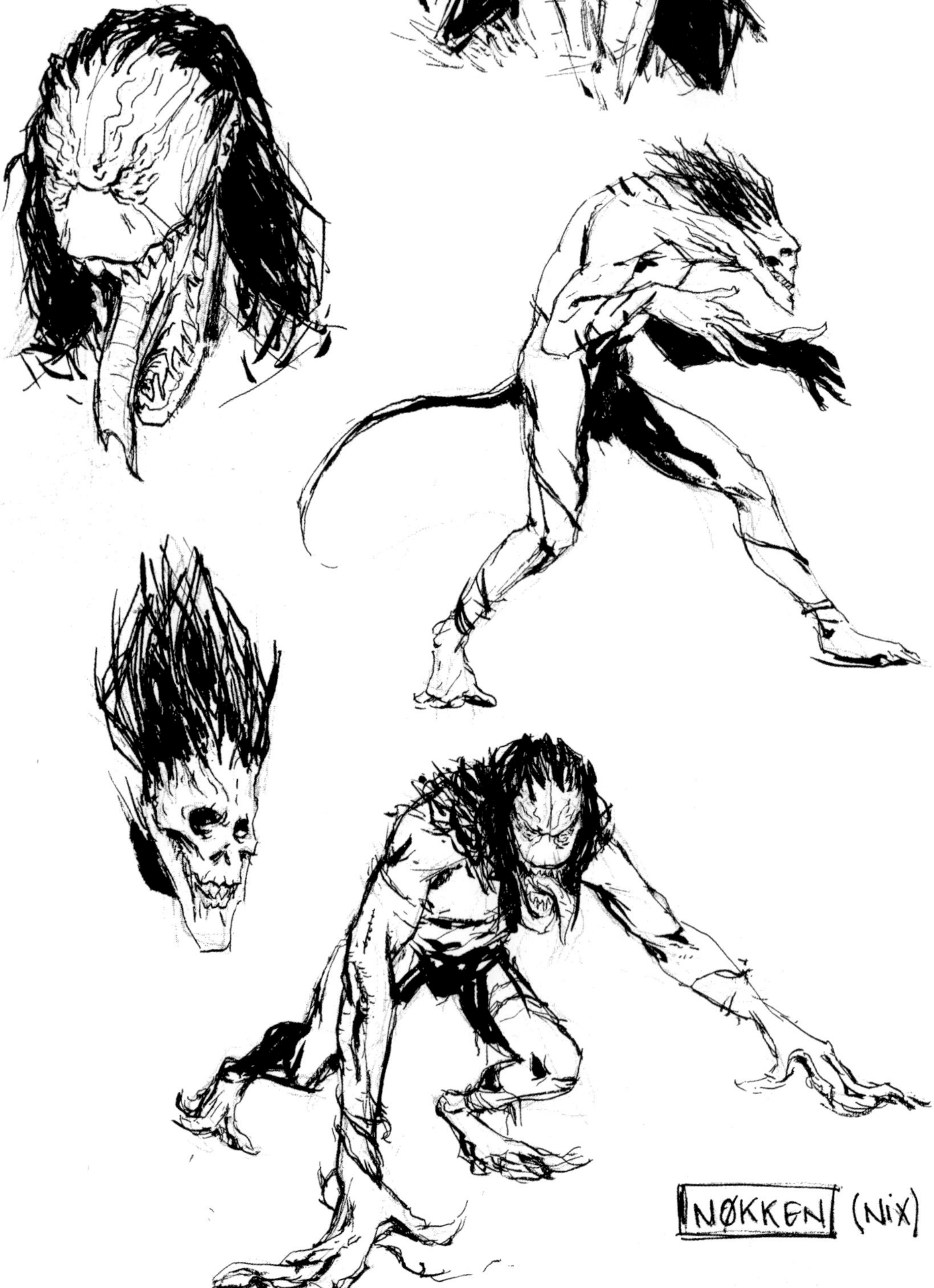
NØKKEN (NIX)

# NØKKEN (NIX)

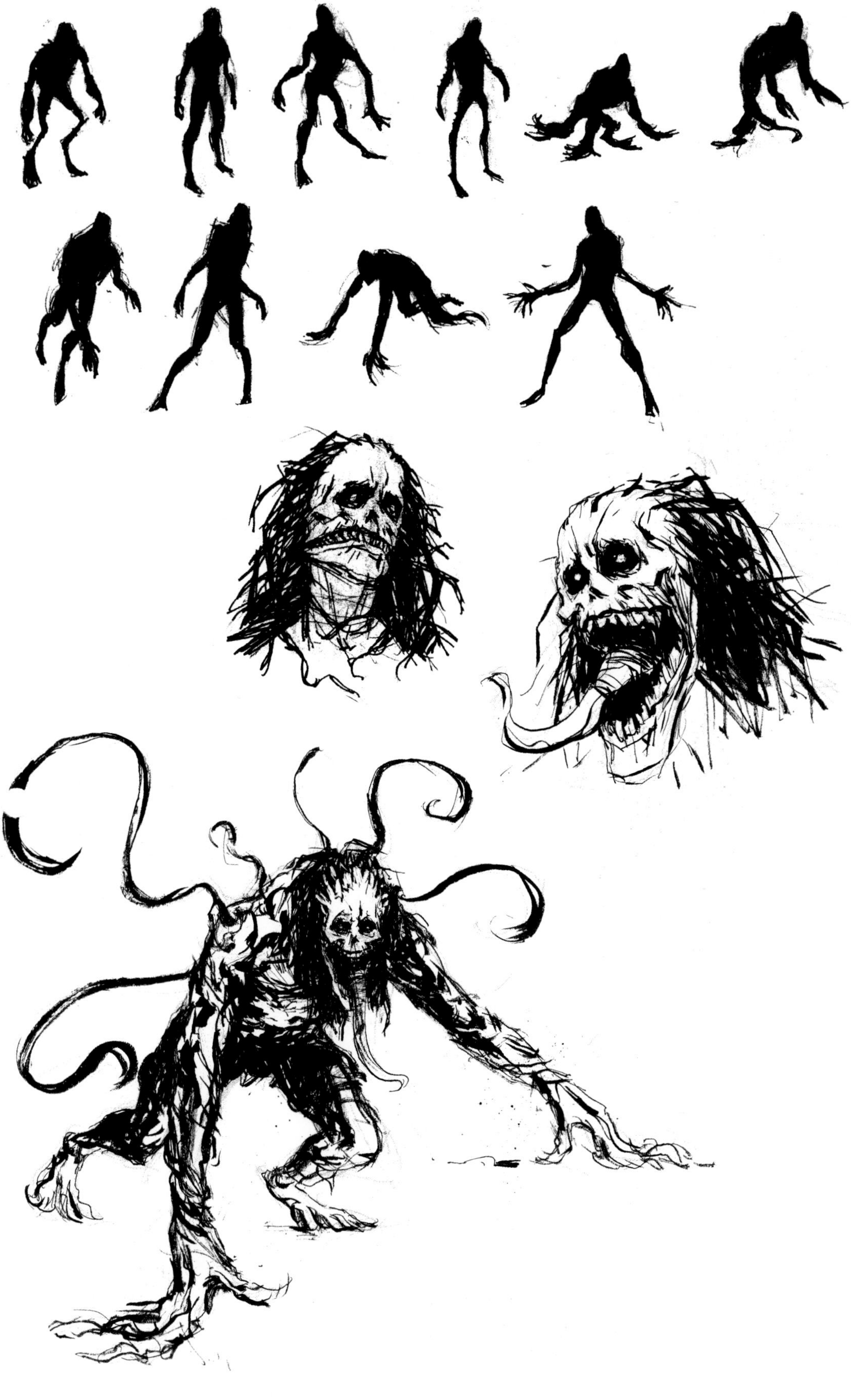

**Peter Snejbjerg's designs for the helmet in *The Abyssal Plain* and studies for the playful demon Varvara.**

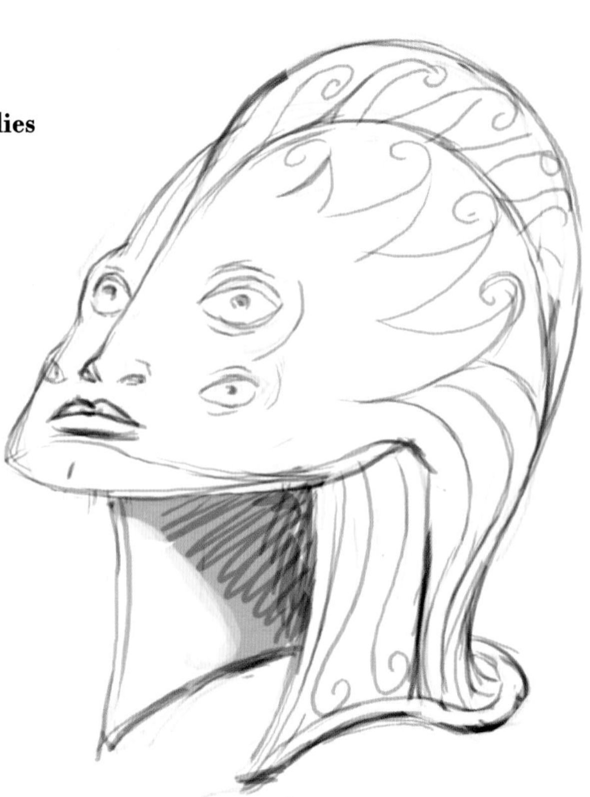

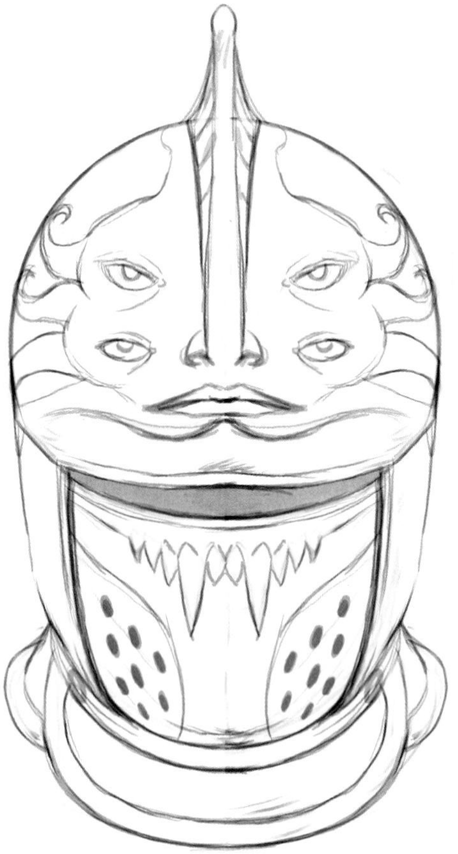

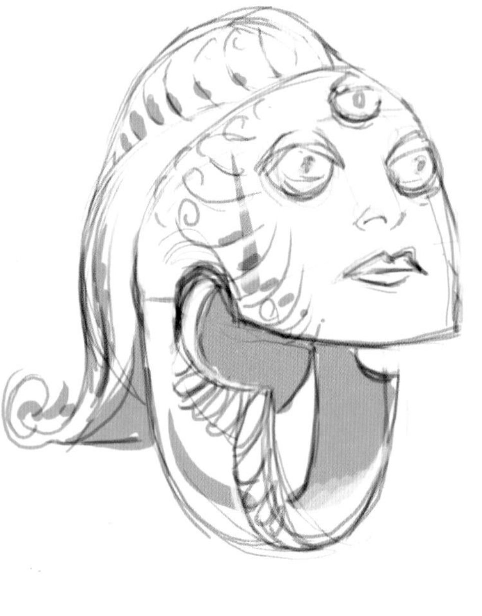

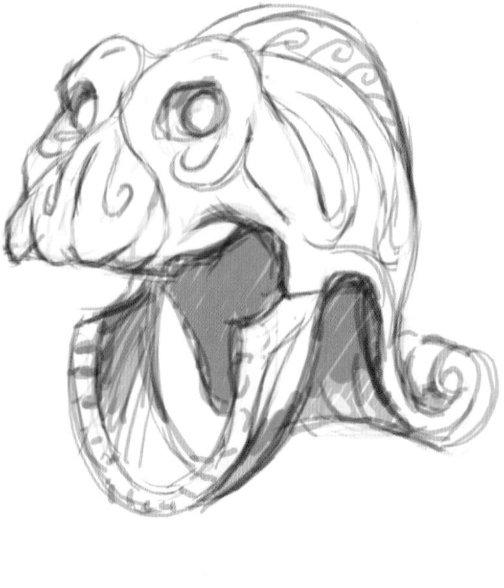

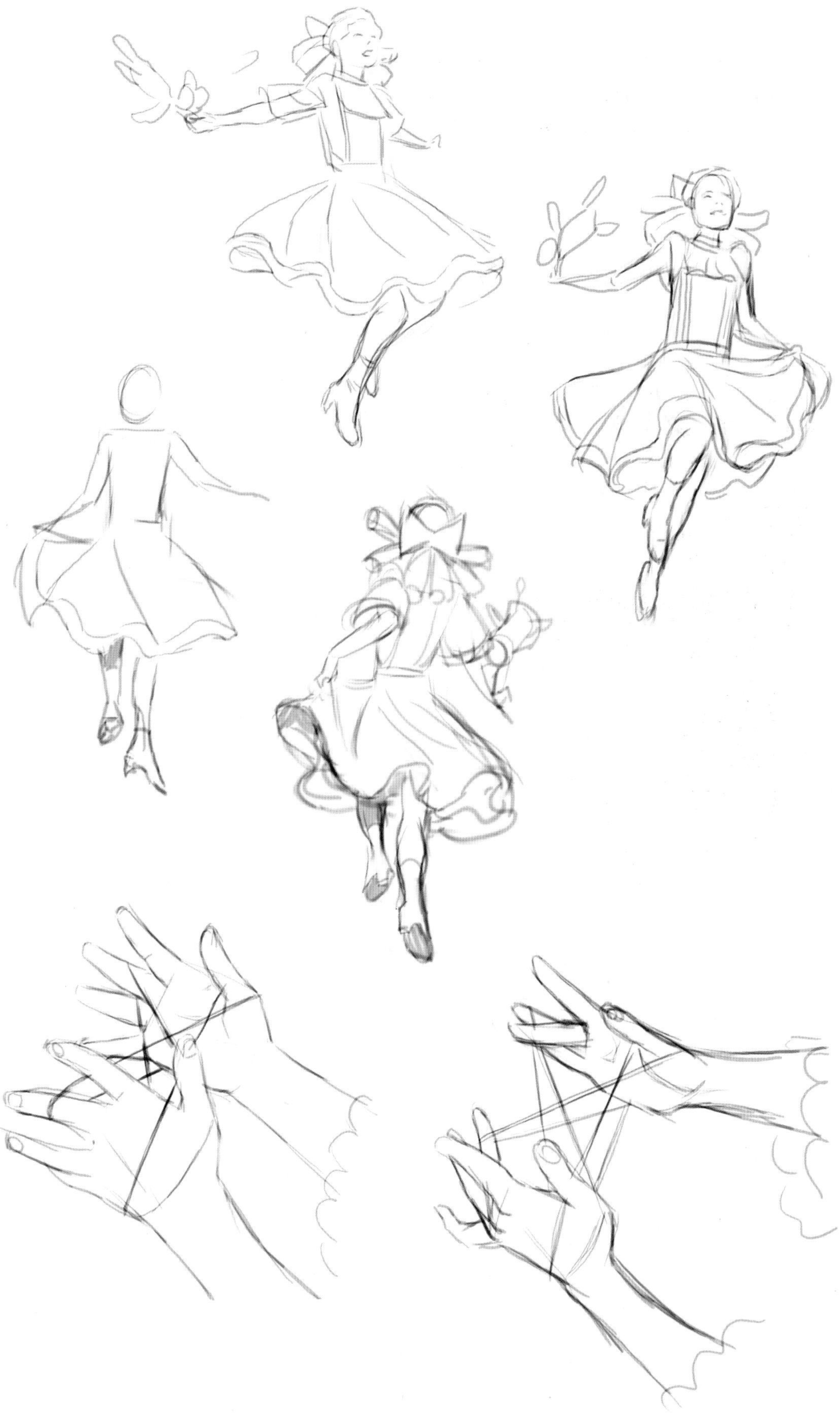

**Peter's sketches, pencils, and finishes for**
*The Abyssal Plain* #1's cover, colored by Dave Stewart.

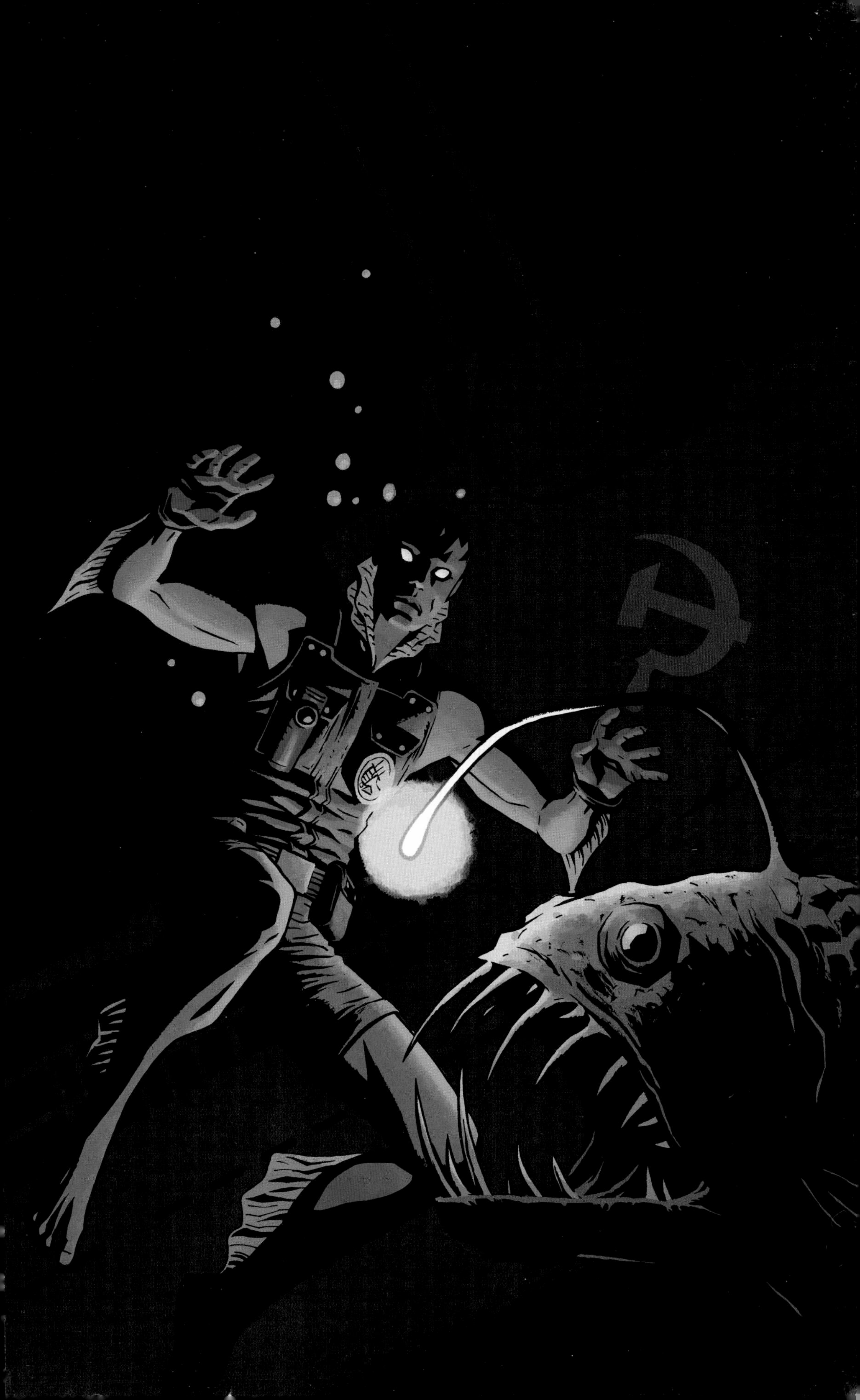

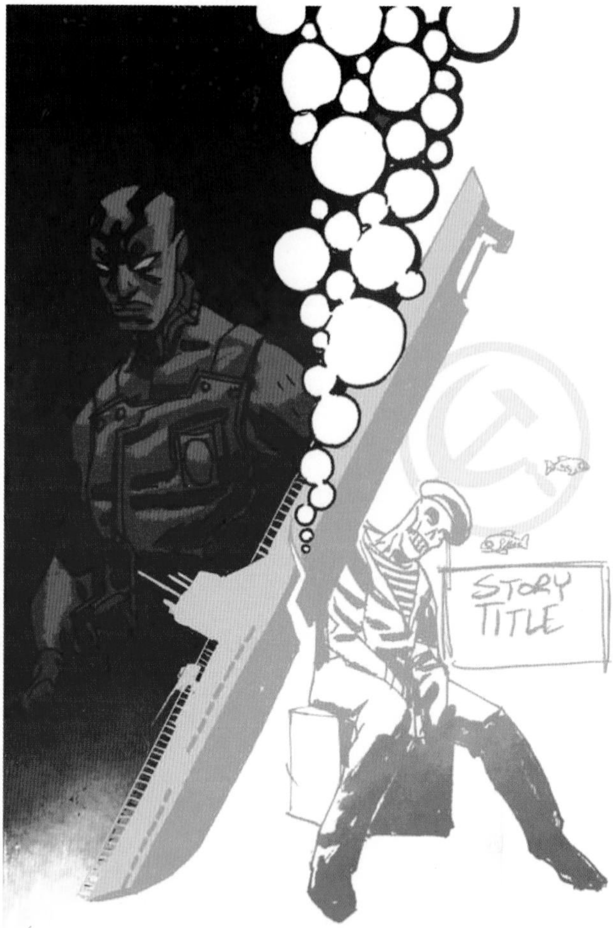
STORY
TITLE

Left: Dave Johnson's cover sketch for *The Abyssal Plain* #1. See the very different final artwork on page 31 of this volume.

Various color options (below) and the final cover (facing) for *The Abyssal Plain* #2.

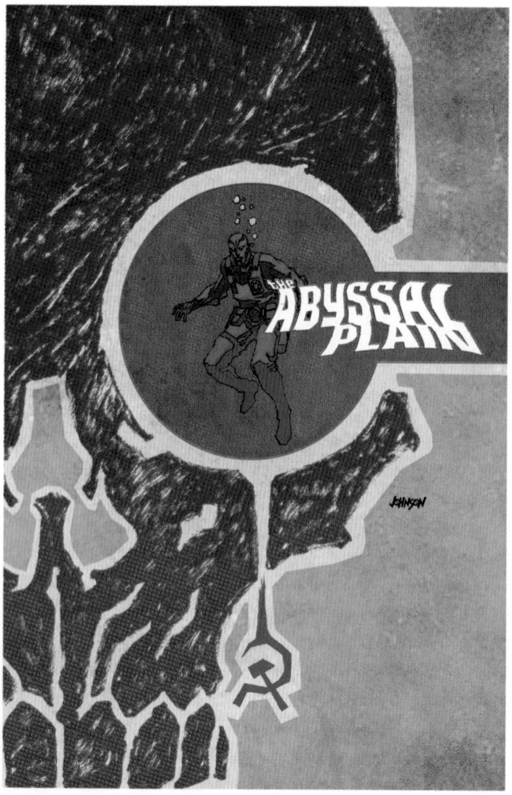
the
ABYSSAL
PLAIN
JOHNSON

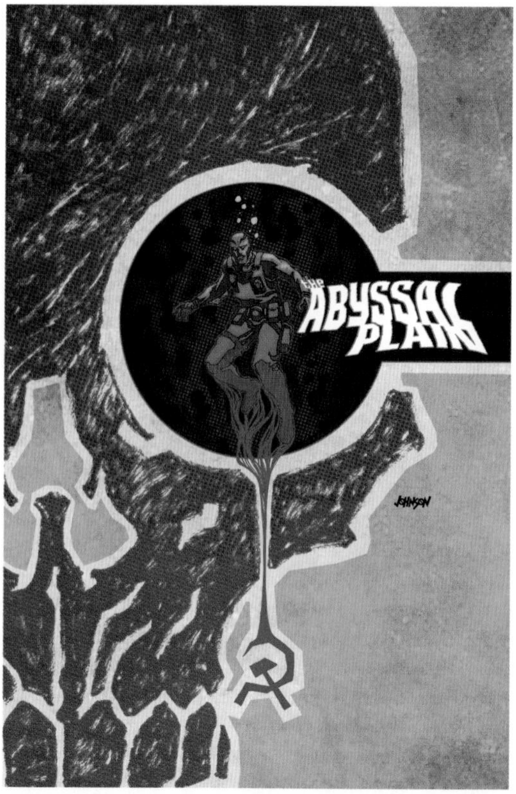
the
ABYSSAL
PLAIN
JOHNSON

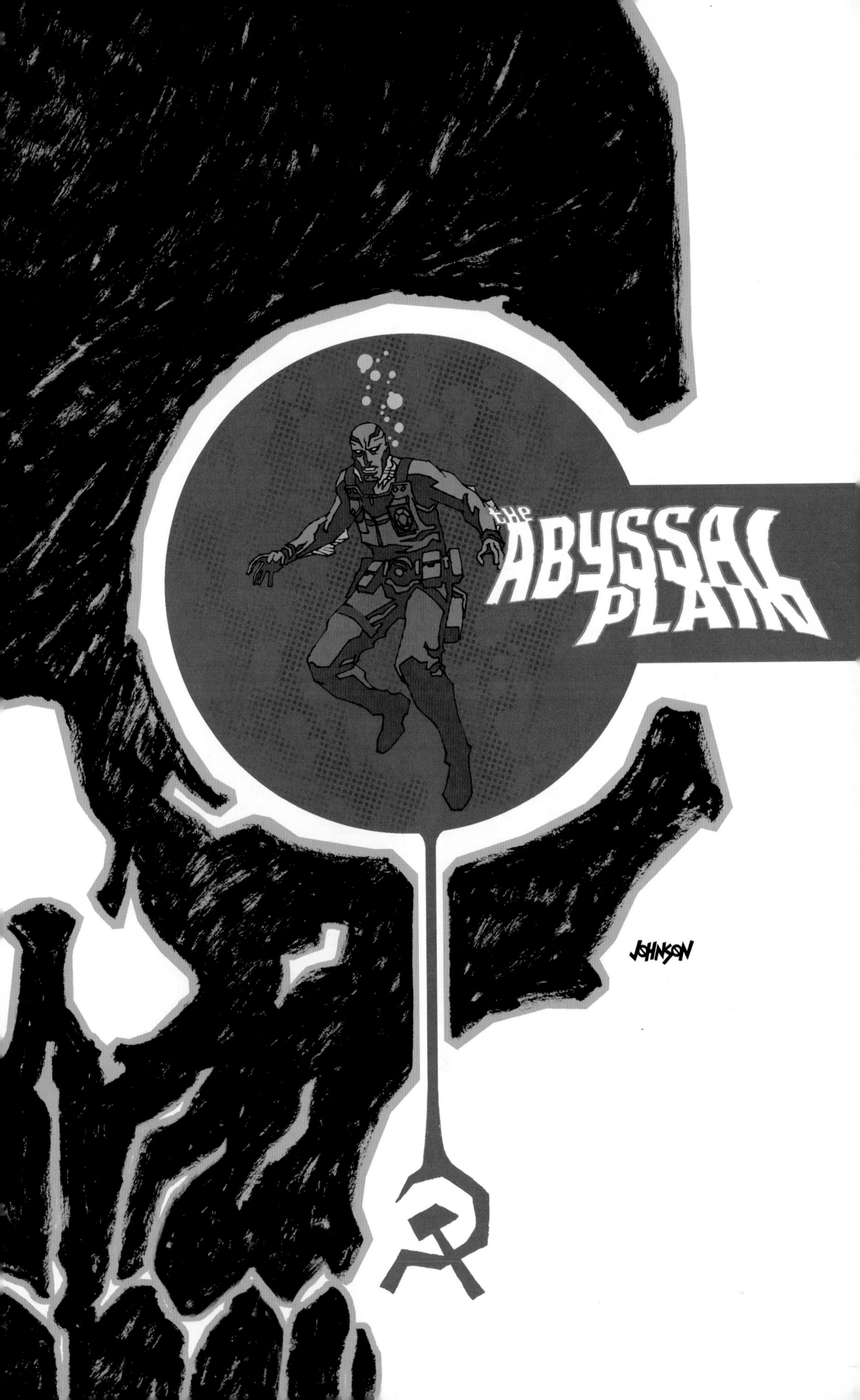
THE ABYSSAL PLAIN
JOHNSON

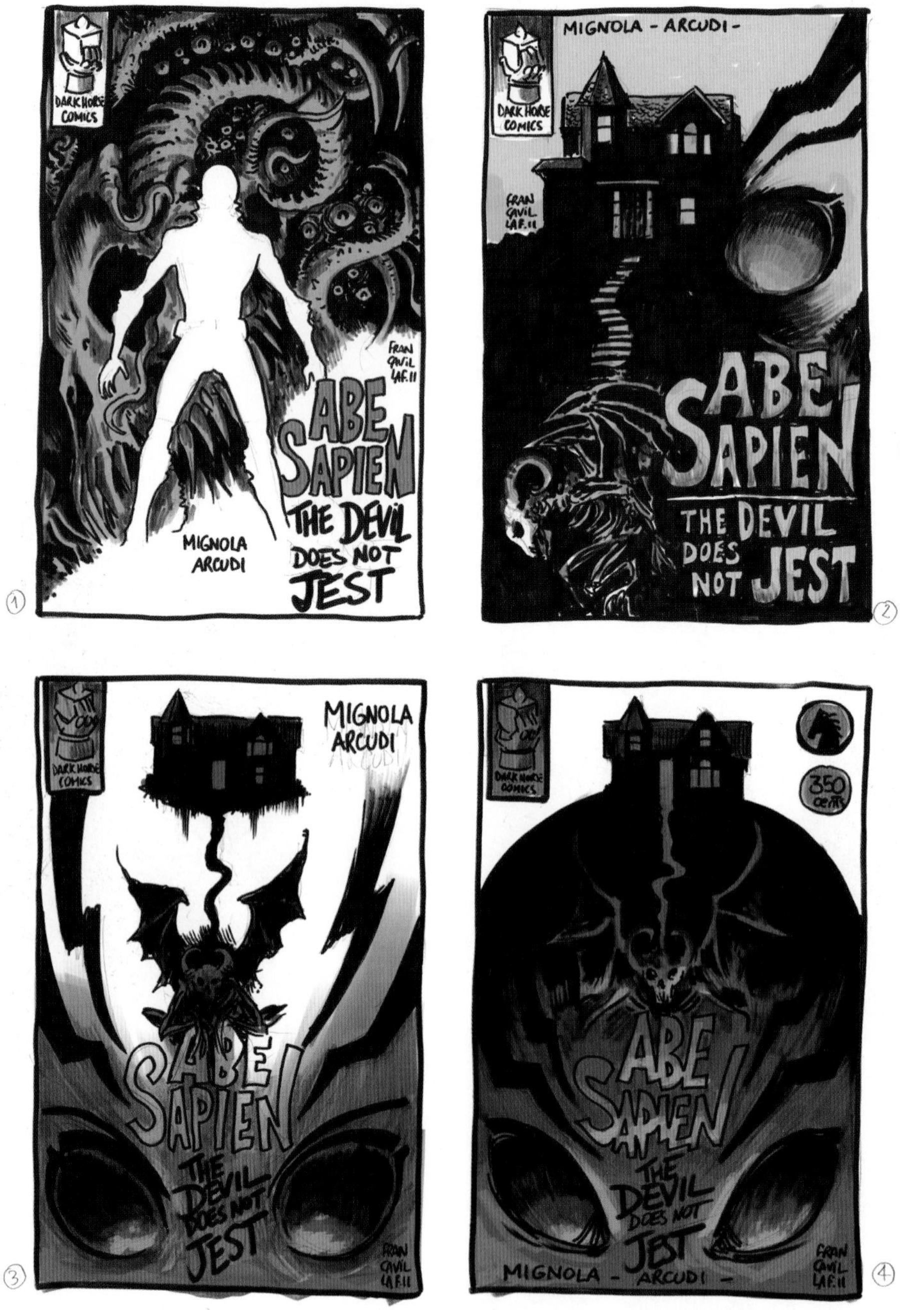
DARK HORSE COMICS
FRAN CAVIL LAF.11
ABE SAPIEN
THE DEVIL DOES NOT JEST
MIGNOLA ARCUDI
1
MIGNOLA - ARCUDI -
DARK HORSE COMICS
FRAN CAVIL LAF.11
ABE SAPIEN
THE DEVIL DOES NOT JEST
2
DARK HORSE COMICS
MIGNOLA ARCUDI
ABE SAPIEN
THE DEVIL DOES NOT JEST
FRAN CAVIL LAF.11
3
DARK HORSE COMICS
350 CENTS
ABE SAPIEN
THE DEVIL DOES NOT JEST
MIGNOLA - ARCUDI -
FRAN CAVIL LAF.11
4

**In 2011 Francesco Francavilla caught Mike Mignola's and my eyes, so we lined him up to do a group of related covers for issues of *Abe Sapien*, *Hellboy: The Fury*, *B.P.R.D. Hell on Earth*, and *Baltimore* that were all coming out in early summer. Here are the sketches (above) and final (facing) for the Abe cover. When he was doing the sketches he didn't know who was drawing the issues, though the story was written for James Harren.**

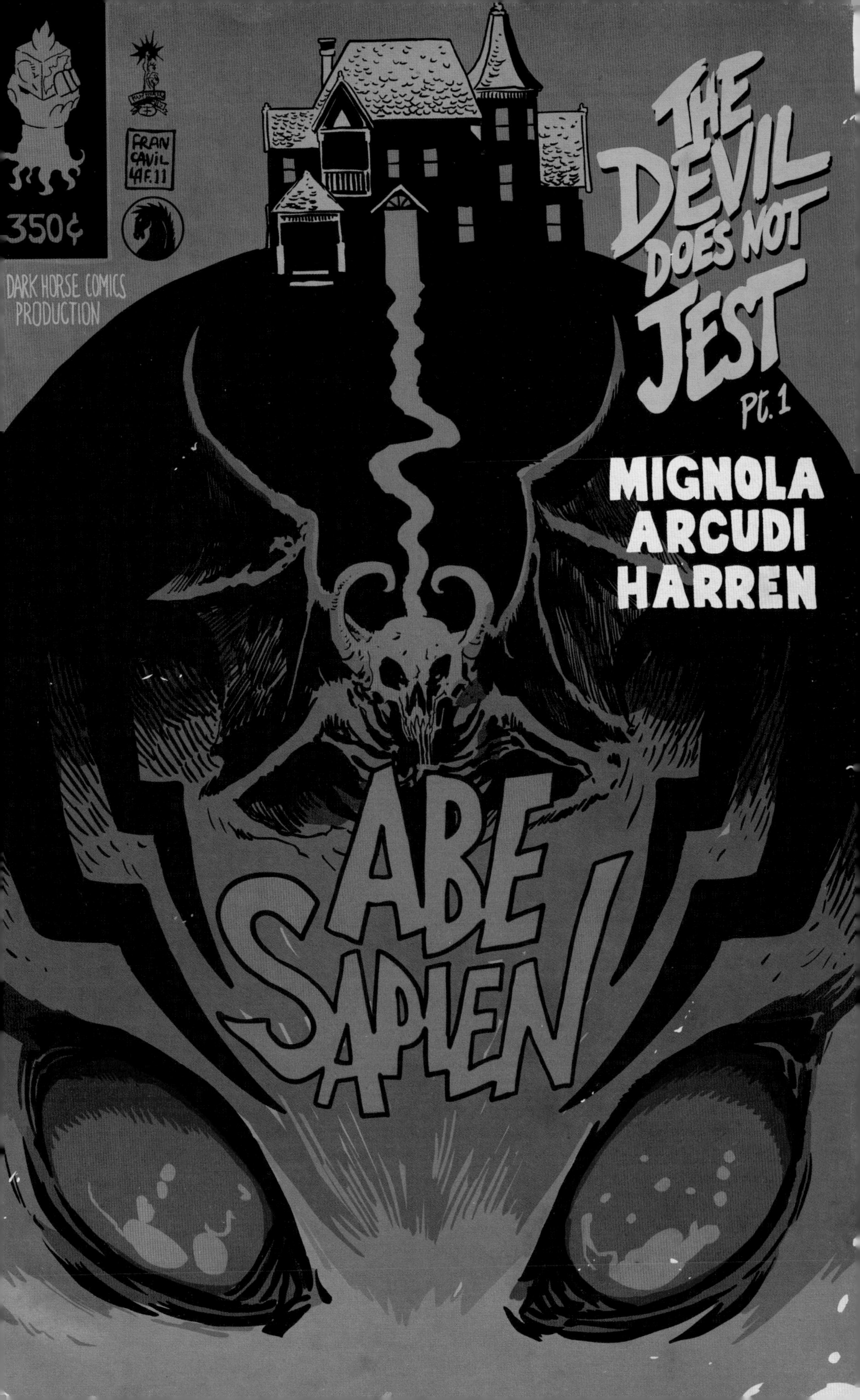
350¢
DARK HORSE COMICS
PRODUCTION
THE DEVIL DOES NOT JEST
Pt. 1
MIGNOLA
ARCUDI
HARREN
ABE SAPIEN

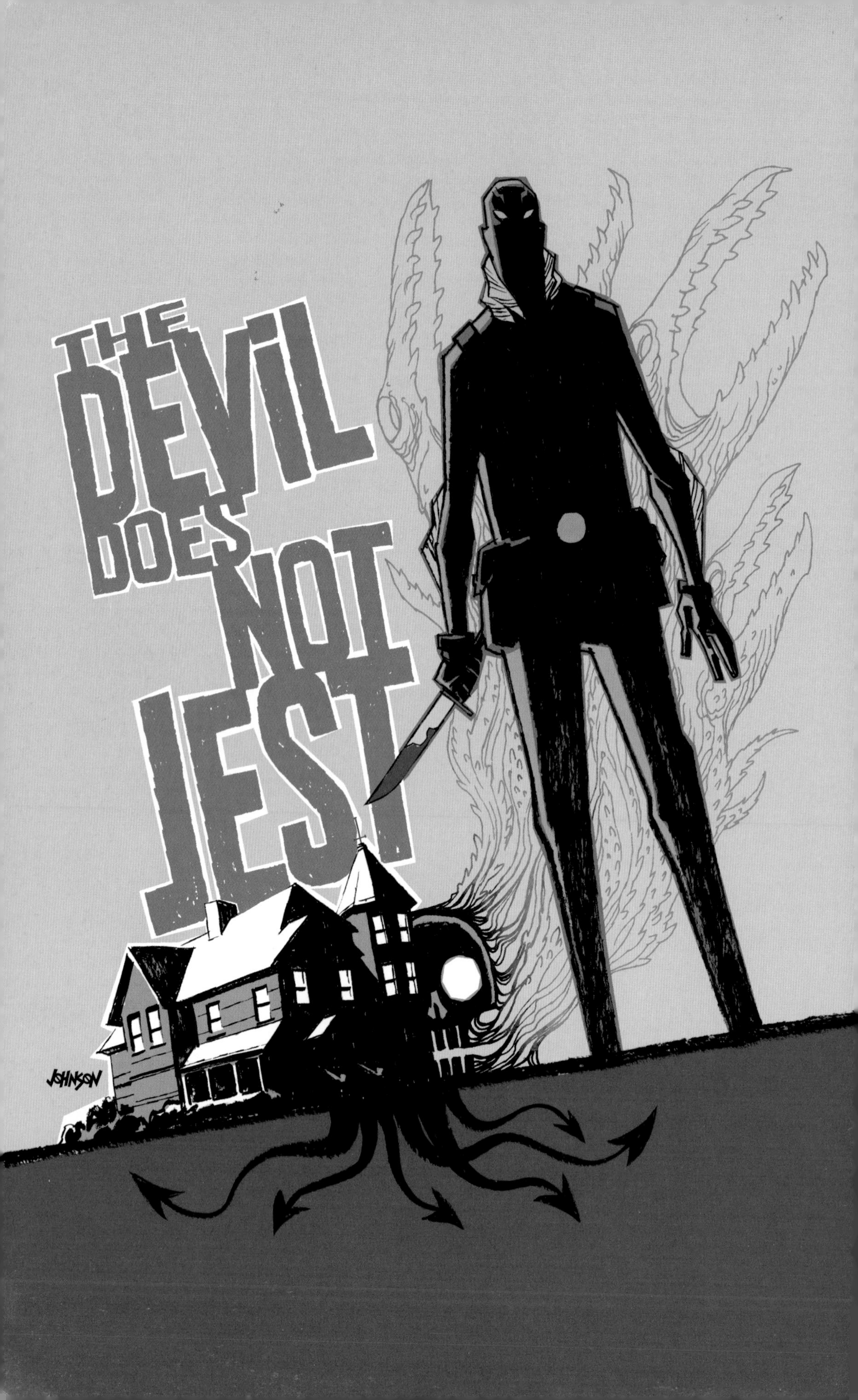
THE DEVIL DOES NOT JEST
JOHNSON

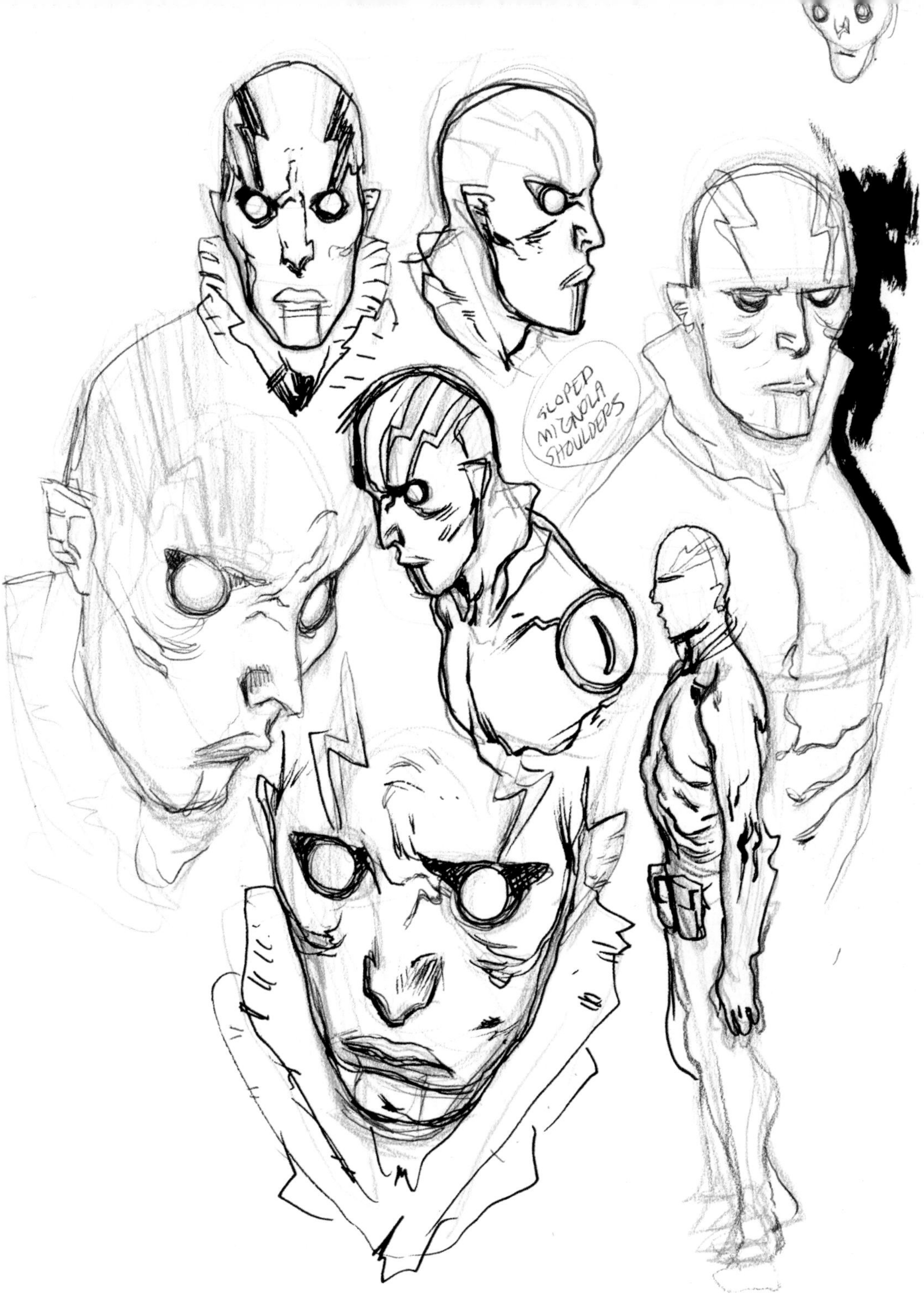
SLOPED MIGNOLA SHOULDERS

James Harren's first studies of Abe.

Facing: Dave Johnson's cover for *The Devil Does Not Jest* #1. Dave dug up one of his alternate sketches for this concept and finished it for the frontispiece on page 2 of this volume.

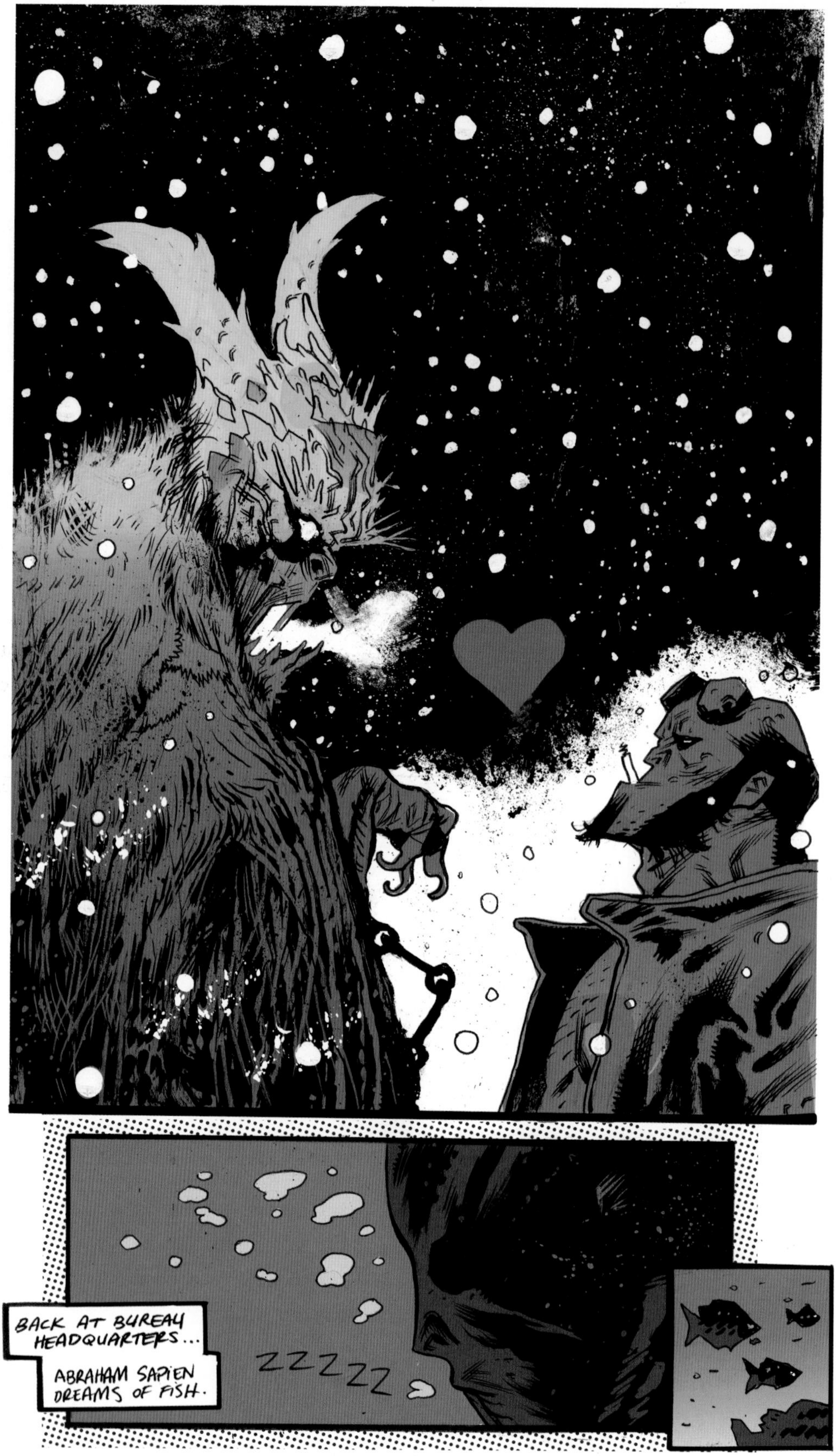
BACK AT BUREAU HEADQUARTERS...
ABRAHAM SAPIEN DREAMS OF FISH.
ZZZZZZ

MERRY CHRISTMAS! HAPPY HOLIDAYS! -JAMES

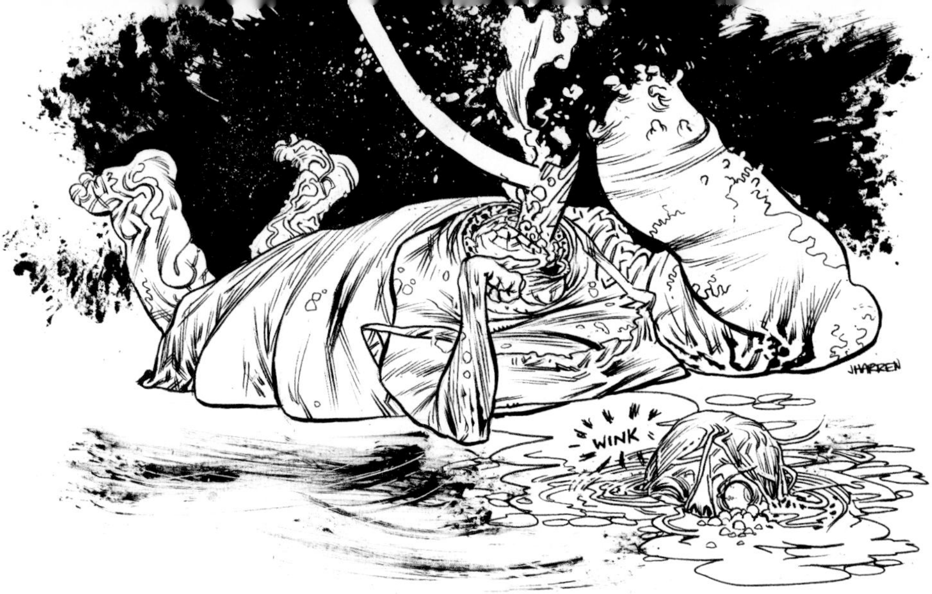
JHARREN
WINK

Facing: James Harren's 2011 season's greetings.

James's designs for the "Momster," the creature in the basement, and, on the following pages, other horrible things from *The Devil Does Not Jest*.

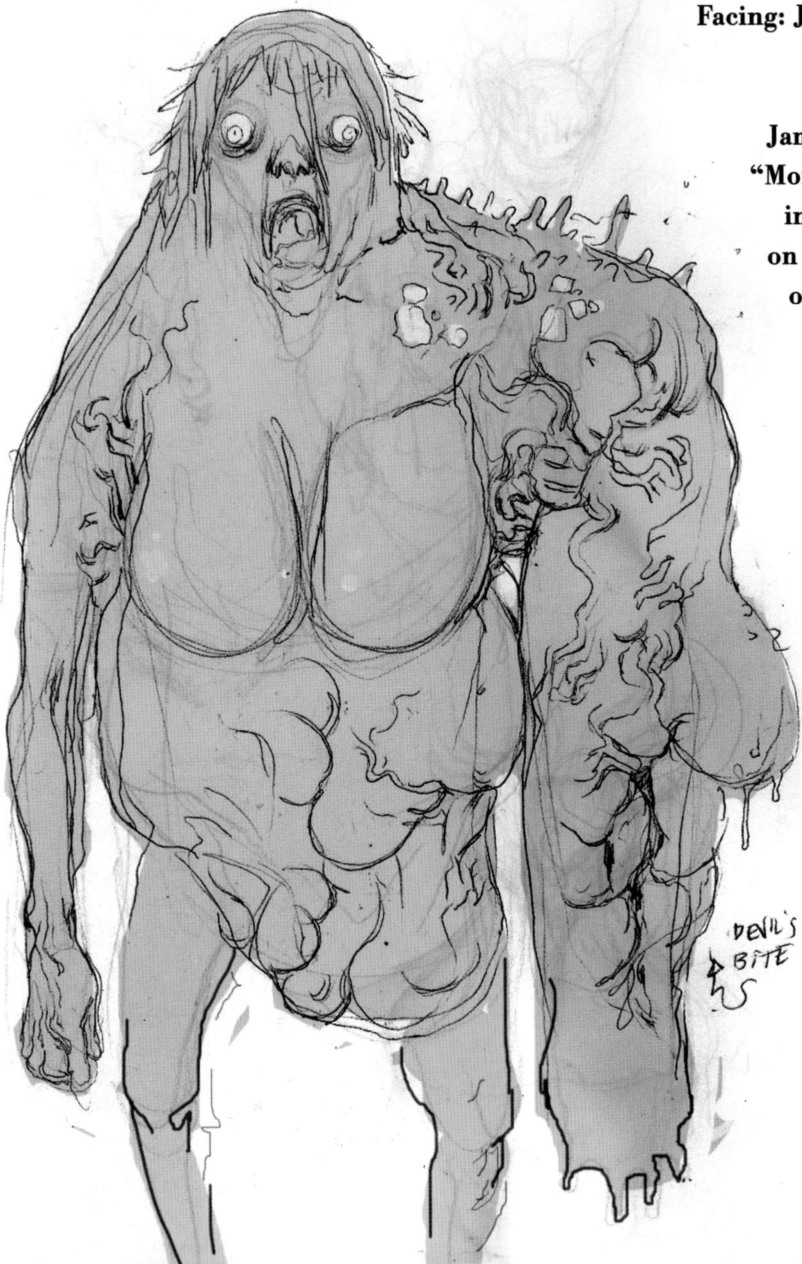
DEVIL'S BITE

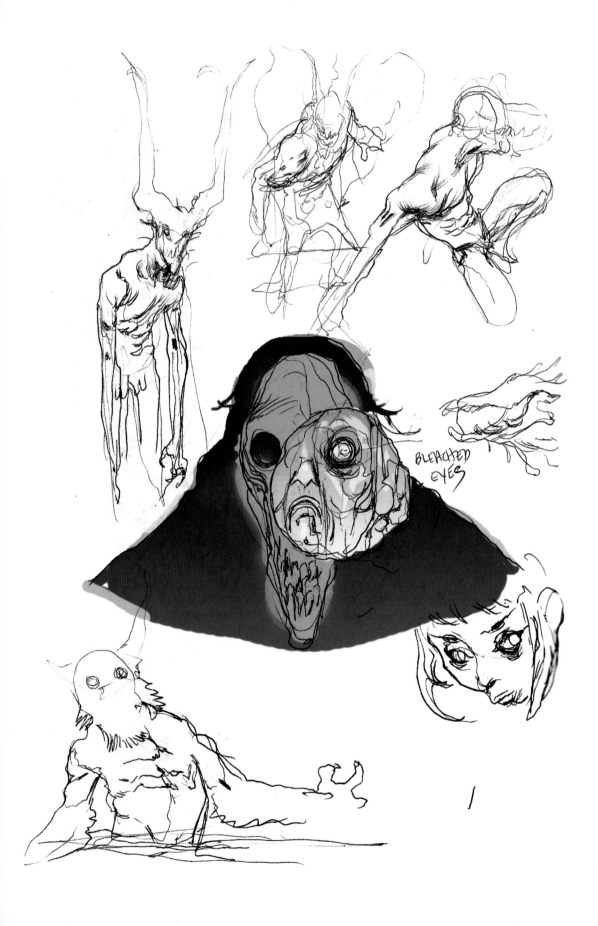

BLEACHED EYES

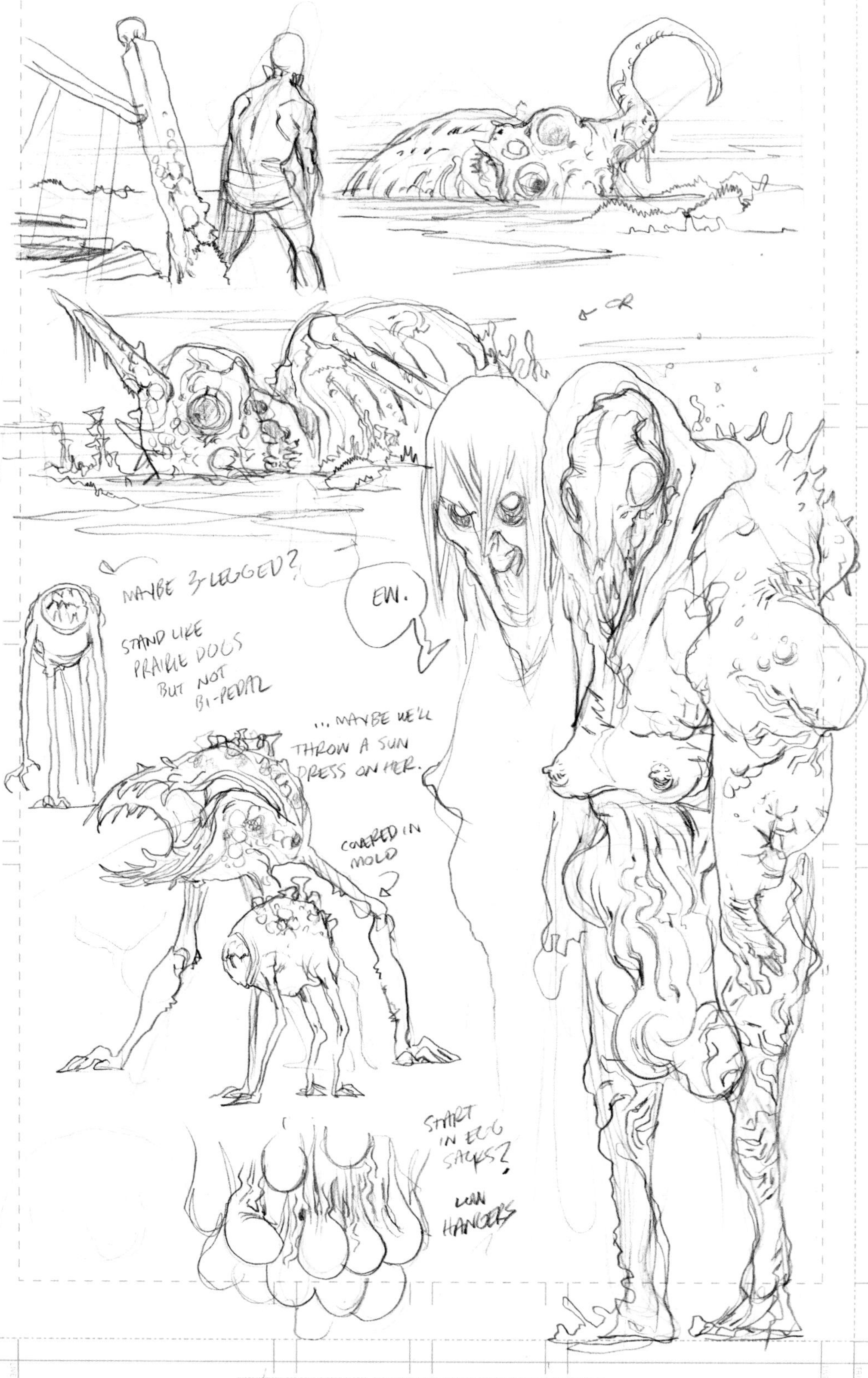
MAYBE 3-LEGGED?
STAND LIKE PRAIRIE DOGS BUT NOT BI-PEDAL
EW.
...MAYBE WE'LL THROW A SUN DRESS ON HER.
COVERED IN MOLD
START IN EGG SACKS?
LOW HANGERS

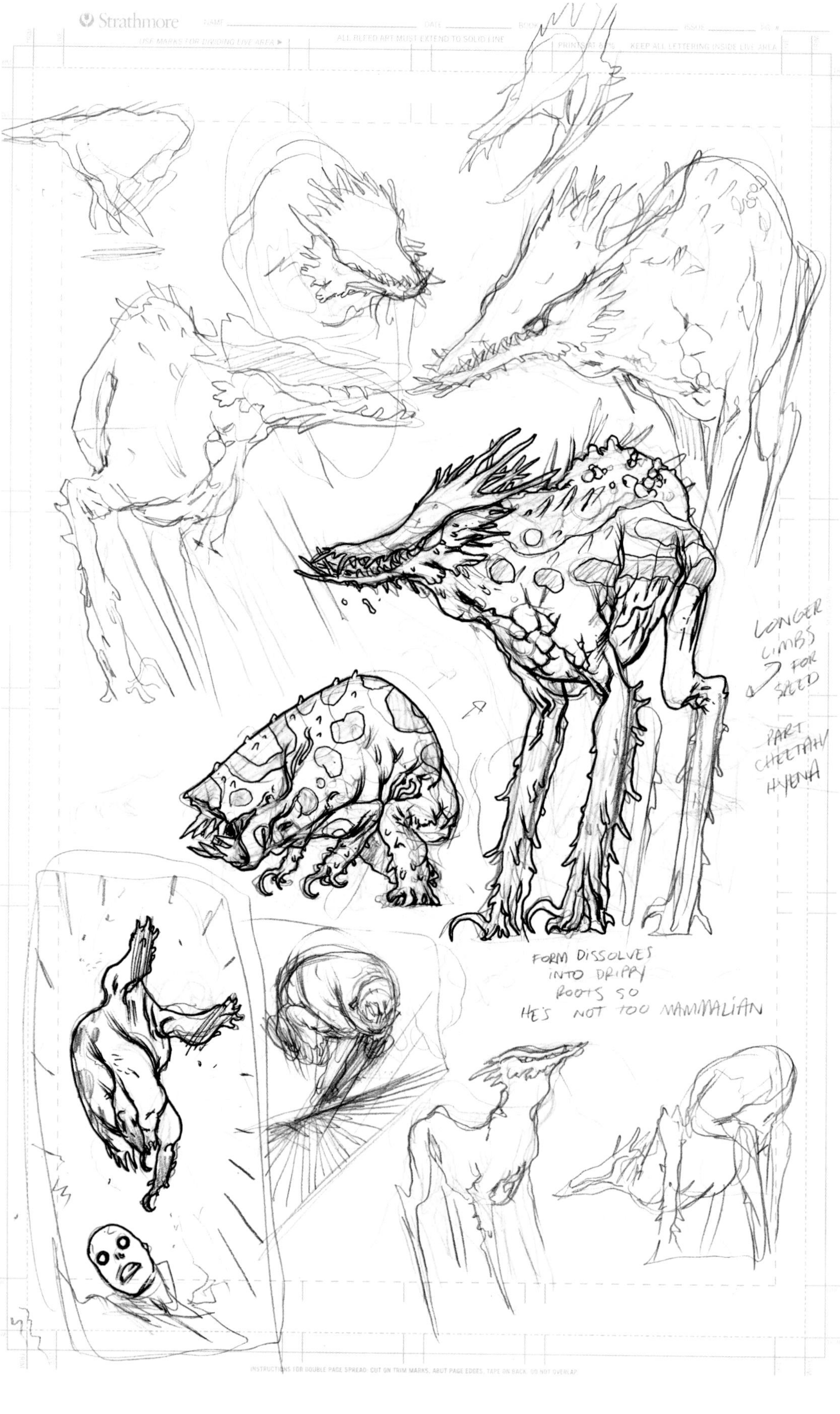
LONGER LIMBS → FOR SPEED
PART CHEETAH/ HYENA
FORM DISSOLVES INTO DRIPPY ROOTS SO HE'S NOT TOO MAMMALIAN

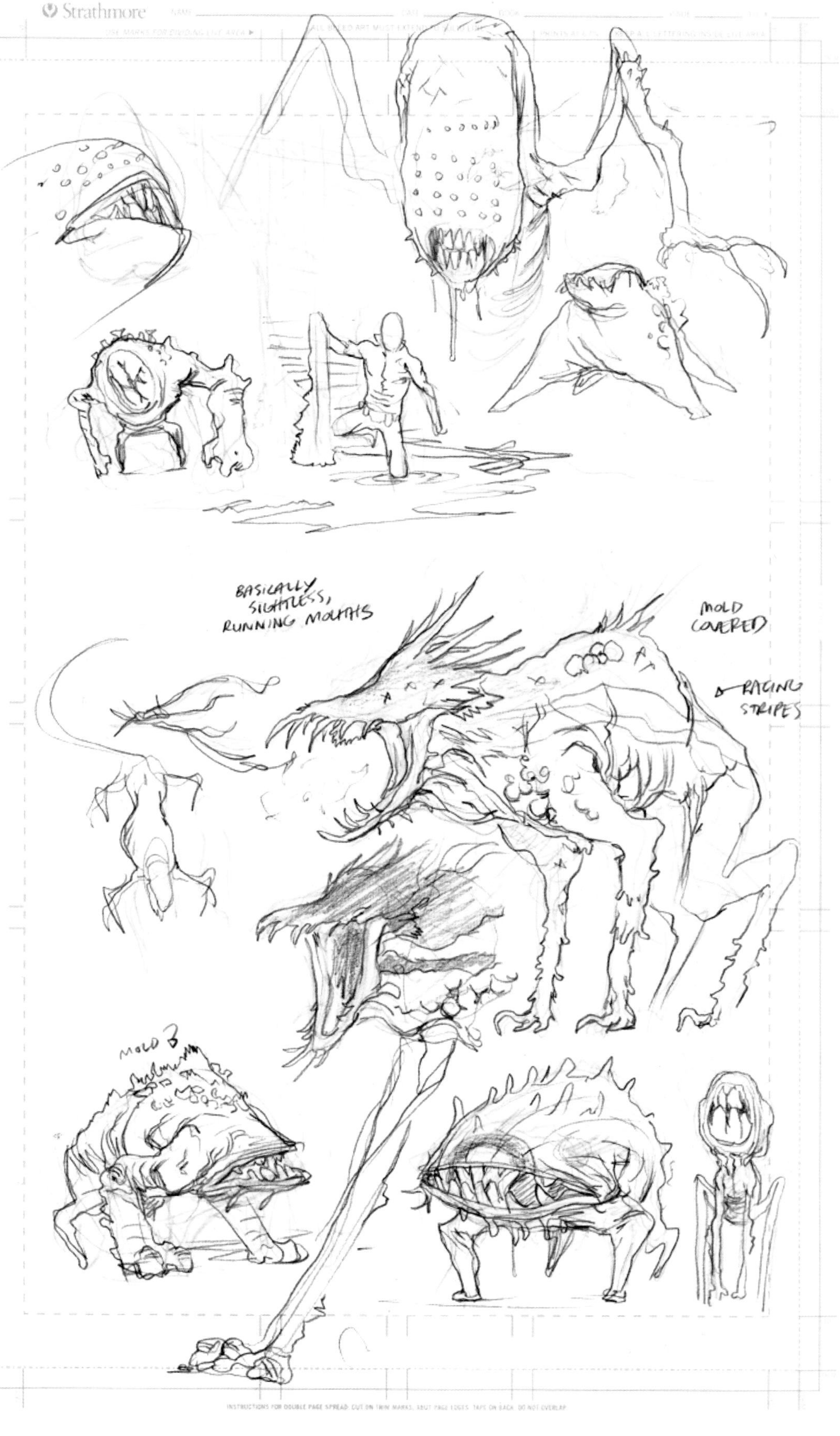

BASICALLY SIGHTLESS, RUNNING MOUTHS
MOLD COVERED
RAGING STRIPES
MOLD

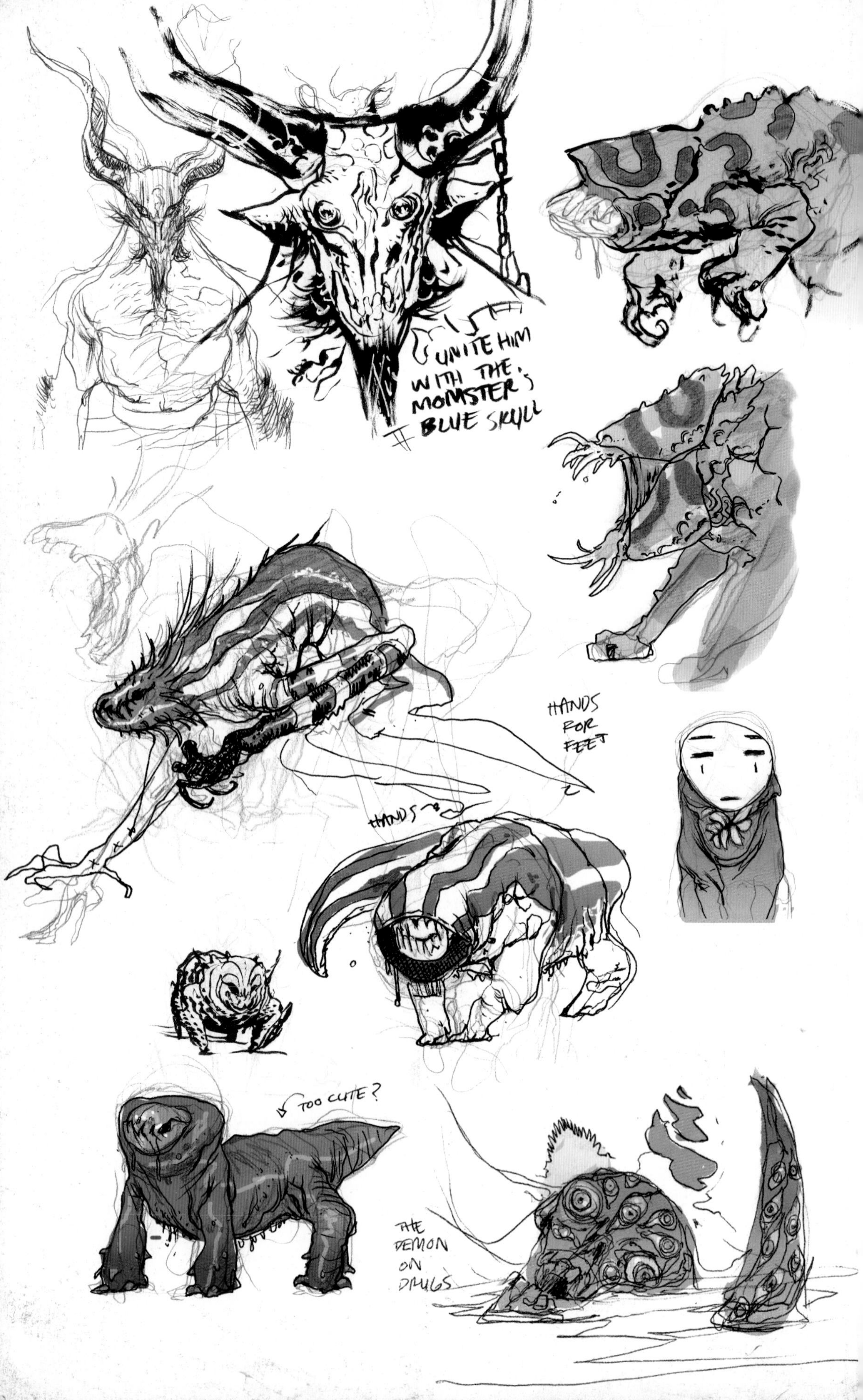
UNITE HIM WITH THE MONSTER'S BLUE SKULL
HANDS FOR FEET
HANDS
TOO CUTE?
THE DEMON ON DRUGS